THE GOLDEN HONEYCOMB

VINCENT CRONIN is well known for his historical biographies and for his two-volume history of the Renaissance ("Probably the best book that has ever been written on the Renaissance" *Times Educational Supplement*). His historical biographies include *Louis and Antoinette, Catherine, Empress of All the Russias, Louis XIV* and *Napoleon,* the last of which is a standard biography both in Britain and in France ("To present Napoleon plausibly. . . takes nerve, originality, prodigious powers of research and a true historical imagination" Michael Foot, *Standard*). His most recent book is *Paris on the Eve 1900-1914*, a collective portrait of the key figures in art, literature, science and politics in the cultural capital of Europe on the eve of World War I. His dual biography of Louis and Antoinette ("painstaking historical detective work" *Sunday Express*) and his biographies of Catherine the Great ("A quite overpowering portrait of a great and admirable woman" *Spectator*) and of Louis XIV ("The best-balanced of the whole reign to appear in years" *The Times*) are also available as Harvill Paperbacks.

Vincent Cronin

THE
GOLDEN
HONEYCOMB

A Sicilian Quest

HARVILL
An Imprint of HarperCollins*Publishers*

First published in Great Britain by Rupert Hart-Davis 1954
This revised edition first published in Great Britain 1980
by Granada Publishing Ltd

This paperback of the revised edition
with photographs by Werner Forman
first issued by Harvill
an imprint of HarperCollins Publishers,
77/85 Fulham Palace Road,
Hammersmith, London W6 8JB

1 3 5 7 9 10 8 6 4 2

A CIP catalogue record for this title
is available from the British Library

ISBN 0 00 272172 4

Made and printed in Great Britain by
HarperCollins Manufacturing, Glasgow

CONTENTS

FOR
Chantal

INTRODUCTION TO
THE SECOND EDITION

In 1951 I was working in London as assistant to the editor of *The Month*, a journal of the arts, philosophy and religion. I took dictation, typed letters, corrected proofs and occasionally committed gaffes. Once I allowed the typescript of Evelyn Waugh's *Helena*, which *The Month* was serialising, to leave the office for parts unknown, where it was read and broadcast prior to publication: a simultaneous breach of several conventions which Evelyn Waugh was not the man to overlook. Nor did he.

Since the age of twelve I had wanted to earn my living as a writer; three years on *The Month* had taught me the rudiments of concision and lucidity, and I had now saved enough money to take the leap of one year's freedom. I decided to give up my job, leave England with my wife and four-month-old daughter, and write a book about Sicily.

Most English people had been denied foreign travel during the war and even for some years afterwards limited foreign currency restricted their movements to sorties across the Channel. So travel books were much in favour. The other reason for my choice of the travel genre was that since boyhood I had been attracted to foreign countries; at school I eagerly read the *Geographical Magazine* and Sunday afternoons would find me in the Imperial Institute turning a handle to work the model gold mines and cocoa plantations.

But why Sicily? Though I am by no means sure, I believe I felt instinctively that it would be a good idea to go to an island, for that would give my book boundaries and a unity. Sicily in particular appeared to possess a wealth of artefacts as well as natural beauty, and these attributes, again instinctively, I felt I could put into words. I bought the Touring Club Italiano Guide to Sicily – it is still on my bookshelves, stoutly bound for the journey in blue canvas by my wife – and every evening when I returned from *The Month* I would read a few pages. As I moved from the Greeks to the Romans and on to the Normans I became more and more excited, and began to sketch to Chantal what was in store for her. Even before I bought our tickets I felt we had made a good choice.

We let our flat, 186 Ashley Gardens, to Persian students, and spent our last night in England – it was early January 1952 – at the St Ermin's Hotel, where Sylvelie protested at this change of surroundings by crying for six hours in the middle of the night, a contretemps made much worse by the fact that a thin communicating door separated our bedroom from the bedroom adjoining, where our unfortunate, unknown but much to be pitied neighbour was obviously spending a wakeful night.

Our route lay through Folkestone, Dieppe and Paris, and I remember the boat train had one whole carriage full of Chinese on a trade delegation; their presence made our grand Sicilian expedition seem quite tame. We slept a little in our second-class compartment and woke on the Italian Riviera, where the sun shone on palms and mimosa. We arrived in Rome but had time only to change trains. In Naples that evening we caught the overnight steamer for Palermo.

We landed in the Conca d'Oro on a cold, far from golden morning, but even light rain could not wholly dim the robust and dappled splendour of Monte Pellegrino. We took a taxi to the inexpensive Pensione Vinci, in a poor district, too modest to be listed in our Touring Club Guide.

Our room was unheated. We had a big double bed with only one blanket, and Sylvelie slept beside it in her trim French Moses basket. We were the only lodgers and the lady proprietor spent much of her time trying to interest us in a very large crocheted tablecloth, which she was prepared to let us have at a bargain price. Most of our time seemed to be spent in heating milk and preparing Nestlé baby food. In spare moments we would watch the unceasing rain fall into a none too clean street and wonder why on earth we had come.

The first building I went to see was the cathedral. It has a fine Norman apse with bold blind arcading on the outside, and contains the marble tombs of Roger II and his daughter. But its porch is late Gothic, and the cupola was added in the eighteenth century. Such a motley of styles interested but also dismayed me. I did not as yet have the remotest idea how I should be able to deal with it. I limited myself to taking conscientiously full notes about the building's appearance and the feelings it induced in me.

Cold and rain are not the best introduction to a Mediterranean island. Cold water that declines to lather in austerity soap is not the ideal medium for washing baby clothes and nappies, and the portable plastic child's bath we had brought from London took a great many kettles to fill. Only Chantal's courage saved our expedition.

Yet we could tell that given reasonably normal meteorological conditions there was much here of supreme beauty: the Cappella Palatina with its mosaics of Gospel scenes and stalactite ceiling; the stuccoed oratorios of Serpotta. All they needed was a new *Fiat lux*.

In February we took a train to Erice, a mountain village in the island's north-west corner with panoramic views of the Mediterranean, where the bread was baked in ovens heated with orange-wood and tasted a little of orange. We immediately took to this place with its clear mountain air, and it was to become a cornerstone of my book, the place near heaven where Daedalus laid his masterpiece before Aphrodite.

On the way back to Palermo we visited Segesta: another place of revelation, this time of the Greek genius for siting buildings in a fold of the hills within sight of the sea.

We continued to Catania, again by train. Sylvelie was a typical northern baby, with fair skin and very blonde hair. These characteristics are highly esteemed in Sicily and are imparted, for example, to the Christ-child of Nativity cribs. Any Sicilian mothers happening to be travelling in our compartment considered Sylvelie a highly eligible *partie* – possibly even a princess – and on on every one of our many train journeys Sicilian parents insisted on arranging an "engagement" between our daughter and any dark-complexioned boy of similar age who happened to be at hand.

Sicilian women, however, became very worried indeed when they saw us leave our paragon of northern beauty exposed to what they considered the baneful vapours present in all fresh air. Whenever they spied even part of one cheek indecently exposed, they hastened to cover it with her shawl. They also considered us unloving, unnatural and potential child-murderers for leaving Sylvelie to sleep in the hotel bedroom while we went out for our evening omelette and insalata verde. Once, when it began to grow warmer, we left Sylvelie on the balcony, and returned to find a mothers' meeting in the street underneath, many a plump arm raised in righteous indignation that this snow-complexioned infant had been left exposed to nocturnal perils and businesses.

While trying to find a factor common to the not very inspiring lava-built monuments of Catania, I began to be badgered by a succession of little dark men carrying large brown cardboard suitcases. Each invited me into a side street and there confided that he had disembarked within the hour from a cargo ship having in his possession a length of valuable cloth on which he had been fortunate enough to pay no duty. No such cloth would come my way again, and I could buy it at a bargain price. He then took out pencil and paper and, in a silence intended to be dramatic, wrote at the top of the paper: 75,000 lire. He paused for a moment to watch my face, then put a pencil line through that figure and wrote underneath it: 60,000 lire. Again he watched my face. Since I had not yet seen the cloth, it probably registered very little. The man then spoke. For me, an American, he would reduce the price even further, and crossing out the second figure, he now wrote: 50,000. With a flourish he opened the suitcase to reveal a length of dark brown serge with a white stripe. The oddest thing about this episode is that it happened on three separate occasions, with different men, the same figures, and cloth that varied only in its degree of unattractiveness. Such are the hazards of travel-writing.

We decided to spend Easter in Taormina. We attended the vigil Mass on Holy Saturday in the little church on the piazza, noticing how the local people came in for half an hour, disappeared for half an hour, and returned in time for the final blessing. All filed out with the grave air of a heavy obligation dutifully discharged.

Here, on the slopes between the town and D.H.Lawrence's house, Fontana Vecchia, we first felt a warm sun. The field we were sitting in was scattered with wild flowers, and small lizards crept from the cracks of rock. We knew that spring had come at last; everyone said it was late that year – is it ever otherwise? – and we were happy.

It was good to warm bodies chilled by two months of unheated *pensione*, and to find white legs and arms slowly acquiring a tan. Now too we could let our imaginations play with the newly inviting landscape and buildings that suddenly had weight and cast a deep shadow.

In Syracuse we made a long stay. Our local hotel stood on the waterfront facing the harbour where the Athenian fleet had been defeated. A short walk brought us to the fountain of Arethusa, and a slightly longer one to the temple of Pallas Athena, which is Syracuse's cathedral. A local marquis happened to be opening his library to the public and kindly asked us to the opening ceremony in a courtyard hung with wistaria in full flower, thus raising the little occasion to the level of an "international event". The marquis's soft-eyed secretary wrote poetry and gave us a book of his verse, the best poem of which is an Ode to a Rat.

I wrote much of my book at the hotel window, bare to the waist, enjoying the by now hot sun. A young well-to-do grocer affiliated to the British Council kindly allowed us to accompany him in his little Fiat on a business visit to Modica, and later we went by train to the other baroque town in this region, honey-stoned Noto.

We travelled to Enna, almost 3,000 feet above sea level, and found winter again: morning mist and peasants huddled into thick dark blue sheep-wool cloaks. Close by we visited Piazza Armerina, where the first mosaics of the imperial hunting villa had recently been uncovered; we were among the first to look at the hunting scenes and bikini-clad ladies disporting themselves in the gymnasium, which for sixteen centuries had been hidden by silt.

We took ship for the Aeolian Islands. On Vulcanello I carried Sylvelie to the top of an intermittently active volcano; happily there were no mothers around to blame me for exposing her satin complexion to baneful sulphurous vapour.

We had let our London flat through a Mayfair estate agent. At first we received neatly typed letters saying that the rent had been received and paid into my bank. Presently the letters began to be badly typed and full of misspellings. They announced that the rent was slow in coming through, then that it had not been paid at all. Finally the letters began to be handwritten; we surmised that the estate agency was collapsing – indeed this proved to be so – and that instead of returning to a small credit balance the only money we should have would be what I could earn from my still only half-written book.

Throughout our travels we were looking for distinctively Sicilian values and modes of expression. This kind of quest did not go easily into words, and most Sicilians thought we were interested in folklore, as to some extent we were. They took us to a puppet show in a back-street Palermo hall, and to watch the panels of horse-carts being carved with Orlando's feats and painted in bright primary colours. But they did not show us what we were seeking. In the end we had to find it, painfully, for ourselves.

We left Sicily in May and for the rest of 1952 lived with my wife's parents in their house in southern Normandy. There I completed the first version of my book. Using Gerard Manley Hopkins's word, I entitled it *Sicilian Inscapes*.

We returned to 186 Ashley Gardens in January 1953 to find, literally, a skeleton in our cupboard – left by one of our Persians, a medical student, perhaps in lieu of unpaid rent. The Persians had slept seven in our double bed and broken the mattress springs. They had also shattered the legs of a small antique table – by piling a lot of heavy books on it, they explained. These little disasters did not deter us later from choosing Iran as the destination of our second journey, described in *The Last Migration*.

The father of my successor at *The Month* happened to be Milton Waldman, who after many years as chief literary editor at Collins had gone into partnership with Rupert Hart-Davis at the sign of the fox in Soho Square. Milton asked to see my typescript. A historian, he was interested in Sicily's rich cultural texture, and accepted the book mainly on the strength of two pages describing the singing of a nightingale. He asked me to revise the book, to correct a centrifugal tendency by strengthening the main theme of quest. I did as he advised. Rupert Hart-Davis then read the typescript, became excited about it and thereafter took charge of the editing. He also passed the typescript to his young production assistant, who summed up his impressions in the memorably laconic phrase: "Everything's chthonic." It is true that I have a predilection for the k sound, and had overindulged in that booming adjective.

When proofs arrived I worked through them in Soho Square over numerous teas, which always included little chocolate-covered Swiss rolls in silver paper, while Rupert, with a tact my novice cockiness was far from deserving, gently coaxed me into improving some of my more infelicitous phrasing. He liked the preposition "in" before a place, and disapproved of my use of "at". Once the typesetter made a happy slip. My typescript phrase compared the snow on Mount Etna "to the white pain on a clown's face", which at Rupert's prompting I retained.

The Golden Honeycomb was published on 25 January 1954 in a first edition of 3,000 copies. No young author could have been more fortunate with reviews. In the *Observer* on the day before publication Harold Nicolson wrote that mine was the best travel book he had read for two years: that is, we surmised, since James Pope-Hennessy's book on Provence, while the following Sunday Cyril Connolly, again in a lead review, wrote with enthusiasm for *Sunday Times* readers. Other good notices followed, including one by John Lehmann on the BBC in which he complained that I hadn't given much space to the Sicilians. That is true. I cannot honestly claim that I hit it off with the Sicilians. They kept expecting me to be a rich, free-spending American, while I found them lacking in vigour and self-reliance, though perhaps it was unfair to ask those qualities at that moment, since they were emerging from the miseries of war, followed by near-secession and its backlash in the sternly unsympathetic hand of Rome.

One reviewer complained that in 260 pages I did not once mention the Mafia. *The Month* generously gave the book two reviews, a short interim notice and, much later when it finally arrived from the wilds of Greece, a review-article by Patrick Leigh Fermor entitled "Honey from Hybla".

My subject was fairly fresh, though not completely so, for Peter Quennell had published *Spring in Sicily* two years before. It struck a chord in the many English people who dreamed of Mediterranean sun but were unable to make the journey south. My book went into three more impressions, totalling 7,000 copies. Heinrich Harrer's *Seven Years in Tibet* had been published shortly before and was breaking records, but Rupert gave as much attention to my small offering as to the best-seller, and advertised it attractively with a small line-drawing of the church of San Giorgio, Modica.

An American edition was published by Dutton in the same year as the first English edition. A French translation followed from Albin Michel and a German translation from Scherz & Goverts.

My book came second for the Citta di Palermo prize, which was won by a German publication. Perhaps there were only two entries! The British Council kindly accepted on my behalf a sum of money and an inscribed medal of Arethusa. The book also won the first Richard Hillary Award. This was a great encouragement to me, for I was midway in my second book, *The Wise Man from the West*, and in a period of economic uncertainty had committed myself to being a professional writer.

I have not revisited Sicily. The island has changed, I hear, in many ways. The Conca d'Oro is much built-up, and the roads in summer are thronged by bus-loads of group tourists, who see the island in air-conditioned comfort through panoramic tinted windows to the accompaniment of a spoken commentary. But tourism and the discovery of oil have brought one extremely important gain. There is much less poverty than twenty-five years ago.

London, February 1980

PREFACE TO
THE PRESENT EDITION

This new edition is illustrated with photographs specially taken by Werner Forman. Most depict places or works of art I write about in the book, while a few, such as his photographs of Segesta, show buildings which, given the plan of my book, I could not specifically describe, but which exemplify visually one or more of my main themes.

Mr Forman does not seek to startle by juxtaposing ancient and modern, rustic and urban. His is a classical approach, in that he allows his subjects to speak for themselves, directly or indirectly. He has a particular feeling for the texture of Sicily's bedrock, that powerful, often forbidding limestone pummelled for millenia by Mediterranean waves before at last achieving a serene and useful role at the hands of craftsmen in walls and columns and lintels for fortresses, temples, cathedrals, theatres and private dwellings. By his careful contrasts of light and shadow, by subtly eliciting detail and pattern, Mr Forman suggests what is hidden and puts us in the imaginative mood to discover secrets.

Marbella, February 1992

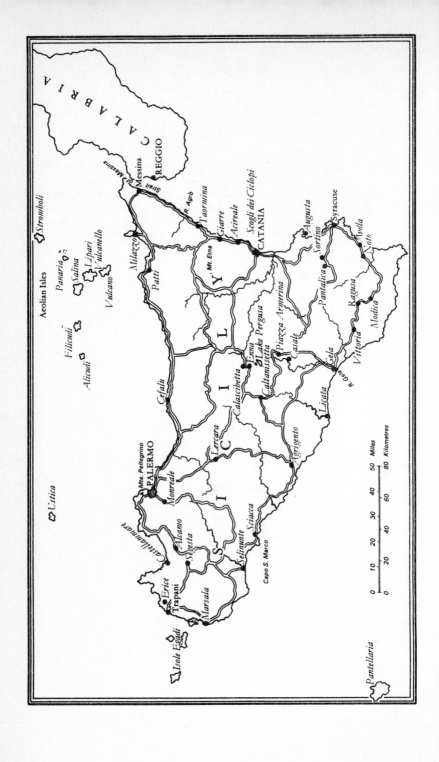

CHAPTER ONE

The Legend

OF ALL the men who have ever lived those most powerful to excite the imagination are the figures looming out of the twilight world where history and legend meet. Precisely because it is uncertain whether they ever really lived at all, they exert the attraction of a mirage or a half-forgotten song. In the earliest historical documents these figures are mentioned as having existed centuries before, in a golden age that was also dark, and their names even for these first recorders already had a legendary ring. They are spoken of now as gods, now as men: they weave an ambiguous path between heaven and earth, myth and fact. They merge with the everlasting archetypes at the depths of the human mind, these early kings and heroes, so as to be almost indistinguishable from them. But were they, in the last analysis, projections or not, real or unreal, the impatient inquirer asks, and the disappointing answer is that the question cannot be put so bluntly. They must be tracked by a more subtle trail, these wraiths that are perhaps real.

Daedalus was such a figure, perhaps the most interesting of them all, for he is said to have been the first artist who ever lived, if not in the flesh at least in the minds of men. As Orpheus first invented music and poetry, so Daedalus first carved statues and constructed buildings that were beautiful as well as habitable. He was the original, primeval craftsman, the first who redeemed man from bare existence. If inventors are memorable and the arts worthy of esteem, then this discoverer named Daedalus, whose works, Plato says, were tinged with divinity, deserves praise in the highest.

The historian who tells us most about him is Diodorus, a

Sicilian who lived shortly before the time of Christ. He relates that Daedalus, of royal descent, lived in Athens, where he gained fame as a builder and sculptor of unparalleled genius. He was the first to represent the open eye and to fashion the legs separated in a stride and the arms and hands as extended. The tradition grew up that his statues were so lifelike that they had to be chained to prevent them from running away. Daedalus employed his nephew as apprentice, and when the boy proved himself adept at inventing technical devices, Daedalus out of envy killed him. Hastily leaving Athens in order to avoid punishment, he went first to Crete, where his works included a labyrinth in which to house the Minotaur. Soon, however, the artist incurred the jealousy of Minos, King of Crete, and was obliged to leave with his son Icarus, who was drowned on the journey. Landing in Sicily, he was favourably received on account of his artistic fame by Cocalus, king of the island, and his daughters. He constructed several wonderful works for the king, and enjoyed royal patronage. Not long afterwards, however, Minos, who was at that time master of the seas, decided to make a campaign in order to capture and punish Daedalus. Landing in Sicily, Minos was killed by Cocalus and his body handed over to the Cretan soldiers, who buried it on the island. Diodorus says that Daedalus remained a considerable time in Sicily, where he accomplished many masterpieces still visible in the historian's day, and he mentions in particular that the artist is said to have fashioned a golden honeycomb, working it with such skill that it was indistinguishable from a real honeycomb. This work of art he gave in offering to Aphrodite of Erice, whose shrine was the most famous in all Sicily.

Diodorus is not a particularly trustworthy writer, but the story of the honeycomb fits appropriately into the wider context of Daedalus's own life, for which we have other confirmatory evidence. Herodotus, for instance, who lived four centuries before Diodorus, relates a tradition which brings Minos from Crete to Sicily in search of Daedalus the craftsman, and the theme was well enough known to be developed by Ovid. Another reason for trusting Diodorus's story of Daedalus is this. In his account the historian gives a detailed description of the tomb in which Minos was buried. It was in two parts, the upper storey consisting of a shrine to Aphrodite, the lower of a grave. This unusual tomb was destroyed in the fifth century before Christ, so that Diodorus himself could not have seen it. Nevertheless, his description of the type of tomb used for the burial of a Cretan king is strikingly confirmed by an actual royal tomb of the Minoan age in Crete, excavated by Sir Arthur Evans. The tomb in Crete takes just such a dual form as that described by Diodorus. If the historian was correct to the last detail in his account of a grave demolished four centuries before his birth, it is likely that he was also correct in regard to other, less obscure details of the same story. Furthermore, that Diodorus, in this particular section of his history, believes he is recording historical fact is shown by his comments on an alternative version of Daedalus's journey from Crete. Some people, he points out, say that Daedalus made his escape on wings of wax, but this, Diodorus declares, is a mere myth. The implication is that the rest of his account is historically true.

Daedalus, if he is a historical figure, lived before the Trojan War, about the fourteenth century before Christ, during an age of Mediterranean history concerning which very little is known. At that time Crete was a dominant power, having built up, under Egyptian influence, a civilisation of great complexity. Cretan ships, as Diodorus mentions, ranged far and wide over the Mediterranean. Athens, on the other hand, if the place existed at all, was at that time only a minor town, uncivilised and unlikely to have originated an artistic tradition. It is probable, therefore, that Daedalus's Athenian origin was a later accretion to the basic legend, and that Crete, in fact, was his native country. After the rise of Athens it became customary to trace the birth of most heroes and many of the gods to Attica, and in this particular story the murder of a relative is clearly a mere device for bringing the hero to Crete, the scene of most of his known activities and therefore, probably, his birthplace.

Apart from this single alteration, there are no certain reasons why Diodorus's account should not be accepted in its entirety, for it fits in well with the pattern of history in the latter half of the second millennium. In an age of kings, artists enjoyed court patronage. They turned their talents to the production of jewellery and fibulas for the ladies, strongholds and shrines for the king. At this time poetry was first beginning to be sung in the Mediterranean, and the artist worked side by side with the first singers of epic. Confirmation of the Cretan period of Daedalus's life is found in the depiction of a labyrinth on Cretan coins and the conspicuous part which the bull played in Cretan religion.

No part of the story fits in better with the known historical facts than Daedalus's tribute to the goddess of Erice. Diodorus, for the benefit of readers who knew only the Greek and Roman pantheon, calls her Aphrodite but at such an early date she must have been Astarte, or a local equivalent of that goddess, whose worship took place in Crete as elsewhere throughout the Mediterranean. Her shrine at Erice is known to be very ancient, and at such an early period the artist's religious obligations would have demanded an offering from one who had found safety and hospitality in a strange country.

That Daedalus should have offered to the goddess a golden honeycomb is, however, curious and unparalleled. In the days before wine was invented it is true that honey was offered to the gods, but it was always real honey, the symbolic product of earth and sky, not a representation. Gold, an easy metal to work, would have been a natural material in which to construct a votive offering, but such presents usually took the form of figurines and statuettes. Thus, gold, ivory, and wooden statues with a religious function and belonging to the Minoan age have been found in Crete. But the combination of the two ideas as in a golden honeycomb is exceptional. Once again the nearest known equivalent, ritual jars in the shape of a wild honeycomb, entwined by a snake, have been found at Cnossus. If the idea was brought from Crete to Sicily, who better than Daedalus could have carried it?

Yet it has been customary to deny the existence of a historical Daedalus. Most historians have been inclined to believe that the legend sprang up at a late period to account, in simple fashion, for primitive works of art, whether in Attica, Crete, or Sicily. An artistic Odysseus, travelling and working in many different countries, was invented to account for early works which during the course of centuries had come to receive the epithet Daedalean, another word for primitive. It would be absurd, argue the historians, to take Diodorus's word for the existence of a man who lived 1300 years earlier; even more absurd to take his word for the existence of a particular golden honeycomb.

Is Daedalus a man or a myth? There seems no better way of discovering whether or not there has been such a historical figure than by attempting to find one of his masterpieces. Of these none is so distinctive as the golden honeycomb. If such a unique work can be found and dated to the second millennium before Christ, Diodorus's story will be substantiated to the point of truth.

Yet the one certain way of arriving at the truth also appears to be the most difficult. If such a honeycomb existed in Diodorus' day, it has never been mentioned, and therefore perhaps never seen, during the Christian era. So distinctive and fine a work can hardly have been mislaid or ignored. On the other hand, it can scarcely have been destroyed. Beauty has a strong and stubborn tendency to survive, and, as though perfect style itself acts as a preservative, the most beautiful things often last longest. In recent times modelled skulls four thousand years older than the honeycomb have been discovered, and the paintings in neolithic caves are as vivid now as though they had been executed yesterday.

Without engaging in archaeology, without excavating anew, is a quest for the honeycomb still possible? And if so, will it prove anything but a wild-goose chase? Sicily has already been dug; its coins and pottery, temples and shrines unearthed and classified. The need now is not for more digging but for a roving eye and a definite object in view. A new searcher, like Jason with a particular treasure to find and secure, will have all the advantages imparted by single-minded ambition and an ideal.

Whether or not the golden honeycomb fashioned by Daedalus is finally discovered, the quest will prove rewarding in itself. It will involve the exploration of a complex country, ancient in descent, a treasure-house of artistic and natural beauty; the sifting of many civilisations and the deciphering of many symbols; and like most journeys its course will doubtless prove as satisfying as arrival at the final destination. Sicily will be a prize no less precious than the golden honeycomb.

The starting-point of the search will be Erice, as it is today, more than three thousand years after the time of Daedalus. Yet it will be foolish to expect, even there, any obvious clues to the secret. The people will assume blank expressions and deny all knowledge of the masterpiece—this is the procedure in all treasure-hunts. Even the buildings will assume a misleading appearance. For this reason everything will require a scrutiny which looks beyond the evident and attempts to elicit secrets. A work of art lost to view for so many centuries will not yield itself to the first questing lover. The object belonged to a goddess and if the goddess is dead her property is none the less sacrosanct. It will have been hedged about not with dragons, for those would at once have revealed its position, but with all the odds and ends of everyday life, just as a nightingale's nest and eggs are so blended with the surrounding twigs and grasses that they altogether escape notice.

But the treasure is of a sort to justify an arduous search: holy, and of gold, and fashioned by a man who, in the judgment of the people most sensitive to artistic beauty, was the first and greatest of all artists. An object of such splendour will cast excitement on every stage of the quest.

CHAPTER TWO

Erice

To THE south and centre of Western Sicily mountains are cultivated to their summit and interspersed with vines: there is a profusion of oaks, poplars and acacias which in Greek times covered most of the island: numerous springs and streams that water a garden of wild flowers, geraniums, bougainvillea, mallows, mustard, fields of red clover like Persian carpets, thyme and asphodel, perhaps more abundant here than anywhere else in the island. Mile after mile stretches a dense El Dorado where armful upon armful of flowers can be picked without encroaching upon the treasure.

By contrast, further north in this western province, the island is flatter, marguerites are the only flowers, trees have dwindled and the lizard-littered ground, dry as desert, is dotted with stocky vines that yield the syrupy Marsala. Amid these surroundings, crowning a high, isolated hill-top on the coast and conspicuous by land and sea for miles around, stands Erice, sanctuary of the goddess of love.

A dusty road winds zigzag up the pyramidal hill, as though recording on its slope the change of temperature from the parched plain below to the cloud-capped crest, refreshed by every sea breeze. Part of the mountain lies exposed in gashes and caves, some of which have yielded tusks of elephants, evidence that Sicily was conceived in the womb of Africa. The earliest people who inhabited these slopes gained their livelihood by fishing: indeed, the sea once covered all this region and its receding level is marked by thin layers of rock, in which fossilised sea-shells are intermingled with neolithic bones. The sea is still retreating, and the long, artificial antenna which is the neighbouring port of

Trapani will one day project no longer into the Mediterranean but into fields of waving corn. Farming will supersede tunny fishing and salt-collecting, as Sicily continues to make her way slowly back to her mother.

Like a snake mounting a boulder, the road finally reaches and rounds the peak, two thousand feet above sea and land. Here is the watchtower of Sicily, almost of the entire Mediterranean, for even Africa is not the farthest visible stretch of land. The panoramas at all points of the compass are bewilderingly remote, and the heady air endows them with the qualities of a vision. Through the centuries, from its very origin which is steeped in myth, this summit has assumed religious importance, radiating as far as the eastern and western verges of the Mediterranean. It dominates the sea and the' western tracts of the island, and for mariner and rustic alike it has always stood as the point of communication between man and the immortal gods. The primitive inhabitants who took the pains to build on this intractable rock did so because they believed they were reinforcing at the supernatural level their impregnable natural position.

The present village is medieval, built of grey stone, a maze of silent cloisters among the clouds. As befits a village built at such a height, Erice, for much of its history, is encircled by mist. For a millennium after its great days as a sanctuary it disappears from recorded history, to rise again in the twelfth century as Monte San Giuliano, so christened by Count Roger, who in a dream had seen that saint putting the Saracen to flight with a pack of hounds, while he and his Norman army were vainly laying siege to the place. From that period dates the present village, a network of alleyways and passages clinging to the bare rock, and little grey medieval houses, distinguished by courtyards. None of them gives directly on to the street, so that there drifts about the place a note of secrecy, almost of barrenness. It seems another Germelshausen, whose period of sleep is a thousand years.

During the thirteenth and fourteenth centuries the town enjoyed prosperity: its numerous churches and castles were built in those grand days. Ever since that period Erice has been forgotten, a living relic, its large population eroded, as it were, to the lowlands and especially to Trapani. This town had formerly been dependent on the great mountain stronghold, but with the coming of the Spanish kings and an era of peace it began to assume an important role as the chief port linking the island to the mother country. Since then, Trapani has steadily increased in importance so that it is now a bustling, thoroughly commercial city of practically no aesthetic interest, while Erice lingers on, a village now, no longer a great town, curious perhaps but quite useless in these practical days. In that fact lies its special form of beauty, for now, deserted almost, it distils the atmosphere of another age.

About the late Norman churches in the village there is an air of abandonment: built for a flourishing centre, many are now falling into ruin, and the village is surrounded on all sides by crumbling houses on which the pine forest has encroached. The place seems to be retreating into itself in protection against a disrespectful century: the outposts have already been abandoned, and many citizens have deserted. Those who live here still are for most of the day out on the mountainside with their flocks of sheep and goats, but a few villagers pass through the streets having about them an otherworldly grace, bowing with a rare spirit of benevolence and welcome to strangers, as though their appearance were something of an event.

The men wear thick hoods against the violence of the wind, and the women black silk shawls. The young girls are slim and have well-formed heads, large eyes and fine noses, beautiful now as when the Arab chronicler Ibn Jubair described the women of Erice, descendants perhaps of the priestesses of Astarte, as the loveliest in the whole island—and asked God to make them slaves of the Moslem. Neither the men nor the women possess the usual Sicilian openness: they do not stand about the streets, but walk with purpose to and from their little low houses. Even the bread they

bake here has a flavour which could be imagined medieval:
it is scented with orange, for their ovens are heated with
branches of citrus trees, and the nectar-laden sap rises to
pervade the flour.

As the bread is interlaced with this evocative perfume, so
too the village is inseparable from the view it commands on
every side: to the west lie Trapani and its salt marshes, and,
far off, the Isole Egadi pretending to be clouds; to the south
the coast of Sicily, Capo S. Marco, Pantellaria and the verge
of Africa; to the east the mountains above Sciacca; to the
north the island of Ustica. Erice is, in its own small compass,
all these remote points; it concentrates in itself, as a lyric
poem crystallises many levels of feeling and many varieties
of experience, the whole of Western Sicily, that primitive
province with the yearning for Africa, that Carthaginian
corner which never quite felt the restraining hand of
Greece.

The site of the temple proves to be just as Diodorus
describes, the highest, precipitous tip of the rock, but it is
dominated now by the remains of a Saracen castle. Not only
the town but the very sanctuary of Astarte has been metamorphosed into a medieval village. The deception is complete: the scene has been shifted for a later act, and there
remains almost nothing of the original background, only a
little uncemented masonry bearing witness to the sanctuary
which Daedalus is said to have visited. This pretence of
medievalism only the imagination has power to unmask,
and from these tell-tale stones reshape, behind the Norman
houses and ruined castle, the original, archaic Erice.

The temple must have been crudely built, imposing only
on account of its position, and its plain, uncemented walls,
devoid of columns, were serviceable without interesting the
eye. Here, in springtime, Daedalus came with the royal
court, to pay homage to the national deity and perhaps to
give thanks for his safe escape from the hands of Minos.
Given the essential conservatism of religion, the rites which
took place then can have differed little from those barbarian

observances at Erice known to later writers: they offered a
striking contrast to the purifying mysteries of Greek religion.
In spring the chief ceremony took place, when a group of
doves was released from Erice and took flight in the direction
of Africa. Nine days later they returned, preceded now by
a red dove, a bird whose care for its young made it a symbol
of fertility. The red dove was Astarte, and her return to the
island signified the return of spring to all living creatures
in Sicily. The cult cannot have been altogether new to
Daedalus, for a comparable goddess was worshipped in
Crete, but the sublime position of Erice perhaps made the
ceremony more moving than any other he had known. The
light air and position of the temple would have imparted a
strong sense of awe: he would have felt himself in a holy
place, that he was partaking of the divine, as he saw all the
world, or so it appeared, stretched out at his feet.

Pilgrims proved their devotion by bringing presents which
were laid in the sanctuary under guard, and to these
Daedalus added an offering which combined in unique
fashion riches with artistic skill. Then, to those pilgrims
who had brought the fairest gifts, whether they came from
near or far, the temple priestesses gave themselves in the
cause of the laughter-loving goddess. In a single rite, at once
natural and supernatural, which seemed to satisfy primitive
vague notions about the sublime rock, the miraculous return
of spring, and a deep desire to participate in the divine, worship was paid to the passionate goddess of Erice. The honeycomb remained in the sanctuary, divine property now, while
its maker returned to the valley.

The remains which have been excavated from the temple
are laid out within the walls: columns and a cornice belonging to a much later reconstruction, for the goddess was taken
up by the Romans, Virgil going so far as to declare Aeneas
founder of the temple. Of the original sanctuary, apart from
the few fragments of masonry, only a round pit called the
Well of Venus remains distinct: no one knows what purpose
it served, for it seems both too wide and too shallow to have

yielded water. Some say it was a fishpond sacred to the goddess, into which pilgrims dropped offerings of money and
jewellery; others claim that corn was stored there against a
siege. It remains now as the one certain feature of that
earliest of all Sicilian cults. But of Daedalus's original offering there is no trace. Scholars, local and national, are certain that no such object has ever been discovered at Erice, and
it is equally certain that the honeycomb could not now remain hidden here, where all is bare rock, refusing burial to
even the smallest object.

Erice reveals a beauty past all bounds, a beauty which
seems to embrace the heights and depths of all creation, of
heaven and earth and the waters under the earth. The village
is the prism of the Mediterranean, where the onlooker can
distinguish all the shades of land, sea, and sky, but it refuses
to yield up its secret, the one treasure that matters. The loss
is all the greater since the town in other respects confirms the
truth of Diodorus's story. Here are the remains of a temple
which clearly dates back to an age when Daedalus was supposed to have lived; here stands the sanctuary on the very
pinnacle of Sicily, open to heaven, but empty of his offering.
The temple has been excavated to the rock; the antechambers
combed; the débris sifted, but no one, since Diodorus's day,
has set eyes on the honeycomb.

It may well be, simply, that the object has never existed.
But to make such an admission, after so summary a search,
would hardly be in the spirit of the quest. Moreover,
Diodorus's statement will have to be explained. If it does not
correspond to fact, then it must presumably have corre-
sponded to myth. Someone at some stage must in that case
have invented a honeycomb and attributed it to Daedalus.
The difficulties are as formidable in this as in the other
interpretation, for a golden honeycomb, alien to Greek
religious rites, is the most unlikely object to have found its
way into a legend unless there had been some basis for it
in reality. No, a denial of the treasure's existence is not a
satisfactory solution to the problem.

But the fact that the treasure cannot apparently be found at Erice does not mean that it is not somewhere to be found. Erice had been the great national shrine of the island until Roman times: when the cult of Aphrodite was superseded by Christianity, the mountain town lost its pre-eminence. It became a place of pilgrimage without pilgrims, and even its own population drifted down into the valley and across the island. No doubt, when the old religions were being stamped out, one of the townsmen, perhaps a priest of the dying cult, secretly took with him the temple treasure—not abroad, for in the days when the Roman Empire was crumbling piracy forbade a sea voyage, and besides, the honeycomb was a national treasure of high antiquity—but to another less obvious part of the island. In Sicily there may yet be hidden the treasure sacred to Aphrodite. But where? There seem no direct clues to its present hiding place, no thread through a labyrinth of time and place which Daedalus himself might have constructed. About the honeycomb nothing more is known, but about its maker Diodorus provides further information. Among the works executed by Daedalus the historian mentions a fortress which he built for King Cocalus at Camicus, the strongest of any in Sicily and altogether impregnable. Here Cocalus established his residence and stored his treasure.

A study of this place may well reveal more about Daedalus and throw light on the honeycomb of Erice. The difficulty is that the site of Camicus is still unidentified. Diodorus says that it is in the territory of Acragas, and it is possible that the present town of Agrigento, which stands high on a hill, may occupy the site of Camicus. Whether or not this is so, a visit to the town, which in Greek times was among the richest and most flourishing in the whole known world, and with which Daedalus's name is associated, seems to be the most likely way of pursuing the search. Its beliefs in early Greek times can have developed little since Daedalus's day (for at that epoch intellectual advance was still painfully slow), so that by exploring primitive forms, by entering into the spirit of its religion and art, it may be possible to recapture some of the sights and sounds, some of the beliefs and customs which Daedalus, if he lived, must doubtless have known. To discover his world will be one stage on the road towards discovering the man himself.

CHAPTER THREE

Agrigento

THE little town of Agrigento looks across a valley of almond blossom to the acropolis of Acragas, the most magnificent and beautiful, according to Pindar, of all the Greek cities of Sicily. Along the line of a hill the temple columns, of yellow sandstone, stand out against the sea, a silent violet-strewn plain some three miles away. If the history of mountains can be deciphered in their different layers of stones, so too can the history of cities. The ruined temples and sanctuaries, the graves and churches, mark the rise and fall of Acragas as articulately as any history book. Her great buildings, and especially her great religious buildings, reveal the quality of the city's spirit and her degree of refinement as surely now as when they were first erected.

Even before the Greeks founded their colony, the gods were worshipped in primitive fashion. Beneath the ruins of the city walls at the eastern extremity, the ground falls away in a precipice of sheer rock. At the bottom of this, in the cliff itself, the early inhabitants of the place, Sicels, built a sanctuary to their corn-goddess. It is a dark and barbarous chapel, dedicated to the worship of earth and water in their immediate forms, and represents the next stage after Erice in the development of Sicilian religion. A long, thin, rectangular building serves as a vestibule to the sanctuary, which is composed of two long passages in the rock, the walls of which were originally hung with lamps and vases and busts of the deities who came to be known as Demeter and Persephone. From the right-hand passage terracotta pipes draw off the water into a channel which runs through the vestibule into a great system of inter-connecting stone containers, of massive construction. In this sanctuary the peasants bowed down and abased themselves before the forces of nature, the chthonic gods. Here, where the cliff falls sheer and overwhelming, they felt themselves subservient; here, where the cave and passages lead into the darkness of earth, they cringed in terror; here, where earth and water meet, they performed rites which would ensure fertility for their crops.

One of the distinctive features of the sanctuary is the un-importance of the buildings—the vestibule is of the meanest dimensions and huddled close against the rock. It could have held no more than three or four people at one time, shoulder to shoulder. Perhaps a priest officiated here, puri-fying with water those who were allowed to enter the lugu-brious labyrinths in the rock. The imposing square con-tainers, since they are too large to have served merely for washing, probably held water enthroned for adoration. In summer when rain was needed for the crops, nothing seemed more fitting to the peasant than to approach a source of water and importune it to beshower his parched fields. The whole ritual remained at every level a natural one, a worship of Nature, yet it was not thereby deprived of all supernatural elements, for earth and air, sky and sea were at this stage considered divine forces. The cult of the corn-goddess which was spreading across the Mediterranean would have provided a focal point and a myth for that instinctive earth-worship characteristic of uncivilised tribes in this region. The gloomy cave, they believed, was the one through which Aidoneus had stolen Persephone away to the underworld: to recall the spring, Demeter must enter and bring back her daughter to light. The lamps to illumine the dark, sterile rock, and the little heads of the goddess and her child which were left in the sanctuary served as tangible expressions of their hope and at the same time as gifts to the presiding deity. The passages themselves are so low and narrow, so winding and irregular, that they bear more resemblance to huge rabbit warrens than to human constructions. It was not that their architects and engineers could achieve no better building, for the vestibule is methodically constructed from huge blocks of stone and the water conduits are artfully contrived, but rather that just such primitive passages were required of them—a warren through which the peasants could return, crouched double, to the womb, to the great, dark, mysterious earth-mother.

So for centuries the primitive rites might have continued, a religion directly based on man's two fundamental instincts: fear and hunger. In such a society every man was a tiller of the soil: his role was the production of food for himself and his family. Even in a land as rich as Sicily primitive tools and methods made life tenuous, so that leisure, the condition of civilisation, was a physical impossibility. Since there was no time for wonder, art and poetry, music and song were denied to them, and denied, too, were all speculation about the purpose of existence, any Virgilian foreshadowing of the true religion. They might have remained in this static condition for centuries, men of almost infinite potentialities compelled to drag out the lives of beasts. Then the Greeks came and within a generation these people had been raised to a level of civilisation which has never been surpassed.

The colony which settled in Acragas in the sixth century before Christ was sent out by the nearby city of Gela, and consisted of citizens of the island of Rhodes, descendants of those who had founded Gela a century before. Thucydides, from whom nearly all certain knowledge about early Sicily derives, gives exact dates for the various Greek foundations in the island but provides no precise definition of their purpose. From the middle of the eighth century colonies were sent out by the chief cities of Greece and Ionia, perhaps for reasons of trade, perhaps as the first stage in a plan of expansion, perhaps simply because certain citizens were taken by the spirit of adventure. Most likely of all, the colonists were drawn by the rich soil of Sicily. Because Greece has a poor, rocky surface which gives low yields over a small area, this fertility would have made Sicily appear an attractive destination. The Greeks, however, were not the first to be

drawn by the riches of the island. For many centuries after
the coming of Daedalus (if Daedalus can be proved ever to
have come) Myceneans and Phoenicians, those merchants of
the whole Mediterranean, had carried on trade with Sicily, and
after the foundation of Carthage in the ninth century Phoenician settlements were established in the island. But these were
exclusively trading posts, made up of merchants and business-
men; their sole purpose was to buy and sell at a profit. In-
asmuch as they could outwit the Sicels and Sicanians in
commercial transactions, they were a superior people. But in
other respects they represented no advance on the indigenous
races. The Greeks, however, though the occasion of their
coming was the wealth of the country, came not to trade but
to settle, not to swindle but to civilise.

The first Greek foundations had been on the coast, not
only the most easily defensible position, but the one which
provided speediest communication with the mother city.
This filial affection, which was reinforced by and found expression in a multitude of myths, continued for centuries and
was to prove the determining factor in war-time alliances.
Later, when the initial foundations had gained sufficient
strength, they sent out in their turn further colonies. Of these,
Acragas was unusual in having a hill-top site, some distance
from the sea. Nevertheless, the colonists chose for their new
foundation a position of great natural strength, on a plateau
which slopes from a height of over a thousand feet on the
north side to three hundred feet on the south, entirely surrounded by more or less steep cliffs and, beyond, by rivers.

At the south side stand the Greek temples, five of them
still existing in whole or in part, most belonging to the fifth
century. This row of buildings, each one consecrated to a
different divinity, bears witness to one of the most remarkable features of that Greek religion which now took possession of Sicily: its multiplicity of gods. The pantheon was
made up of primitive forces and pagan idols, nymphs and
maenads, demigods and heroes, assimilated without pattern
from countries all over the eastern Mediterranean. Local

divinities were given Greek names, and the goddess of Erice now became known as Aphrodite. No order harmonised the myths pertaining to the various deities, yet this did not seem to perplex a people renowned for their methodical minds. There was little except their immortality to distinguish them from men, and they were certainly lacking in omnipotence, yet they were all unreservedly addressed as gods. Part of the explanation lies in the fact that the Greek divinities were gods of the imagination, created by man. By now he had got the better of his surroundings; he was lord of the world, capable of indefinite progress; what more natural than that he should gradually re-create the primitive forces of nature as gods in his own image, indiscriminately and as many as he wished. They satisfied the imagination and, partially, the growing pride of the people, but they did not altogether satisfy that part of the personality which demands a mysterious, an infinite quality in its deity. For this reason, the Orphic rites, the Bacchanalian orgies and the cult at Erice continued side by side with the nominal religion. The people still mingled with the temple priestesses; still plunged themselves with wild abandon into frenzied dances at the prospect of a simple ear of corn or bunch of grapes, unveiled in secret ritual. Thus the old religion of earth, similar to that of the Sicels, lived on.

In what way, then, had there been an advance? In one sense it is impossible to speak of an advance towards a revealed religion, but on the natural level it cannot be denied that the Greek contribution represents an important development. It is not that the gods had been taken out of the winding caves and exposed to the sunlight and wind of Mount Olympus, though this is symbolic of what occurred. Rather, the Greeks made the drastic discovery that beauty is a vital element in religion, and that magnificent buildings not only praise by their beauty but can also draw the mind to spiritual, even divine concerns. More important still, the mind was directed, perhaps for the first time, towards fathoming as opposed to worshipping the unseen and eternal. If the

Greeks' purely imaginative endeavour to construct a theology ended in failure, the failure nevertheless stimulated their philosophers to make a purely discursive attempt. That, too, was destined to be an incomplete interpretation, but it carried the intellect as far as it could go on the purely natural level. Thus the forms were gradually elaborated, the words found, the atmosphere adjusted for the crucial, unique intersection of time and eternity. The role of the Greek pantheon was therefore at this stage negative in so far as theology was concerned. Indeed it was perhaps during the Renaissance that the Greek deities found their most ardent worshippers, who saw them for the first time for what they really were: a glorification not of God but of man himself. This was the untold secret of Greek religion: this explained the ease with which heroes became demi-gods, this explained the human weakness of the Olympians, and accounted for the pale and insignificant character of the after-life, a life which because it did not take place in man's world could arouse little enthusiasm.

But from the Greeks themselves, and especially from the early Greeks, all this lay hidden: in the sixth and fifth centuries the gods still had numinous and protective functions. Zeus was still the thunderer and bearer of lightning; Poseidon lord of the seas, and Hera still presided over all the phases of a woman's life. Thus the line of temples at Acragas, to Zeus and Heracles and a host of other gods and goddesses, assured the patronage and protection of the most important members of the pantheon. Each reinforced, rather than opposed, the others. There were also less spiritual motives for such an array of buildings. A city's status could be judged by the number and wealth of her temples: they were a talisman of her treasure, on the crown of the hill visible to all.

Because the temple was so vital and fundamental a feature of the city, it is not surprising that it figures largely in the early history of many colonies. The first two tyrants of Acragas rose to power in connection with the building of temples. Within twelve years of the colony's foundation, the people of the still incomplete city decided to erect a temple to Zeus. The complex undertaking, which even with modern methods and machines would still prove a formidable one, was naturally entrusted to a powerful man controlling a large number of slaves. The money donated by devout citizens was handed over to this contractor, and with it also the city's freedom, for instead of buying building materials he used the sacred money to hire mercenaries and immediately seized power. Thus began the rule of Phalaris of Acragas, most famous of early Sicilian tyrants, whose cruelty became so proverbial that a century later Pindar felt bound to censure it. He was only one of many tyrants, evil and benevolent, who rose to power in the early history of the colonies. Disorganised groups in a strange country, without any stable means of government but the aristocracy of the original settlers, were a natural prey to the ambitions of a single man, and that series of tyrannies which in the mother-country had already given way to democracy now became a feature of Sicily.

The great men of remote antiquity attain immortality in remarkable fashion: their heads are not depicted in sculpture or painting or on coins for future generations to admire or criticise, their sayings are not transcribed, their qualities are not tabulated: instead they are identified with one or more stories which have a universal appeal, stories which may or may not be transmuted into legends, and which are handed down, like the early myths and epics, from mother to son. As with Daedalus so with Phalaris; almost nothing at all is known about him except that he constructed a brazen bull in which he roasted his enemies, their cries of suffering being transformed by the cunning design of the machine to issue forth in sound like the roaring of a bull. That was the one important piece of information the people of Acragas chose to hand down to posterity about their first tyrant: the inessentials were filtered away, and his character epitomised in this one typical story. It is a horrible fashion in which to be immortalised, but since these legends, when they can be verified, usually prove accurate, doubtless the cruelty of Phalaris was revolting enough to merit this fate. The story is in many respects a puzzling one. The first and most obvious difficulty is that Greeks never indulged in torture. Though they might sack cities and sell the women and children into slavery, though they took life indiscriminately on the battlefield, to prolong the sufferings of the dying was considered the mark of a barbarian. Yet Phalaris, to have become tyrant of a Greek city, must have been Greek. Perhaps, coming from Rhodes, he had some Persian blood, or had been given an opportunity of studying Persian customs. Another puzzling feature is that the instrument of torture should take the form of a bull. Was the whole bloody ritual human sacrifice in the worship of Moloch? The roaring of the bull suggests a feature of worship rather than a refinement designed to satisfy the tyrant's streak of cruelty, yet to have entrusted the building of a temple to someone whose orthodoxy was in doubt would have been unthinkable. So the simple legend becomes a riddle, just as many nursery rhymes do, a starting-point for poetry and monographs by erudite scholars. The fact remains that for fifteen years Phalaris exercised his monstrous tyranny. Whether or not he ever built the temple to Zeus is a matter for speculation; no ruins of such a building remain, and in general Greek tyrants did not hedge their power with religious trappings.

One other detail is known about Phalaris, one which in the circumstances proves significant. The tyrant offered to Athena a bronze krater inscribed with the words "Daedalus gave me as a present to his host Cocalus." Since Phalaris is supposed to have found this bowl when he captured Camicus, about the middle of the sixth century, here is evidence for the existence of a Daedalus of flesh and blood, an artist whose signed works were in existence seven centuries after his death. More encouraging still, if so inconsiderable an object as a krater was preserved over this period, there may well be hope of discovering a work of gold, the property of a goddess.

Acragas did not learn the lesson of her first tyranny. Less

than a hundred years later a wealthy nobleman, Theron by name, assumed power by exactly the same means as Phalaris. Theron however was a benevolent tyrant and his skill as a general brought Acragas victory and unprecedented wealth in the great war against Carthage. Shortly before 480 the Persians and Carthaginians formed an alliance whereby the Greek world was to be jointly attacked: while Xerxes bridged the Hellespont and marched across Macedonia to attack the cities of the Greek mainland, Hamilcar, using as a pretext the reinstatement of the tyrant of Himera, whom Theron had banished, was to land on the north coast of Sicily. Theron opposed his attack with large forces but suffered an initial defeat. Urgent messages for help were sent to his ally, Gelon of Syracuse, who arrived promptly with reinforcements, and on the same day as Salamis put an end to Persian ambitions in Greece, the Carthaginians were defeated at Himera. As many as 150,000 of their men were killed and Hamilcar took his own life by leaping on to a blazing pyre. It was the proudest day in Greek history: on two fronts the in-numerable barbarian hosts had been routed: for the rest of the fifth century, until the Peloponnesian War broke out, Greece was free to bring her civilisation to fulfilment.

For Acragas the victory meant an increase in fame, wealth and slaves: henceforward she was second only to Syracuse among the cities of Sicily. In the flush of unexpected, total glory an enormous temple to Olympian Zeus was planned and started. A multitude of Carthaginian slaves were set to work quarrying stone and hauling it up to the acropolis, cut-ting and shaping the colossal blocks from which the columns would be constituted, raising them into position with pulleys mounted on wooden scaffolding. It was to be twice the size of Doric temples, a monument worthy of the battle it would commemorate, over a hundred yards in length and half that in width: with the exception of two other buildings, one at Ephesus, the other at Miletus, it would be the most colossal achievement of all Greek architecture, and its style would be unique. So heavy was the superstructure that great caryatids, giant figures over twenty feet high, were set on stone bases between the columns to take part of the weight of the entablature.

One year, five years, ten years passed and still the ropes groaned in the U-shaped grooves of the stone, as block upon block was added to the columns with their cedar-like girth, and the slaves grew sick and old under the weight of work. Building continued, but at a slightly slower rate: it was only a question of time before the roof would be completed. But meanwhile other more pressing affairs had diminished the glory of Himera, and the treasury was called upon to provide money for more essential needs. The proponents of the temple claimed that very soon now it would be completed, but even they had their doubts. They had not envisaged quite such a crushing labour. If it was to be a temple worthy of Olympian Zeus, the great god surely should lend his aid to this titanic work, whereas, on the contrary, he seemed to have turned against his worshippers. Like an infernal machine the great building exacted an increasing toll of human sacrifice: cords broke, obliterating an overseer under a weight of stone; one of the giant caryatids toppled and fell, killing two slaves, and, worse still, this was taken by the rest of the labour force as an ill omen. The cost of building materials rose; interest flagged, doubts began to prevail as to whether the temple would ever be completed. In conception it had been a sort of Tower of Babel: hubris, not homage, had promoted it.

Only a god could have completed a work so superhuman, and without divine assistance the temple did in fact remain uncompleted, only a small portion of the roof being covered over. It satisfied no one except the moralisers of antiquity, who found it a perfect illustration of some of their platitudes. It was from the very start an outlandish monster, a clumsy pterodactyl of enormous dimensions but little strength, and as such it could not survive for long. In a country of frequent earthquakes it did not possess adequate weapons of defence. The earth heaved, and with as little resistance as a

castle of cards, the giants and their intolerable burden, walls
and entablature, ornaments and the partial roof disinte-
grated, flew apart, fell and lay still. The work of decades,
the skill and labour of tens of thousands of men, was undone
in half a minute. So the monster lies today, while little men
from the town of Agrigento dig and probe among the skeleton, dwarfed even by the minor bones. In the centre of the
temple area, among the foundations which delve twenty feet
deep, one of the giants lies stretched out in death, his face
worn by time to impassivity. Others were borne away by the
little men to be interred in their local museum; this one alone
lay quiet on the spot where he had fallen.

That beauty is often a function of strength is illustrated by
the building erected immediately after the uncompleted tribute to Zeus. The temple of Lacinian Hera, as it is incor-
rectly named through confusion with a temple dedicated to
the same goddess at Lacinium in Croton, stands at the eastern
end of the acropolis, twenty-five columns and part of the
architrave still erect. Beside it, at the extreme edge of the
hill, are the remains of the altar, a hundred feet long, on
which the blood of countless sheep and bulls was shed to
appease the patron divinity. It was surely dedicated to some
god or goddess of earth or water, for of all the temples it is
most directly in touch with nature, looking over the valley
and river to the hills and sea beyond. This is gentle country,
tamed and softened to man's needs. All along the valley in
February stretch almond trees in blossom, an indefinable
shade between white and rose, like snow at sunrise or sunset,
acting as a link between the dark brown fruitful earth, with
its cactus and olive trees of similar tone, and the pale blue
spring sky. If the almond blossom bridges the difference of
colour, the temple provides a formal connection. Above the
architrave the sky forms a pediment and roof to the ruined
temple; while the stylobate remains completely earthbound,
the fluted columns have in them something of earth and air,
so that they lead on quite naturally to the open sky: they
almost seem built to support it.

The neighbouring temple, similar in style, was the next to be completed, in the middle of that opulent, glorious fifth century. It is called the Temple of Concordia for no other reason than that an inscription to this Roman divinity was found in the vicinity: its original patron is unknown. But the name is imaginatively correct, for of all the Greek temples in Sicily this has the most harmonious lines. The outer structure is complete, having survived like the soul of the city after death. Four steps lead up to the fluted columns, six on the façades, thirteen on the long sides, and further steps precede the cella, each side of which is pierced by twelve arches. This structural alteration was carried out in the sixth century after Christ, when the temple was transformed into a church dedicated to SS. Peter and Paul, but more commonly called S. Gregory of the Turnips, after a Bishop of Agrigento. At the same time the wall between cella and opisthodomos was removed, and the spaces between the columns walled up. For twelve hundred years the temple served the Christian faith until, in 1748, the Prince of Torremuzza, a local nobleman, restored it to its original form.

The building so satisfies the eye that there is no tendency to question the principles underlying its design, which seems the logical, even the unique way in which a building could be conceived. This impression derives partly from the fact that the temple exactly serves its purpose without going beyond it, partly from artful contrivance: the space, for instance, between the columns varies in order to provide, at a distance, the effect of uniformity. The Temple of Concordia is inevitable as an Aristotelian syllogism, yet lilting as a Pindaric ode: it alone stands complete in a row of ruins, the ideal to which all the other, more earthly buildings are trying to attain.

This triumph of temples along the crest of the acropolis is more eloquent of the greatness and riches of Acragas than all the stories of her wealthy men. They endorse the saying that while her people gave themselves to pleasure as if they would die tomorrow, they built as though they would live for ever. Through the greater part of the fifth century her twenty thousand citizens cultivated the graces and refinements of life, games and hunting, poetry and art, while as many as two hundred thousand slaves, the bulk of them descendants of those captured at Himera, made possible a calm and carefree existence.

Of the great cities of Sicily, only Acragas remained neutral during the war between Athens and Syracuse. By nature she was not militant and she had an additional reason in this case for refusing to participate against the invader: Syracuse was her rival as the leading city of the island: should Syracuse drive out the Athenians, her hegemony in Sicily would be beyond dispute. So Acragas anxiously looked on, hoping that both sides would exhaust themselves in a struggle which would benefit no one but herself. Her wealth continued to increase, not as a trading city, for she had no port, but from the sale of goods manufactured by her slaves. Of these the most famous, the emblems of her luxury, were beds and cushions, which became celebrated throughout the Greek world.

With refinement and abandon she cultivated the delicacies of the table, inventing new sauces and dishes, and preferred, above all other foods, fish—the traditional Greek luxury—especially tunny and lampreys, sea-urchins and eels. One of her citizens—a certain Gellias—built himself a wine cellar: three hundred jars, each holding a hundred amphorae, were cut out of the rock, and these jars were fed from a great pool which held as many as a thousand more. Here and there in Greek literature, wherever a particular instance of luxury is cited, the setting is usually Acragas. In the gymnasium, the utensils were of gold; noble girls built costly tombs for their favourite song-birds; at weddings the guests were numbered by thousands. The greatest extravagance was reserved for those who brought fame to their city in the Greek games: thus a certain Exainetus who won a race at Olympia was welcomed home by three hundred chariots, drawn by milk-white steeds. Because this opulent life was unchallenged, either from within or without, for two generations, it declined into sheer luxury for the sake of luxury; the citizens became soft and undisciplined. At Athens, the only other contemporary city comparable in wealth, the ever-present danger of attack and the frequent sacrifice of the flower of her manhood disciplined and mortified any tendency towards indulgence or softness. Thus, when danger threatened and finally struck, Acragas was unprepared. A directive of the time decreed that soldiers on watch were not to have more than two pillows or three blankets: such conditions proved that the city was already lost. Moreover, she confided the bulk of her defence to mercenaries and a Spartan general who did not hesitate to accept a bribe from the Carthaginians in exchange for abandoning the city. In 406 the Carthaginians entered Acragas, sacked it outrageously and burned it: the stones of the Temple of Hera still bear traces of this disaster, the yellow sandstone being flushed rose-red where the flames desecrated the holy place.

The city never recovered, and under Byzantine rule declined to such an extent that when the Arabs occupied the island, deeming the Greek site unworthy of settlement or defence, they fortified the present town, in a stronger position on the landward side of the valley. If this was the original Camicus where Daedalus built, no traces of his work or the treasure of Cocalus have been brought to light and the town in its present form is essentially Saracen: tortuous alleyways and steps serving as gutters for the fawn-tiled, sloping roofs rather than as streets. Here the Greek city's life has been continued under another, meaner form, with no more slaves to build on a colossal scale, no golden utensils, no gymnasium, no milk-white steeds, no vast wine-cellars: all that is part of the wild and glorious past, and the little old town is content to look across the almond blossom at the silhouetted temples, symbols of youth, and in February, when the blossom is at its best, to cross the valley coloured like mother-of-pearl and dance on the bare stone floors, among the broken columns. That annual commemoration, together with the sending of a few labourers to turn up the past in the Temple of Zeus, are Agrigento's only gestures towards its former self, made neither in deference nor with regret, but simply because the golden days of youth are too magnificent to be quite forgotten.

Yet the glory of the Greek city is preserved once and for all time in another form of art besides that of her temples. In the odes of Pindar the heroes of Acragas still win their Olympian victories, still move gracefully in a world of ivory and gold. Though not a native Sicilian, this poet sang of the island and above all of Acragas better than anyone has done before or since.

Pindar was a poet who glorified men willing and wealthy enough to patronise him. In the new aristocratic society of his day such men were not as in Homer's time warrior princes but victors in the Olympic games, founders of cities and astute statesmen. Occasionally soldiers of exceptional renown, like Gelon, tyrant of Syracuse and victor of Himera, might be lauded by the poets, but the virtues of peace, not war, were the typical subject of the age. Pindar, by force of circumstance, was pledged to that interstellar space which lay between an Olympic victor's ancestors and the gods themselves: his task was to extend his subject's family history back through the centuries until it merged with an appropriate deity. In one sense, therefore, Pindar was a poetical propagandist, his purpose to stabilise by myth-making a comparatively recent aristocracy. He fulfilled this task in supreme fashion. Hieron, who had been successful several times in the Olympic games, was extolled as lord of Syracuse, founder of Etna, mild towards his citizens and without envy towards the good, in language of beaten gold as convoluted as a cup by Benvenuto Cellini. Reading Pindar's odes, no one would suspect that this tyrant razed Greek cities to the ground, used an espionage system at Syracuse and as an individual was depraved, greedy, and cruel.

Pindar, it is already clear, was possessed of a remarkable imagination: of all poets he is the supreme idealist. The coarsest material is grist to his mill: emerging as fine and fanciful fable. But it is not to be supposed that in singing odes to despicable tyrants he deliberately compromised himself. On the contrary, he considered his office one of sacred dignity and did not fail to moralise when occasion offered. Rather, Pindar was so completely a poet, so in thrall to his imagination which, by bold metaphor and similes drawn from every sphere of activity, glorified what to the uninspired might seem most ordinary, that the less pleasant aspects of tyranny were transcended in the splendour of the whole poem. His piety to the gods was outstanding in an age of devout religion: he believed that from the gods are all means of human excellence, and therefore by celebrating human virtue and achievement he was indirectly performing a religious rite. In Pindar's time, therefore the poet possessed both a religious and a political function, and, in addition, his social position was assured by the patronage of men of wealth and influence. These circumstances were reflected in poetry charged at all points with religious and social significance. The individual man, the aristocrat, Nature's pride was its subject, for he controlled the destiny of an entire city: he stood only a little lower than the gods: in fact, as history and legend showed, the blood of heroes ran in his veins: let him display mildness and wise judgment in his rule, qualities to match his physical strength and beauty.

"It was not idly, Pindar, that the swarm of bees fashioned the honeycomb about thy tender lips." A poet of the Greek Anthology wrote these words under Pindar's portrait, and they can be matched by many other passages in which the Muses and the bees bring the gift of song to mankind. Theocritus, for instance, in one of his idylls, mentions a goatherd, Comatas, who devoutly served the Muses and used to offer them his master's goats. His master to punish him shut him up in a cedar chest, but the bees came and fed him with honey, and when at the end of a year the master opened the chest, he found Comatas alive.

There is only one close parallel to this symbolism: in northern countries the gifts of song and prophecy are said to be imparted by the honey-drink, mead. But there the connecting idea is the exaltation felt after taking a fermented drink, whereas in Greek literature the symbolism is probably based on the "sweetness" of the poet's words. Yet that idea could have been conveyed merely by calling his words, as Homer does, "honey-sweet." The truth seems to be more elaborate. The Greeks knew more about poetry than any people before or since: when they describe the Muses sending their bees to a poet's mouth and producing there a dripping honeycomb, they clearly intend that as an exact analogy of the poetic process. They mean that the poet is, first and foremost, a man inspired, and since his inspiration comes from the Muses, who are goddesses, his poetry has a religious quality: it partakes of the absolute. Furthermore, honey is the food of the gods, and the poet, tasting the Muses' honey when he composes, feels himself divine, and indeed, through his song, may achieve immortality.

The symbolism extends even further. Just as bees form honey from flowers, so the poet makes his song from the beauty around him and above all from natural beauty. He casts it in symmetrical pattern, and in Greek times the basic form was the six-stress line, to which the hexagonal cells of a honeycomb clearly correspond. Again, the comb designates the wax tablets on which the Greek poets inscribed their honey-sweet verses.

Did Daedalus, in offering his golden honeycomb to Aphrodite, intend his gift as a representation of the art of poetry? There can be no certain answer, but the fact that the honeycomb possessed this symbolic significance for the Greeks, and for Diodorus too, suggests that Daedalus may have been offering all art, from sculpture to poetry, as a gift to the goddess.

Agrigento has shown that the original artefact may possess a wider significance. Apart from Pindar's odes and the inscription on the krater dedicated by Phalaris, the town has no further clues to offer. But there remains another town, Selinunte, the Greek Selinus, with which Daedalus's name is associated—in that territory he is said to have designed thermal baths—and a visit there may throw brighter light on the man and the myth.

CHAPTER FOUR

Selinus

ON THE south coast, within sight of Africa, lies scattered what might be the wreckage of an ancient fleet, blanched by the sun, eroded by the sea air. With the fragmented, fluted shells and intricate seaweed, the birds with broken wings and cork floats lost from fishing-nets, the larger ruin is united in death: it too seems to have been pulverised by the waves which now lap, a stone's throw away, so placidly and lazily under the unmasked sun. The wreckage is not strewn haphazardly, but heaped in two extensive graveyards: there has been a certain order even about the act of annihilation. One group lies on a slight eminence directly at the sea's edge; the other half a mile away to the east, a short distance inland. There is neither mountain nor tree to stand sentinel over the place of destruction—all the surrounding country is flat enough to be a continuation of the sea—but the sky itself, ampler here than anywhere else in the island and loftier, too, so intense is the light, acts both as shroud and tombstone to the ruins and, when the sun is at the meridian, as a consuming pyre. The extent of the remains is as vast as the devastation is complete. On all sides, as though in the whole world's cemetery, the grey-white debris, levelled like cut hay, stretches across the original valley of death.

These desolate ruins—since there is no visible proof the fact must be taken on trust—constitute the last remaining vestiges of Selinus, once a thriving city of many thousand inhabitants. This silent wilderness was one of the great Greek colonies of Sicily, a bustling commercial metropolis possessing four ports, and as a maritime power second only to Syracuse. Being the most westerly of the Greek cities it was an important trading centre especially with Carthage, towards whom it preserved good relations until, urged on by Segesta, Selinus's commercial rival, Hannibal was induced to destroy the city with great slaughter at the end of the fifth century. (This general is unrelated to the celebrated Hannibal who later fought against Rome in the Second Punic War; the name, meaning "Grace of Baal," was common among the Carthaginians.) The wealth and size of Selinus are attested in death by the large number of temples—seven in all—which constitute the extensive ruins. Since in only two cases are the patron deities known, each is designated by a letter of the alphabet: a curious arrangement in which science has got the better of art, and unnecessary, for even in death each building has an individual character. The eastern group is composed of three temples, a wide collection of gigantic stones among which not a single column remains standing. The buildings have been subject to a systematic destruction such as can be accomplished only by natural means: the earth swallowed these magnificent works of art and regurgitated them in the form of broken, intractable bones, between which grow marguerites, occasional *selinon*, the golden parsley which gave its name to the city, and agave, its tall stem vertical against the sky, mocking the fragmented fallen columns.

Temple G, among Sicilian buildings exceeded in size only by the temple of Zeus at Acragas, underwent the most spectacular death. Spread-eagled drums, some fluted, others smooth, have smashed against each other and crumbled like sea-shells; the monolithic capitals, constituting a small fraction of the total mass, are almost as large as a circus ring; columns have the girth of a castle tower. Fragments of the architrave rear up like the hull of a sinking vessel and the smaller fragments of stone would serve as the foundation for a palace. It is no wonder the temple was a hundred and fifty years in course of construction—archaic and classical styles can be detected in the various sections—yet, like most such buildings, never completed. Close to the master lie buried the servants.

While the ruins of Temple F, an archaic construction, have been devoured by dog and bird of prey, so that only joints and minor limbs remain, the neighbouring building, Temple E, is well preserved. Like a wedding-cake which has melted under the sun, it has toppled in a line, to constitute on the ground a bas-relief of its former self. It belongs to the fifth century and shows the Doric style at its best, the metopes, now in the museum at Palermo, being amongst the finest in existence.

Of these metopes the most consummate shows Heracles in combat with the Amazon. The demi-god draped in a tiger's skin, the head of which lolls back behind his own, is lunging obliquely at the Amazon's helmet, his left foot covering her right to prevent escape. In a complementary bas-relief of dogs attacking Actaeon, similar diagonal lines, this time sloping the other way, again suggest the intensity of the conflict. The artist has achieved that well-defined, vigorous movement necessary in sculptures which are to be viewed from a considerable distance. Yet action did not preclude subtlety of expression. In the metope depicting Zeus and Hera, the god is seated leaning backwards, his face eager with passion, his right arm outstretched, grasping the goddess by the wrist, while Hera stands beside him absolutely impassive, her garments neatly pleated, the personification of sulky fire.

To appreciate the excellence of these metopes they should be compared with the sculptures, a century earlier in date, taken from Temple C, in the western group of ruins at Selinus. Here the figures are still static: the breath of life has not yet blown through them. In a bas-relief of Heracles holding two dwarfs upside down by the hair, the hero's body is too long for his neck and head, which have been ingenuously compressed to fit the allotted space, while in the representation of Perseus decapitating the Gorgon, the artist's limitations are revealed in the faces, which he was able to depict only staring directly to the front, and the feet, which he could represent only sideways. There is an artificiality of posture, action and expression about these archaic bas-reliefs which is reminiscent of tableaux: they are child's drawings which prepare a way for adult art a century later.

Yet despite their crudity they are well in advance of their age, and recall Diodorus's remarks that Daedalus first gave statues open eyes and parted legs and outstretched arms. These proofs of a flourishing school of sculpture in an island remote from the mainstream of Greek art suggest that a local school was then in existence which doubtless traced its origin to some more advanced culture. Perhaps that culture was Cretan, and the connecting link a historical Daedalus: as yet these can be little more than guesses.

Temple C, with forty-two columns, was the largest of the temples on the acropolis. Under its fallen pillars lie buried several houses of a Byzantine village of the fifth century after Christ, for following upon its sack by the Carthaginians Selinus decayed and was generally inhabited only by hermits and nomads. The chief interest of this village is that it provides the means of dating the destruction of Selinus. The earthquake which rocked the city to its grave must have occurred after the fifth century but before the time when the Spaniards began to keep regular annals. Twelve columns of this same temple were recently re-erected in a row, crowned by their architrave. In no sense do they detract from the effect of total destruction; on the contrary, by providing an echo of the city's former glory they serve only to accentuate the disaster and present ruin. The remaining temples of the acropolis are separated one from another by wide, straight streets, intersecting at right angles. The careful planning which was lavished on the city's construction evidently did not extend to defensive fortifications; as Hannibal said, after having put sixteen thousand of the city's inhabitants to the sword: "Since the Selinuntines do not know how to defend their liberty, they deserve to become slaves."

When the past triumphs of Selinus are known, its works of sculpture viewed and its streets frequented, the full magnitude of the destruction becomes evident. Neither fire nor pillage nor decay could so utterly annihilate: earth and sea alone are capable of overthrowing buildings conceived on such a grand scale and constructed with such titanic materials, until not one of the megalithic blocks is left upon another. This city, which for the Selinuntines as for the Greeks was not a mere place of habitation, but a work of art and beauty to house citizens as the body houses the soul, should have been treated less wantonly, or at least veiled in its shame. As it is, the outrage, the total destruction lie revealed, now, as for centuries past, uneffaced by the activity of a later age.

Selinus yields no evidence of Daedalus's work or even of his existence. The gigantic stones which, piled high and at random like a child's blocks, once constituted the temple pillars, are now overthrown and in some cases pulverised. The harbours are silted up, the site harrowed by earthquake. What hope could there be of finding an artist's imprint here where everything bears the stamp of disaster? Even the metopes, safely in the Palermo museum, provide only the slightest clue to the riddle of Daedalus: as for the ungarnered ruins, they merely gape at the inquirer with an empty, desolate stare.

Yet perhaps, after all, the toppled town does hold a solution, not in the ruins, but in its situation and its own name. Selinus means the place where the *selinon* flourishes. Here and there, scattered across the fields which formerly were streets and temple precincts flowers the wild celery which the Greeks gave as an emblem to the city. Its stout, furrowed stem bears greenish-white flowers between large, smooth, pinnate leaves. The clue perhaps lies in its botanical name, *apium graveolens*, the strong-scented flower of the bees. Soon, now, when the flowers are fully opened, bees will come down from the hills to fertilise the only survivors of the ruined city, and in doing so obtain their by-product of honey.

Bee-keeping is an art usually unknown to primitive people and Homer, for instance, is acquainted only with wild bees. Yet in the heyday of Cretan civilisation bee-keeping was practised, and the bee appears to have played an important part in the island's religious ritual. Some of the earliest Greek myths about bees and honey, which were probably indigenous to Crete, are those connected with the Mother-goddess Rhea and the birth of her son Zeus, who was concealed in a cave full of sacred bees which fed him on honey. The ancients believed that bees were born spontaneously from the decaying flesh of oxen, and in Crete, where the bull had a religious significance, honey was probably considered a sacred substance, and the bee seems to have been a royal emblem.

In classical times Sicily was famed for its honey and it is not unlikely, therefore, that bee-keeping was introduced from Crete to Sicily at an early date, perhaps by a historical figure named Daedalus. Such a supposition would demand a new and more high-handed approach to the problem of the golden honeycomb.

In the first place, its artificial nature would mean no more than that it had been formed regularly by bees in a man-made hive, as opposed to the usual wild honey stolen perilously from rock or tree-trunk. To a people unacquainted with the art it might well have seemed that the bee-keeper himself made the symmetrical object which he withdrew from the hive like a masterpiece from his workshop. The honeycomb was then offered to the great goddess of the island. Honey was a sacred substance; in Cretan rites it was probably offered to the Earth-mother; what more natural than that Daedalus, a Cretan, should have continued this time-honoured ceremony in the country of his exile? The occasion would have represented a unique and memorable innovation in Sicilian religion, the sort of event which finds its way into oral tradition. Diodorus's story, translated from mythological to factual terms, means simply that Daedalus introduced bee-keeping to Sicily and offered hive-honey, in Cretan fashion, to the local goddess. The masterpiece in gold was simply a poetic description of something else: to seek it would be as absurd as to try to locate the gates of heaven.

Yet such an explanation, however recondite, does not in

the last resort prove satisfying or convince. First and most important, it does not fulfil an instinctive preference for the concrete rather than the abstract. Wistaria, caught for an instant on a hot day both as scent and perceptible waves rebounding from a sun-lit wall, spells happiness better than a library of dusty volumes on the subject. Diodorus spoke of a honeycomb fashioned in gold: to be fobbed off with the introduction of a new industry is to lose the honey and retain only the wax. Explanations of the unverifiable can claim acceptance only by satisfying completely and at all levels: this particular explanation fails to meet the expectations aroused by Diodorus's text.

Secondly, bee-keeping does not seem to tally with Daedalus's other activities. As an artist and craftsman, his role is to imitate nature, but only by circumventing and thwarting natural processes. Nature is the artist's enemy, not his ally. Daedalus moreover is a technician and engineer— he is said to have invented carpentry and the masts and yards of boats—but he is never conceived as a countryman, whereas bee-keeping is a highly skilled work which demands, before everything, familiarity with a particular part of the country, its seasons, flowers, hiding-places, and also the habits of the insect in its wild state. Furthermore there is no good reason why an innovation such as bee-raising should not have been transmitted as such, instead of being recorded under the cryptic form of allegory and attached to the name of a man famed for totally different achievements.

The best way to disprove any such interpretation will be to find Daedalus's original work of art. The search must continue, but along what lines? Only one other work by Daedalus in Sicily is mentioned by Diodorus, a reservoir near Megara Iblea on the east coast, of which no trace remains. The thread attached to the artist's name has come to an end: for a while the passage through Sicily will have to be random and intuitive. Erice had been the point of departure: only one other place in the island bears any similarity to Aphrodite's shrine: Taormina, Erice's twin, on the east coast, within sight of Etna. This town, perhaps by contrast, perhaps by a negative quality, may give Erice a new significance, and even if it does not, can, as well as any other place, disclose the country of Daedalus's adoption and open up a path to the treasure.

CHAPTER FIVE

Taormina

THE brow of Taormina is wreathed by its theatre. Even if certain evidence from other sources were lacking, the position alone of the building would attest a Hellenistic origin. Where the other Greek theatres of Sicily—all works of the classical period—are sited towards one particularly far-reaching view, usually of the sea or mountains, the theatre of Taormina is on all sides deluged to distraction with multiple beauty. Nor is it only the extent of the surroundings which amazes: the land- and sea-scapes have a rare, closely-worked quality as though specially designed to please a fastidious and highly discriminating eye, tired of all that is obvious. This theatre was sited by connoisseurs, by descendants of a long line of artists so trained in the subtleties of scenery that only the most elaborate and ornate views could any longer satisfy. The theatre of Segesta faces the bare mountains and looks beyond to the sea: in its straightforward, unmannered way the view is unsurpassable. The theatre of Taormina takes the same subject and, like a court poet elaborating a folk ballad, refines it out of all recognition. Straight lines are retained only in the case of Etna, the central point of the background, and this mountain, with its snow and smoke and ever-moving veil of clouds, is already touched with exoticism. The other peaks lie inland to the right, so that their naturally bizarre shapes are seen obliquely: jagged, acute, multiple peaks, some crowned with a cluster of houses, others standing sentinel with a superimposed castle. Not only their form but their texture also has this baroque appearance. Here there are no smooth-grained hills of uniform colour: instead a complex foundation of spurs and re-entrants, of trees and cultivated

ground, of vines in terraces and groves of citrus fruit, in
which green appears in every conceivable shade; as on the
palette of a painter trying in vain to find exactly the right
colour for leaf or hill. In such a variety of shape, surface and
shade the eye loses its way—and that was the intention of the
designers: to bewilder with excess of subtlety.

The same principles determined its position in regard to
the water. Whereas at the theatre of Syracuse, where the
view is centred on the Mediterranean, the sea lies at a mile's
distance, no more than a suggestion, a prosaic line without
vivid appeal, at Taormina the theatre rises sheer out of the
sea to preside over an audience of waves. Like a seagull it
hovers, poised half-way between two elements—the ever-
changing pattern and colour of the water harmonising with
the multiple texture of the adjacent countryside. This tension between earth and sea finds its expression in the smoul-
dering, uncertain pyramid of Etna, which occupies the centre
of the stage, a peak which leads naturally to the third element in the panorama—the Sicilian sky. In spring this provides the variations necessary to show the other scenery to
advantage: long periods of intense sunshine alternate with
cloudy adagios to produce an irregular pattern of light and
shade on land and sea, accentuating their complex, florid
texture. The wind, too, at this season is variable and sets
itself to confuse and elaborate the strong prevailing current
northwards towards the Straits of Messina.

If the theatre dominates the town, the southern hills, and
even Etna itself, it is in turn dominated by the peaks lying
immediately to the west, foremost along which is Monte
Tauro, with its acute-angled summit surmounted by the
ruined castle. This again is an advantage, for an altogether
omnivident view, like a canvas entirely suffused with light
would tend to surfeit the eye. As it is, the towering peaks
accentuate the lofty position of the theatre, place it, and lend
a secretive quality to a landscape which otherwise might seem
too forthright. It is not for nothing that a semaphore has been
established within a stone's throw of the theatre: this is the

most outstanding position in a range renowned for its many
vantage-points. For not only does the view extend without
interruption south and east: it also stretches north, behind
the theatre, completing the circle and revealing the place as
a kind of earthly observatory.

The view northwards is perhaps the most richly endowed
of all. The mountains continue close to the sea in a succession of ridges and valleys as far as the island itself, while out
of the haze which hangs about the horizon emerges the hill-
topped coast of Calabria. In certain lights this coast appears a
mirage, so that one can look at it indefinitely without being
quite sure whether or not it is a construction of sunlight and
clouds. Were the coast a little farther distant, it would be
altogether invisible except on the clearest of days, while,
brought closer, it would lack that ambivalent quality which
makes it fit so well into the scenery of this theatre. The view
has another unique feature. On the fourth mountain to the
north stands another town—Forza d'Agrò—which occupies
a position only a little less dramatic than that of Taormina.
Looking across, as though in a mirror, at this image of herself, the Greek town reflects on her beauty and rank, her
exalted position and incomparable surroundings, and not
without reason yields to self-admiration.

If the choice of site is Greek, the theatre itself is Roman.
The thin, brown bricks and mortar, the arches that have
crumbled, the grandiosity which covered up shoddy workmanship—all these features are the antithesis of Greek art,
so that the actual construction apart from its view fails to
commemorate the original founders. To accommodate the
masses, arches, on which were erected tiers of wooden seats,
were built round the circumference of the Greek structure,
fitted into the natural slope of the mountain, and on either
side of the stage vast parascenia were erected to house the
extraordinary scenic effects which had taken the place of the
actual drama in the audience's favour. As if, in this spot
above all, there were need of wooden painted scenery! These
brick buildings, with their colossal arches, are not in them-

selves unsightly—in fact, their brown terracotta contrasts
well with the prevailing blue and green. Where the Romans
reveal their insensitivity is in the wall which they built across
the diameter of the semicircle, behind the stage. Although
pierced with arches, this effectively destroyed the balance
between sea and mountains, destroyed, in fact, the whole
purpose for which the Greeks had chosen the site. Poor
building contains the seeds of its own decay, and fortunately
the wall is now in ruins, across which the original view is
again visible. Roman columns have been erected in arbitrary
fashion against the ruined wall—they were discovered
piecemeal during the nineteenth century—and these serve
to strengthen the otherwise too dilapidated foreground, and
to give a strong upward line to a view which because of its
seemingly limitless extent might tend to flatness and dissolution.

In the theatre one is in a world apart, a world man seems
to have designed in order to forget himself among scenery
which is totally unrelated to that of workaday life. All that
is human in this place of transformation is rendered remote
and insignificant: the houses which creep impertinently up
the slopes of Etna are too minute, from such a height and
distance, to be treated even as dolls' houses; the fishing-boats
which put out from the cove of Mazzaro are idle and incon-
sequential as miniature water-beetles. In such a theatre the
Olympian gods might have been imagined watching mortal
men engaged in their love-affairs and wars, intervening occasionally to take pity or inflict punishment: spectators who
could take a hand in the performance, or rather puppet-
masters who could manipulate men's lives not in any arbitrary fashion but according to a story written by the Fates.
The sounds and disturbances of the lower world can no more
rise to this auditorium than a fountain with its loftiest jets
can extinguish the stars: the sound of voices sharp-edged in
quarrel, of suffering, of catastrophe, dissolve impotently in
mid-air before they attain these heights. At night more than
ever a world apart, when in the centre of the semicircular

orchestra the heavens form a diadem of constellations about one's head, and the theatre itself seems to have an existence separate from that of the earth, to become one of the innumerable stars. A world apart, where beauty instead of being trampled on is conserved and honoured, where the contemplation of beauty is still deemed not a luxury but a necessity. A world apart, existing in another order of time. The ruined arches and columns which frame the view southwards are the battered rind to fruit which still grows in the garden of Eden. The columns which stand in a row supporting a void, the arches which upheave their half-circle of stones with no apparent reason, the deep T-shaped pit which once gave birth to scenic marvels, all these being now without purpose or urgency in their own right, serve to show off the timeless character of the picture they frame. A world apart, at the intersection of time. Southwards lies the past, in the shape of Etna, still giving form to matter, the world still being created, under the appearance of white-hot lava lying on the mountain slopes, cooling in the Sicilian sun. The theatre itself is the present moment, having no existence in itself: merely the sum of its memories and expectations. Northwards, emerging out of the sky and sea, still precise and idealised, is the future, the coast of Calabria. A world apart, where every thought is touched with the physical characteristics of the place, to participate in the sublime, the ideal, the eternal. The theatre embraces the summit of purely natural beauty, a less remote but more constant half-moon, under whose influence all things human are transcended.

If the theatre belongs to an ideal order, the castle of Monte Tauro, which provides the other magnificent view of Taormina, is so much a part of the terrestrial world that it seems a natural rather than a human construction, and if the theatre takes a poetical view of reality, the castle is altogether precise, military and practical. It has occupied the dominant feature of the surrounding country in accordance with text-book strategy and surveys the approaches to its town from a well-nigh inaccessible position. The building is polygonal in shape, following the contours of the mountain crest, which falls steeply away: directly to the sea on every side but the west, where, after an interval of lower ground, the country again rises to mountains. Monte Tauro is arrow-shaped and the castle is its prey, a bird pierced to the heart, fallen directly on the apex of the sharp formation of rock. It is in every respect a shattered, tumbled thing, its grey stone walls reduced from their former strength and glory to piles of rubble, its towers toppled, its rooms unroofed. It has outlived the days of usefulness: now in its dotage, amid dreams of past battles, it is tolerated, and, worst humiliation of all, daily attacked and captured. North of the ruined V-shaped wall which once protected the vulnerable escarpment at one side of the castle, a zigzag path leads up to the ruins. Near the summit stands a sanctuary dedicated to the Madonna della Rocca, built partly into the mountain-side, for here as elsewhere throughout the island overwhelming natural beauty coupled with a powerful position is deemed hallowed ground. Those who pass this way pick wild flowers, marigolds, campions, marguerites, speedwells, and place them in crannies in the doorway as an offering, so that the chapel at first seems abandoned to nature. So high is this spot that the town below, which itself can claim to command half the Mediterranean, seems built in a deep valley. The occasional sounds of cocks crowing, schoolboys at play, mules braying, fail to animate the rooftops and towers of the town, which gives less the impression of activity than does the mountain-side.

Here all is frantic with spring. Through the faint green foliage of the almond-trees finches and pipits are darting in frenzied love-play, the hens playing at fleeing the cocks, not to escape but simply that there may be a chase; from the crannies of walls scurry lizards, as though spontaneously generated by the heat, their eyes like the jewels in a watch; swallowtail butterflies, their black markings on yellow wings the original pattern for lava and limestone mouldings which are such a feature on the medieval buildings of the town, move to a less urgent rhythm, fluttering like miniature kites in a failing wind. The wild flowers which fill every corner of the landscape undulate slowly in the breeze to the dance of spring, while insects of a thousand kinds and shapes thread the blossoms together according to a pre-arranged labyrinthine pattern. Amid all these rearrangements and renovations the main colours and lines of the landscape (since olives and cypresses are the dominant trees) show little change from winter. There is here none of the sudden green of thrusting buds which makes deciduous trees the very emblem of a northern spring: the change is one of light and shade rather than of colour and line: cypresses put on more uncompromising mourning and alchemist olives add silver to that mixing bowl in which every shade of green has a place; while the change of season in sea and sky is less marked even than in the landscape: their blues become perhaps more than ever interchangeable.

The crucial sign of Sicilian spring is one invisible alike to eye and ear: a sudden, steadily increasing surge of heat. The sun which has never been absent for long all through the winter and on some propitious days has shone uninterruptedly from deep azure skies, like a rocket which suddenly bursts a second time to add golden stars to blue, now gives warmth as well as light. This is a signal for the beginning of the dance, which from the very first assumes such a tempo that it seems the dancer will fall down exhausted before the spectacle is complete. Where in less prodigal countries wild flowers as a special grace are scattered here and there in favoured spots, in this island they are lavished by the meadowful in colours which, were the blossoms less numerous, might clash or appear gaudy but which, in fact, by their very profusion harmonise with the general spirit of opulence. Under the balconies of the town below house-martins build at a prodigious rate, darting backwards and forwards from the nearby fountain with pebbles and pellets of mud, forming an inverted dome of caked clay round their own breasts, choosing invariably the most shaded spot as protection from sunshine which already in this season might crack the mud walls. These birds go to their work methodically and infallibly as master-masons, yet many of them did not even exist a year ago. Without faltering or delaying a moment they lay pebble upon pebble to construct a nest identical with those made by their parents and ancestors, and with those, built at a less urgent rate, in northern countries. If the variety of the wild flowers is astonishing, this uniformity is even more so. In the frenzy and abandon of this southern dance, animal instinct is handed on like a magic baton from one line of partners to the next without ever being dropped or distorted, without ever becoming worn or frayed. That would be less extraordinary were not the constituent parts so complex and intangible, composed of innumerable little graceful actions and flights, each one as remarkable an achievement as the semi-annual marathon migration. The performance is so complicated and extended, the artist so delicate and untutored: it is as though a child prodigy were executing flawlessly and at sight a continuous recital of all the Beethoven sonatas.

The rebuilding which the house-martins are accomplishing in this fashion is taking place across the whole island, and the activity which seems so mammoth on the mountainside of Taormina is being repeated and magnified throughout Sicily. In the fashioning of flowers even the foundations of the island participate: the very rock brings forth a blossom, walls become trellises of wistaria, balconies trail carnations and begonias, steep stairways soften their flight with pots of geraniums. For the towns, too, take part in the rebirth. If the Sicilian people experience none of the northerner's amazement that the world has been re-created out of darkness and deathly cold in a fresh beauty, they give spring as excited a welcome, for winter was never a season to which, like the northerner, they could grow accustomed: no fires, no comfortable homes, no woollen clothing to break the edge of frost and rain, no indoor amusements to while away the long winter evenings. These people have their home in the open air, in the streets or in the fields, and during the first days of spring they return, after a period of exile, to their home. Thus spring, which in colder countries is looked upon as extraordinary and even miraculous, is here treated as an event which in every sense of the word is quite natural. There is consequently no popular bewilderment or awe: the people take up their song where they left it off in late autumn, the young men once more gather round the baroque fountain in the cathedral square to tease pretty girls as they pass, and when darkness falls to make love.

Only at night does Taormina assume a particular existence of its own, for as long as the sun shines it is merely a *nid de pie*, a vantage-point from which vistas radiate in every direction. During the hours of light the town, like a painter, becomes the beauty it regards so intensely and with such mastery: at night it recollects itself and tries to find a meaning for the memories of the day. The flowers on balconies and walls, denied their display of colour, make up for the loss with intensified perfume which permeates the streets and alleyways and flights of steps, giving each a particular identity, so that the traveller can find his way about the town merely by recognising the pattern of the varied scents. Night, too, softens the blatant lines and dulls the showy colours of those buildings which make the town a resort, leaving the medieval palaces to receive the admiration which is their due. For Taormina achieved greatness only after the Norman conquest. It was originally a late Greek foundation for long a vassal of Syracuse, so extensive was the power of the island's capital city, but like those other mountain strongholds, Erice and Enna, it became powerful and wealthy in the Middle Ages, when warfare had reached a stage at which the rock-built fortress was the dominant military factor.

Despite such buildings as the small cathedral and the Palazzo Corvaia, with its courtyard graced by an external staircase, the town remains essentially a vantage-point of natural beauty and of the distant mountain which smokes ominously on the horizon. From Taormina one is drawn naturally there, from the world of ideas to the world of flux and brute matter, by its immense and compelling size and also because all these surrounding towns have taken their origin, at one time or another, from its inextinguishable fire.

CHAPTER SIX

Etna

ETNA is less a single mountain than a whole planet. While Fujiyama, for instance, has been the subject of many paintings, so that in a sense it stands as a figure not only of Japan but of the country's art, Etna never has and probably never will be adequately depicted: one cannot paint a whole new world. Yet of all mountains in Europe it is one of the most renowned: for centuries it has been the great Mediterranean bonfire, a lighthouse to sailors from Phoenicia and Spain, from Crete and Corsica, a symbol of safety and disaster.

The mountain does not stand alone, as so many extinct volcanoes do—mere monuments posing to be admired—but hunts with a whole pack of lesser monsters, their jaws foaming. The whole volcanic mass is, to change metaphor, a military fortress, connected by underground tunnels. Mt. Etna is the highest tower, guarded by a network of subsidiary forts, some dangerous, others ruined; some named—Mt. Leone, Mt. Gemmellaro; others christened—Mt. S. Leo, Mt. S. Maria; others nameless, but none the less formidable for that. The perimeter of the whole military system measures some hundred and fifty miles, and the slope is correspondingly gentle. The ascent is unsensational, considering the mountain's great height: orange groves give way reluctantly to cherry and apple trees, and these in turn to oaks and beeches, which once entirely covered the middle reaches of the mountain but are now sparsely sprinkled. Higher still lies the desert, lava too overwhelming for anyone to clear and pile into neat walls, lava in boulders, fragments, slabs, waves; brute matter, prime substance devoid of all shape and even of all colour, for this dark grey does not merit such a name.

It might seem to be a petrified sea of lava, yet a sea has form, while this nameless stuff has refused all shape. If that ὕλη, dear to the Greek philosophers, could ever be pictured, it would surely be as lava, lying on the extreme verge of nothingness. Here it rises in the shape of a crater, there it falls in a valley, like grey, useless slag; solidified in monstrous chunks, and broken into particles. This, then, is the beginning of everything: this is the world still in creation, this is the underlying enduring substance—cold grey lumps of molten rock, formless as ghosts, crushing as millstones, and all the rest, brown earth, green grass, even the rugged mountains which at one time seemed so forbidding and shapeless but which now appear almost graceful, are mere superficial ornaments which conceal the essential horror. For this scene is horrible—brute, devoid of vegetation or flower, of any animal or human trace whatever—it might be a meteor, it might be the moon. Such a grey wilderness was not designed for men, or is it true that the whole world was once like this before mankind softened and humanised it, giving it a tolerable, inhabitable form? Were the poets of nature, the singers of flower and tree and the beauties of Mother Earth, to look beneath the surface, at the lava of Etna, at the basis of living things, they would be as shocked as a lover confronted with the skeleton of his mistress.

Higher still, above the snowline, the formation assumes an even more unearthly aspect. Drifts of snow, like the white pain on a clown's face, stretch along the mountain-side: within the extinct craters it is heaped high, while the steep verges are black and bare. Not long ago the snow on Etna used to be the principal source of revenue for the Bishop of Catania, in the days when Etna furnished snow and ice not only to the whole island of Sicily but also to Malta and a great part of Italy. Even the peasants in the eighteenth century used to regale themselves with ices in the summer, and the nobles declared that a famine of snow would be more grievous than a famine of either corn or wine. Now it is scorned and allowed to lie side by side with the lava, close to the smoking cone, its surface grey with dust from the volcanoes and with fine particles of embers. From a height of two thousand metres these alternating patches of snow and lava, dotted with minor volcanoes, stretch as far as a perimeter of clouds, which stand like the outer wall of the great fortress, cutting it off from sea and plain. Yet only fifteen miles away, beneath the line of clouds, lies Catania, its network of streets and buildings defenceless as an open city. Fifteen miles is a formidable distance for a huge rock to be hurled, yet Etna has twice in recorded history sent down those fifteen miles such a tremendous torrent of lava as to destroy the city to the last house.

This thought, taken with the authentic descriptions by the Greek poets, gives such a vivid image of the volcano's power that, when one stands on the summit, among the ashes and smoke and gases, the whole rite of eruption is, as it were, enacted. First, like the noisy clanging of scenery from peace to war during the interval of a play, rumblings and subterranean thunder, accompanied by minor earthquakes, a process which may continue for a few days or for whole months at a time. Then, suddenly, a fissure while the throat of the monster fills with murderous foam, and hot ashes are ejected like sighting shots. From the depths of the volcano, accompanied by red shooting flames and smoke, the torrent of molten lava, many million tons of boiling rock, is thrown up to the sky like a new comet, to fall in a wide curve far down the mountain slopes, until an entire white-hot ocean is soon coursing down the incline, slowly but relentlessly, crushing with weight and heat all things, animate or inanimate, which lie in its path. Grass, trees, woods, houses, the least flower with the tallest oak, single house and entire city alike are as though they had never existed—annihilated under the glowing mass. From deluge, from flood, from mere fire there might be some means of escape, some way of resisting and surviving, but this hot, molten stream, which combines the terrors of water, fire, earth, and air, is irresistible—there is nothing to do but to fall down, petrified, and

die. It is a terrestrial rite of purification, a primitive process
of nature which takes no account of man and which man
cannot harness or humanise. Significantly, the Greeks, who
made out of many mountains divinities in human shape,
never deified Etna: it was always the slumbering monster,
the great unpredictable force which seemed to deny man a
right to the earth.

The inexhaustible volcano has remained active through the
centuries, drawing round its outer works a great crowd of
worshippers. The south-eastern slopes are among the most
thickly populated regions in the world—such is the power
of the unknown, the attraction of the catastrophic, and also
the fertilising effect of lava. Along the rich lower slopes row
upon row of vines and fruit trees rise, like an opium dream
out of smoke, from the black soot which is the earth, for this
ugly dark soil is, paradoxically, among the richest in all
Sicily. The wine from these vineyards has a special mineral
flavour, coming from a level deeper than the roots of the vine,
with magical properties, like a love potion compounded by a
wizard. The people in these parts live royally off the refuse
of the monster, but their grey squalid landscape resembles a
rubbish dump. Farther up the slope the houses disappear, but
close to the summit, incorporating that *casa degli Inglesi*
built in 1811 by amateur scientists among the English naval
forces occupying the island, stands the observatory, a minute
encrustation where little men patiently watch the monster's
moods. Here they compile statistics and relevant facts, fill-
ing over the years many thick volumes concerning the temper
of the beast, its exhalations and rumblings, its effusions and
and explosions. Here, close to the wide fatal mouth, they
attempt, scientifically and methodically, to predict the unpredictable, to catch with their subtle nets the last surviving
relic of an age when man went in awe of nature. They have
measured the monster's height and found it two hundred
feet lower than a century ago, while the present depth of the
crater has been computed at some six hundred feet: meanwhile minor eruptions continue, not without casualties. And

still the measurements and calculations proceed in an attempt, as it were, to read the great beast's palm, to foretell its destiny.

This concern to know the monster by means of its physical characteristics, to bring it within the compass of human understanding, even eventually to control it, is as old as the Greeks. Close to the observatory stands a tower of rocks of primitive construction, designated the Philosopher's Tower, where Empedocles of Acragas is said to have lived while studying the volcano. But he was too dangerous because too wise an observer—a philosopher as well as a scientist, who already knew that the world was composed of atoms—and the monster, alarmed for its secret, one day effortlessly swallowed him. Brydone, always anxious to introduce extraordinary scientific theories into his book of travels, did not fail to draw conclusions from his ascent of Etna. The pure and refined air on mountain tops, so he believed, allows the mind and spirit to act with greater freedom. This fact, however, did not prevent him from falling on the ice and spraining his leg, so that he had to stumble his way back with the assistance of friends. A few years after Brydone's visit, an Englishman was lowered down the crater by cords and not surprisingly "immediately lost all his faculties," while in 1805 a certain Monsieur de Foresta climbed down and, covered with fire and ashes—exposed, to use his own expression, to the discharges of a formidable artillery—he had the courage to observe the sublime spectacle for three-quarters of an hour. Fifty years later Miss E. Lowe, as she records in that book of travel which almost lives up to its title—*Unprotected Females in Sicily, Calabria, and on the top of Mount Aetna*—removed her petticoats one by one as she climbed the volcano on foot. Her mother, who accompanied her, wore gutta-percha goloshes, but the snow got inside, and she does not recommend them. So, down the centuries, men and women have approached a trifle ridiculously, paid homage, and departed without solving the riddle of Etna. Modern explorations are less adventurous and colourful, and discoveries tend to be made not by personal observation, but at the desk, by correlating different groups of figures. Meanwhile, the dragon, scornful as ever, stirs in uneasy sleep, surrounded by the wreckage of past eruptions, and at any moment may awaken in fire-breathing fury, to scatter more cities with a single sweep of its tail.

All around its vast perimeter, here in lava which has not yet cooled, there in the streets of Catania and the cathedral apse, built out of the mountain's molten rock, are vestiges of previous eruptions, and among the most striking of such memorials are three large, pointed rocks lying in a row offshore at Aci Castello, between Taormina and Catania, in the region imortalised by Verga.

These rocks are called Scogli dei Ciclopi, because they are said to be the very ones thrown by Polyphemus and described in the *Odyssey*. In the Homeric poems the Cyclopes are a gigantic, insolent, and lawless race of shepherds, who lived in Sicily and devoured human beings. They had no political institutions and each lived with his wives and children in a cave on a mountain crest, reigning over them with arbitrary power. Polyphemus, the principal among them, is described as having only one eye, in the centre of his forehead, a giant who was not like any man that lives by bread, but like a wooded peak of the towering hills, which stand out apart and alone from others.

Homer describes how Odysseus, with a company of men, lands in Sicily and visits the cave of Polyphemus, only to be taken captive. Some of the party are eaten by the Cyclops, who makes it known that they will all sooner or later suffer the same fate. That night the prisoners cut an enormous club of olive wood, heat the point until it is glowing and thrust it into the Cyclops's single eye, while he is sleeping. Blinded and maddened with pain, the giant casts the club from him and calls for help, but Odysseus and his surviving companions hide and later make good their escape. Once on board their ship, and drawing off from shore, Odysseus shouts taunts at Polyphemus, who, in an attempt to sink the ship, breaks off massive rocks from the hill and hurls them in the direction of Odysseus's voice. However, his shots either fall short or overreach the boat, and Odysseus, with his companions, sails away safely to the Aeolian Isles.

The rocks project out of the sea to this day, as Homer described them, just off shore, in a line pointing directly from the peak of Etna. They are of volcanic origin and are totally different in appearance from other off-shore rocks, being lofty, pointed and in one piece: they seem, in fact, to be precisely what Homer says they are, fragments of a mountain-top cast purposefully into the sea. Though Sicily was almost unknown in Homer's day, Greek sailors passing through the Straits of Messina must have noticed these peculiar-shaped rocks and described them to their friends when they returned home.

The story of Polyphemus is clearly a description of Etna in eruption, the natural phenomena being personified, as is the custom of primitive people, and the personification being retained by the poet. Perhaps Homer knew that Sicily possessed a volcano which periodically erupted; perhaps he considered the drama of persons provided a better story. More likely than not he knew the scientific truth yet did not find that knowledge inconsistent with a poetical explanation. For the description of Polyphemus seems purposely ambiguous. The characteristics attributed to him—lawlessness, living with his children (the minor cones) in a mountain cave, his single eye which is burnt out, and the fact that he is compared to a wooded peak of the towering hills—are only those which could also apply to a volcano. Polyphemus is not merely a giant, he is a giant and also Mount Etna, just as for children a pile of blocks can be both blocks and castle at the same time, without any inconsistency. At the imaginative level the blocks are a castle; and that, for children, is more important than their real essence.

Explanations are satisfactory accounts of the unknown in terms of the known. The story of Polyphemus provided Homer and his listeners with an account of what took place

on Mount Etna, even down to such details as the purposeful
line of off-shore rocks—an account which satisfied people
accustomed to view the world in terms of adventure stories,
human conflict, battles and imprisonment. A technical
description of the natural causes underlying a volcanic eruption, even had it been intelligible, would have proved unsatisfactory to men of that age, just as, at the present day, deter-
minism might prove unacceptable to a novelist because he
knows it would drain his works of all suspense.

The Romans, materially more advanced, found one or two
details of Homer's story unacceptable. They regarded the
Cyclopes no longer as shepherds but as the assistants of
Hephaestus, under whose direction they fashioned armour
and ornaments for the gods and heroes, working with such
energy that Sicily and the neighbouring islands resounded
with their hammering. The story has been elaborated to
provide an account which will better satisfy a people more
familiar with the working of metal than were the men of
Homer's day. Similarly, the modern inquirer, possessing a
far more complete pattern of scientific knowledge, seeks an
explanation for the line of volcanic rocks in terms of a sub-
marine eruption of basalt.

But to the searcher for Daedalus, the line of rocks has yet
a fourth story to tell: they are a long-awaited pointer. If
Polyphemus is really Mount Etna and his eye the main
crater, then similar early stories and legends are likely to tell
the truth, but not the literal truth. The legend transmitted
by Diodorus may have to be interpreted as imaginatively as
Homer's; and in that case to be searching for an actual
golden honeycomb it perhaps as naïve as to expect to find a
one-eyed giant on Mount Etna.

By what process is poetic truth melted down or transmuted
into fact? How is it possible to know what Diodorus signified in his account? In the case of the Polyphemus legend,
certain facts, such as the Cyclops's residence in Sicily, nar-
rowed the range of possibilities; then someone with the myth
in mind happened to watch Etna in eruption and, by a pro-

cess exactly comparable to that whereby a poet finds a new and daring metaphor, saw the one in the other and identified the two. Applying that principle to the present myth, the obvious procedure will be to scrutinise Sicily for something which a poet might have imagined or objectified as a honeycomb fashioned of gold. If a tradition relating to such an object was handed down for 1300 years and considered by Diodorus to be worth recording, perhaps, like the myth of Polyphemus, it refers to a permanent not an accidental feature, to something of wide significance. If so, the horizon is unlimited: all Sicily, with its multiple civilisations, will have to be sifted, starting with the earliest known remains. The quest is now no longer for a particular object: instead, the whole island will have to be scanned with the hope of discovering in something, whether person, natural feature, or work of art, the significance of Daedalus and his golden honeycomb.

CHAPTER SEVEN

Carnival

But now it is carnival time in the towns around Mount Etna, and in this week of hectic festivities before Ash Wednesday all work, whether it be olive-tending or a quest through time, must cease. Throughout Sicily the season is being celebrated, but nowhere more frantically than in the shadow of Etna, as though many of the towns remembered still the days of their destruction by fire and were intent at once on compensation and forestalling. Carnival time, the season when meat is put away—not that many of the peasants or townsfolk can afford the price of meat—but the word signifies a farewell to luxury in general. Lent is an austere dam extending for a ninth part of the year, on either side of which, at carnival time and Easter, the flood tides are released in a great pent-up, canalised surge of joy; not at the return of spring, for that suggests a gap between nature and the objective on-looker, but joy which is the seasonal flowering of people attuned to a natural rhythm. Carnival time, with its dressing up and dancing and singing, is the human equivalent of what takes place among flower, grass and bird: lacking all deliberation or self-consciousness, it springs from the vege-table, even the mineral soul.

At Acireale on the slopes of Etna crowds of people from all the country around parade the main streets on Shrove Tuesday, throwing confetti at one another, blowing trumpets, clowning, setting off fireworks, joking, laughing and shouting. Coloured lights decorate the fronts of houses and the piazzas are illuminated, while from the balconies crowds of spectators throw down paper streamers at the passing flood of participants. Here and there small spaces are formed in the crowd to allow a group of masked figures to dance or clown, but apart from these pools the stream of people flows continuously up and down the street and round the piazzas. When twilight falls the parade of carts which the crowds have come to watch moves into the town, down one long street, round the Piazza del Duomo and back by another route. As many as twenty of these fantastic cars form the procession, some pulled by horses or donkeys, others by small trucks, and they move very slowly, stopping every now and again either for admiration or because the crowd will not yield a passage. A few are quite small and simple: one shows a shark swallowing a small girl, another a loathsome green creature, half frog, half humpty-dumpty. But most are massive constructions, built on a platform which runs on wheels, and carrying as many as twenty masked figures, some dancing or joking, others playing musical instruments.

The first to roll slowly into sight shows the Three Musketeers, great, grotesque, drunken figures with swords askew, sitting astride Chianti bottles. Their faces are both awe-inspiring and ridiculously funny, monstrous and clownish, with long red noses and bulging eyes. Their dress like the figures themselves is made from papier mâché, yet in the half-light there seems nothing artificial about either subject or presentation, for that undercurrent of music which comes from the carts themselves steals away all critical sense, so that the rational and absurd become equally acceptable. Next comes a children's playground, with huge overgrown boys and girls see-sawing and riding a roundabout: the animals' heads terrifyingly deformed: the whole tableau decorated in variegated tinsel of riotous colours. Those who are not riding throw streamers at the cars or jump upon the platform beside the monsters to ridicule the musicians with actions and words. No one is a mere spectator: to see a pretty girl is to throw confetti at her, to meet a pompous old man is to steal for a moment his best hat and set it on an unsuspecting head, to come across a friend is to shower him with abuse.

Now a new car rolls into sight. A pukka sahib in tropical

kit is leaning back on cushions somewhere in the jungle, surrounded by his four native wives, two playing the accordion, while one fans him with a palm leaf and another offers him a string of sausages. So debauched he looks, this fat, pink figure, and yet so comical, personifying the impulses underlying the carnival, which reduce man to the level of an animal, but an animal whose every appetite is satisfied. Here is a second car expressing the same theme in a different way: its title is *Sogni Proibiti*, and it is the largest car of all, the one that will eventually be awarded first prize. The background is composed of minarets, in front of which is seated a fat sultan, surrounded by his harem of dancing girls: all these figures are huge papier mâché constructions, vividly coloured in reds and oranges and greens. In the foreground stand real persons, no less gaudy, some dressed in Turkish costume, others wearing animal heads, rife with horns, others playing Oriental music on pipe and drum; one, perfectly expressive of the carnival's irrational principle, has no head at all—in its place is a spinning-top. Still another car continues the motif of sensuous abandon. An Indian snake-charmer, with bulging eyes that wobble grotesquely when he moves his head, is holding spell-bound six giant cobras, which sway back and forward to the sound of the magic pipe, keeping time with the vibrating eyes. Last of all comes the archetype: a vast assortment of horned and leering animals, each degraded beneath its natural level, dancing to native African music, behind which, some twenty feet high, tower the head and torso of a man who is even more loathsome than any of the animals, though all are hideous, so that instead of rising above them, as his predominant position might suggest, he is reduced to a level far beneath the pigs and asses who grovel beneath him. He too keeps time to the wild music, not by dancing but by moving his eyebrows, mouth and ears in unison, and as these are all of enormous size, the effect is less burlesque than abomination.

So the procession moves on, a parade of monsters to the rhythm of primitive music, down the long street into the

Piazza del Duomo, turning in front of the cathedral and then retreating to the outskirts. Under the coloured fairy lights the giants are silhouetted against the towers and rose window of the high cathedral façade, making plain the essential point about the whole carnival. It is true that they are primitive forces expressing all that is base and bestial in man, but they are not entirely out of control, they move under the shadow of the cathedral and tomorrow they will be exorcised. Meanwhile, as the sight and sound of the monsters make their impression on the crowd, people become rowdier and more daring in their jokes. Water is squirted on all sides, smoke let loose and the line of people which before has glided along, now rushes like a torrent down the narrow streets. The lesson has been learned: man is a creature of earth, let him satisfy his earthly appetites, let him become a grotesque beast, with bulbous nose and bulging eyes: since the monsters are compelling, irresistible, it is better to yield now, at once. So they troop into the drinking shops where the dark red wine, the earth's blood, lies stored in its round, wooden kegs. Release it, they cry, and it is released, to fire their bodies and in a few minutes to give them final freedom from their inhibitions. Now they move out, masters of the world if not of themselves, and form a dance in the wide piazza, taking as partners strangers or friends, masked or unmasked, men or women, in a primitive alliance of gesture and step, keeping time to the emphatic music of a band. Those who wear fancy dress and masks give themselves up most freely to the moment: they have lost both inner and outer marks of their personality. They offer no resistance to the wine and pulsing music and to the gleam of their partner's white teeth as she smiles boldly across the dance. They have become princes and cowboys, toreadors and clowns, anything but citizens of Acireale. The town itself has become a prehistoric place, a sort of never-never land.

Here is the Marquese di Geraci, a Spanish grandee, once viceroy of the island, with powdered periwig and golden coat, with white stockings and buckled shoes, so handsome, his skin like olive, his black eyes excited, his cheeks dimpled when he laughs. On the other side of the square, caught up in the dance, whirls a little Arab girl, with dark, curly hair falling on a mauve, long-skirted dress. They have glimpsed each other already and not by chance meet in the next dance. During two successive rounds they are partners, but they keep silence, for words are too rational a form of communication. Their eyes and hands, warm from continual movement, tell all they need. With a nod of his head he beckons her now out of the anonymous crowd, and hand in hand they walk down one of the dark alleyways. After a few minutes they find what they want—a cheap *trattoria*—and the Marquis and the little Moorish girl sit down to eat pasta and meat sauce with a large bottle of red wine. But they neither remove their masks nor utter a word—for fear perhaps of recognising one another. The refined Marquis gulps his food, and the little girl drinks more wine than she has ever drunk before. The bottle is finished and replaced by another: soon this too is emptied. With a flourish the viceroy pays· for their meal and they leave, refreshed and with still higher spirits, to join the dance.

By this time the tempo of the music has become faster, while the older couples have grown tired and returned home, leaving the revelry more spirited than ever. The Marquis and the Moorish girl, partners now in all the different rounds, dance alone, oblivious of their surroundings and the rest of the company. They meet and mingle, unconscious that they are giving expression to that medley of blood, that intermarriage of alien ways which characterises their country. Round and round, on and on, hour after hour they dance together until far too soon midnight is struck by the cathedral bell and the dancing comes to an end. But the Marquis and the little Arab girl move to their own music, out through the alleyways into the fields, still without speaking, still without identity, out at last to the earth, under the shadow of Etna, under the spring stars. Darkness falls on Acireale; the fairy lights have been extinguished; confetti and streamers cover the empty streets like a fall of snow, the music, the drunken shouts, the joking—all are annihilated.

At dawn, a grey, sunless dawn, the crowing cock cracks sleep, and the young dreamer who last night was sandalled and masked wakes to a bare narrow room. She rubs her eyes: where now is her Marquis, where the music of the carnival, where the spell she thought would last a lifetime? Again the cathedral bell tolls, but now with a different note. She jumps up from bed and runs to the window: already old women are making for the church door along the littered streets. Ash Wednesday—she had forgotten. She will go out and receive the ashes. As she dons her black clothes, she sees her pretty fancy dress crumpled on the floor—out of place now, a memory. She joins the congregation in the bare stone cathedral and goes up with the others to be marked with the burnt palms. On this child's curls—the little boy would boast later that he had received more than his friends; on this old woman's head—dust to dust, ashes to ashes. Beside them kneels the carnival girl: *Memento, homo, quia pulvis es, et in pulverem reverteris.* The carnival had ended; after the fire only the ashes remained; the dark earth spirits, last night's monsters, had returned to the soil, to the ashen soil of Etna, and with them her passion and its dusty memory. The grotesque devils were exorcised: the people of Acireale and the little Arab girl were again at peace with themselves and with the earth.

CHAPTER EIGHT

The Sicilians

THE pattern of daily life is once more resumed, in Acireale as in all the other towns of Sicily. Many of the inhabitants here are petty landowners, with small-holdings high up above the town worked not by themselves but by poorly paid serfs. At dawn, here as in every centre across the island, the labourers set off on their mules and donkeys for the mountain slopes, where they spend their day hoeing beans and peas, harvesting oranges or olives, mowing hay with a scythe or reaping corn.

Meanwhile the petty landowner occupies himself not with improving methods or even with extending his holding, but with the far more pressing business of enjoying life, of talking and arguing, of acting the man of leisure among leisured friends. In these small Sicilian towns leisure is attested by a man's pyjamas: the longer he wears them in the morning, the higher his status. That the significance is purely symbolic is shown by the fact that the jacket may just as well be worn over ordinary trousers, or that in the afternoon a man may exchange his shirt for the pyjama top before starting to read his paper.

When the sun climbs higher, he goes out to one of the mirrored *saloni*, where company provides him with the opportunity of a long wait and many-sided conversation before his turn comes to be shaved. This is followed by coffee in tiny cups and more talk in torrents until the hour strikes for the mid-day meal and sleep. In the late afternoon, if there is no wedding or funeral to provide diversion, he sets himself to business, that is to say, enters a further stage of some barter or transaction which will last several weeks before final agreement is reached. As evening comes down, the day's work being finished both for master and servant, he watches the labourers plod slowly back to town, their beasts so heavily laden on either side with produce that each forms a trinity. Tomorrow smallholder and serf will repeat the performance, with minor variations.

This way of life has been variously attributed to the climate, to malnutrition, or to innate carelessness, but none of these interpretations bears scrutiny. Vigour and self-development are found among the tribes of tropical Africa, and in any case the weather in Sicily for three-quarters of the year is no hotter than in Southern France or the deep South of the United States. As for the second alternative, if the average working woman can continue feeding her child at the breast for as long as fifteen months after birth, there can be little cause for speaking of dietary deficiency. Furthermore, that carelessness is not a natural Sicilian failing is proved by the attention lavished on personal apparance and clothes, by the methodical care given to children. No, the true explanation of the Sicilian attitude of *dolce far niente* lies deeper than any of these interpretations—in a personal choice of one particular way of life in preference to any other. The root assumption is that life itself is more valuable than any end to which it can serve as a means. The journey is more important than the destination, and a journey without any destination is best of all, for then one can look out of the window without interruption, eat caramels and continue talking heedless of time or space. To want to arrive in general, and, even more, to want to reach a particular destination, would already entail incompleteness and dissatisfaction —a turning away from the present moment. To take action in order to attain a nearby goal is *a fortiori* undesirable. Since the present moment is of paramount importance, it can on no account be bartered—for no matter how many golden hours in the future. The future is uncertain—the history of Sicily, a series of wars, eruptions and earthquakes, has proved it so —and even unreal, an abstract conception which in Sicilian scales can never outweigh the passing hour, however petty, drab, and meaningless that may appear to the impartial observer. Lack of purpose in life is itself exalted into a kind of purpose, and lack of action into a mode of action. Just as in countries where people are generally ambitious and bent on self-advancement, an obstacle in their path—illness or any other factor which disturbs or impedes their work—is considered catastrophic, in Sicily, the reverse is true, so that all useful employment which detracts from watching the pageant of life is something to be avoided, while on the other hand all that contributes to rest and conversation is diligently fostered and stimulated by every possible means.

In the towns only men parade: the women are almost invariably at home attending to their children. Where physical charms are highly prized, it is natural that the women, as soon as child-bearing has spoiled their early prettiness, should lose their attraction for their husbands. It is the men who retain their looks for a much longer period, and match them with elegant clothes: in this country the cock birds sport the finer plumage and are admired accordingly. Whereas the women are dressed plainly and soberly, young men and old vie to keep up with the fashion, careless of all expense.

Since women in Sicily outnumber men by a considerable margin, the male has become the more valued of the sexes. He is at a premium and is able to take advantage of this fact on every occasion. Thus the woman is continually occupied in her house during the day, looking after her children, making order in the single family room, cooking and washing. Apart from the agricultural labourers, none of the men does an equivalent amount of work. Since self-advancement and ambition are not Sicilian characteristics, the man's aim in life is to perform the least possible amount of labour commensurate with a bare subsistence level. Moreover, since wives are too occupied to indulge in endless talk, the men flock together: they pass most of the day conversing in the streets, looking at newspapers and illustrated magazines, discussing politics, watching the girls pass by. Their faces, expressive of each nuance of emotion without check or disguise, are as variable as the waters of a mill-stream. Yet, five centuries ago, a great painter caught once and for all time this multiple character of the Sicilian face.

The portrait of an unknown man by Antonello da Messina is a late work, painted when the artist was forty. It hangs now in Cefalù museum. In technique it shows the influence of Van Eyck and Fouquet, but apart from its intrinsic merit as a work of art it is profoundly interesting because it reveals how little the Sicilian physiognomy has changed in the five hundred years since the portrait was painted. Apart from an increase of Spanish blood, chiefly among the nobles, all the main racial characteristics had been assimilated and fused in Antonello's time, and his picture might represent any one of countless Sicilians living today. The head and top of the breast are shown from three-quarters, in great detail, against a dark background. Low over his forehead the man is wearing a black, brimless hat, beneath which, at the nape, can just be distinguished a mass of dark, curly hair. The face is fat, with a two days' beard, and the neck thick; small, very alert dark eyes are looking crossways at the spectator. The eyelids fall low over the eyes, the sides of which are wrinkled, and wrinkles, too, mark the corners of the mouth, which is wide and thick-lipped. The one ear which is visible is unusually small, with a suggestion of deformity, but since it lies in deep shadow this cannot be verified. The rather thick nose is straight and rounded at the end. The man is wearing black clothes turned back at the neck to reveal a white lining and white shirt, immaculately clean. He is a Sicilian countryman, a peasant: that much is evident, but his character Antonello has declined immediately to reveal.

The artist's most brilliant stroke has been almost entirely to hide the brow under the dark hat, which is indistinguishable from the background, thus centring attention on eyes, nose and mouth. But this barbarously low brow, which robs the head of intelligence, appears contradicted by the sharp expression of the eyes, which, peering obliquely, reveal a malicious glint. The nose and mouth reaffirm coarseness and stupidity, but the smiling lips once again betray a contradiction, for they lack the eyes' purposeful intent. This subtle balancing of opposites constitutes Antonello's mastery: the quality which gives his paintings a perennial interest. No matter how familiar one is with his portraits, they continually surprise by this unresolved complexity. The subtlety of his brushwork, which holds back essential details in the shade, almost out of sight, is the technical counterpart of that psychological insight which uncovers the conflicting elements in a peasant's face, sensuousness and simplicity, laughter and robust self-interest. To these he has added another typically Sicilian trait: the subject seems to be in communication with at least one other person. He is laughing at someone else's joke, and in turn preparing his own: one can imagine the hands gesticulating, or clasping a friend's shoulders.

This suggestion of others in a portrait of a single man shows how well Antonello understood the essential character of his countrymen. For the basic Sicilian unit is not the individual but the group, and for this reason all life is public life. Everything that is, is known, and everything that is known is communicated, immediately and in its entirety, by word of mouth and gesture to the family and the community as a whole. Not only is the Sicilian always in company; he is also physically linked to the other members of his group, as though he formed one of a party of mountaineers, for whom isolation spelt disaster. Solitude is emptiness, stagnation; only in the constantly changing stream of human intercourse are reality and enjoyment to be found. If there is no news to impart, provoke an argument or start a scuffle; if there are no friends to be found, address a stranger; if there is not even a stranger, the only recourse is to sleep. Just as there is no clearly defined division between work and play, between the hours of employment and leisure, so that all action seems to glide slowly and agreeably along on an undercurrent of amusement, in the same way there is no marked division between the hours of sleep and waking. During the hot months, night is the only tolerable period, and the laughter, singing and general commotion, checked by the heat of the day, finds expression under the stars, while much of the afternoon is spent in sleep. Thus, at three o'clock in the morning it is natural for a Sicilian confectioner to discover that his caramels are the most succulent in the world and equally natural for him to shout this news at the pitch of his voice all round the town. Sleep, too, is taken in short snatches, like gulps of water when the sun is intolerably hot —in doorways, on an empty cart, wherever a little shade suggests oblivion. More often, sitting on benches or on the pavement in the sun, men relapse into a form of semi-drowsiness, neither sleep nor waking, in which life can be enjoyed quite passively and coloured with dreams. Certainly there is no appreciable difference between the rhythms of Sicilian night and day. All through the hours of darkness the animated conversation continues, at an even intenser rate as though breeding by night; carts transfer their loads; vendors prepare their wares for early morning; and the young men who are in love break into song. The angelus which strikes at dawn from the cathedral towers is like the sounding of eight bells on board ship—a division of a continuous cycle rather than the beginning of an absolutely new period of time.

Perhaps as an expression of their communal nature, all Sicilians are, to a greater or lesser extent, traders, whose chief principle is that the price of goods is not an objective, absolute quality, but a variable figure imposed according to mood, need, weather, and other circumstances. Here man is still master of the goods he offers for sale: he is not merely a passive link in an exchange of articles each with a price predetermined by officials. The way is left open both for generosity and rapacity. The vendor is always able to believe he possesses the former virtue, for the opening price he demands is invariably fantastic—a daydreamer's price, far higher than the object is worth and very often two or three times its actual value. By thus showing how exceedingly he treasures his goods, he appears generous in offering them for sale at all, and even more open-handed in selling them, as he always does, at a price far below the first he quoted. But this is not the only pleasure which a vendor enjoys during a transaction. The actual dispute over prices is an occasion for displaying that rhetoric and repertoire of facial expressions and gestures in which all Sicilians delight, a sign language which an increasing complexity of dialects consequent upon foreign invasion may originally have necessitated. The salesman becomes the leading actor in his own play, his shop a theatre, the passers-by an appreciative audience. Moreover, the long duration of each particular bargain is able to compensate for the fact that only a few customers present themselves in the course of a day: they must therefore be played carefully and subtly to provide the greatest amount of amusement commensurate with suitable profit.

The Sicilian sense of humour is best described as Aristophanic, earthy and bordering on the gross. It is comedy of persons and situations, never of manners or wit. Anxiety and pomposity—in fact almost any form of seriousness—are its favourite targets, but it treats them spontaneously and without venom. It is the precise opposite of that sudden spasmodic preoccupation with the grotesque and monstrous which characterises countries where the people are not naturally gay. In Sicily laughter is never silent; night and day it bubbles up like a spring, providing an undercurrent of rippling sound which softens and transmutes all hostile elements. The grand no less than the mean, exceptional beauty as well as exceptional ugliness, sanctity and immorality, liberality and thieving, and above all an unsmiling face—these, because they represent a challenge to society, are laughter's sources.

The most exact definition of the structure of Sicilian society would be that it constitutes a benevolent paedocracy: a society in which children hold the dominant power. They are the final cause of almost everything; towards them most actions tend; being most loved, they are most powerful. No single characteristic of the people is more striking than their affection for children. It extends to all classes, to both sexes and to people of every age. Nor is it merely a family affair: all children, no matter whose, receive fervent and immediate tenderness as an inalienable right. A wealthy and respectable man, should he see a woman in the street carrying a baby insufficiently wrapped, will at once, as a matter of course, go up to her and himself put matters right. If a baby starts to cry, it is the duty of everyone within sound to rally to amuse it. If strangers with a child enter a house, it is the child who receives the first welcome and attention. But within the family this affection naturally assumes its most intense form. A mother spends every moment of the day in taking care of her children. She continues to feed her baby at the breast for well over a year, although meanwhile she herself is eating little more than bread, pasta, fruit, and cheese. As it grows older, she is continually amusing it, never on any account leaving it alone for a moment, while the care lavished on its clothes is in inverse proportion to that spent on her own wardrobe. Babies and children, even in comparatively poor homes, are well washed and dressed in neat, clean clothes, while their parents may be wearing patched and repatched rags.

These are the material signs of great affection, which in the intangibles of domestic life becomes even more evident. In the home it is neither the mother nor the father who is the dominant figure, but the children, not because the parents feel a sense of duty towards them or wish purposely to sacrifice themselves for the next generation, but because children are wholeheartedly loved in and for themselves. They are loved for their innocence, their gaiety, their helplessness, but most of all for their pretty faces. In a country where life is soon worn out, where the period of flowering is pathetically short, youth and beauty are prized above all other goods. Women begin to lose their beauty at the age of twenty-two or three and by the time they are thirty, having given birth to perhaps seven children, are so occupied with their family that they have no time to care for their appearance. Thus children usurp the position of honour accorded to beauty, which in other countries is generally occupied by women. They receive the tributes and affection which a pretty smile always evokes, and in a correspondingly greater degree as beauty is seen to be fleeting. As for the children's gaiety, it provides the chief amusement within the family. Whenever parents stay home together, a relatively rare event, it is usually in order to play with the children. The amusement extends to both sides, for if the chief purpose is to make the child happy, success sets the adults laughing. It is never clear who precisely plays the part of the toy, nor is the father any less adept at fondling and amusing than the mother. The single room which constitutes the home is before all else a nursery, where the adults kneel in adoration.

The effect of all this attention on the children themselves is not noticeably bad. Since they are not nervous by nature, they develop without precocity or complexes, and since they have no toys, since limited space restricts their freedom, and because of the large families, there is no danger that they grow spoiled. The admiration they receive as children, however, is the cause of that supreme self-confidence which marks the Sicilians, a quality which often tends to degenerate into self-complacency. This same admiration of children is perhaps also responsible for the great respect accorded to innocence and purity, the distinctive virtues of childhood, and for that satisfaction with a handsome appearance and new clothes felt by so many Sicilian men. As for the women, their inbred love of children is satisfied in child-bearing. In a country so prodigal of sunshine and where the standard of living is so low, the sacrifice involved in providing for a child is not very great, and is more than compensated for by the joy it brings the parents and relatives. If there are already older children in the family, these adopt the new child, again not out of duty but because they enjoy it. This co-operation is absolutely necessary in a country where it is not unusual for a mother to have to look after a family of as many as fourteen or fifteen. No sight is more characteristic or more engaging than that of a very small boy caring for his younger brother, amusing him when he is cross and teaching him first not to talk but to gesticulate.

The consequences of such large families are overpopulation within the island and widespread emigration, chiefly to South America, the United States and Australia. One member of a family will save sufficient money for his passage and, once arrived in the new country, will begin to put aside his earnings, so that within a few years he is able to bring his family from Sicily to join him. The effect of overcrowding on the island itself is that schools are swamped, educational progress hampered and primitive habits perpetuated. Shopkeepers even in the large towns can count only with difficulty and make mistakes in the simplest sums. Reading is a labour seldom indulged in, and when unavoidable is accomplished slowly, the words being articulated one by one. Not that the people are naturally dull or stupid: on the contrary, they are sharp and observant and in many ways clever, but it is altogether an outward cleverness, an astuteness of perception rather than an intellectual quality. It is part of their pattern of life, which treats existence, the mere fact of existence, as an end in itself. The physical enjoyment of life requires not great intelligence but quick sensations and to this end an alert response is stimulated by continual companionship and incessant talking. Only the shepherds in Sicily are ever alone: the rest of the population are always in company, usually parading the streets or, since the houses are inadequate, sitting at a *caffè*. It is a civic life, a life of talk and laughter which always takes place out of doors, and this fact is itself a reflection of the external and extrovert quality of the people. People in the streets, people continually passing, people talking and laughing and joking—this is the life of a Sicilian small town. In a country where comparatively little is actually achieved, where action is minimal, a flood of conversation acts to redress the balance. It is a play in which all the countless characters talk simultaneously and interminably, where the lighting is at full blaze against the most beautiful back-drop imaginable, and where nothing ever happens.

Nowhere is this essential inactivity more clearly reflected than in the number of public holidays in Sicily. The island naturally observes all the Italian national holidays, which are numerous, and the great feasts of the Church, which are even more numerous. In addition, the name-days of all local saints are counted as days of rest, together with any other local historical incident worthy of commemoration. All these are regular annual *feste*, which can be counted upon and anticipated. But during the year the number may be considerably increased by local decree. A civic success or disaster will result in cessation of work, either as a holiday or as part of the *lutto cittadino*; and civic elections of whatever nature also bring the town to a standstill. Such are the public *feste*; within the family there are naturally additional holidays to celebrate births and weddings, and days of rest to honour the dead, so that at any given moment during the year it is likely either that the whole town or at least a considerable part of it is observing a holiday. In this way, for all classes of society, always excluding the paid agricultural labourers, who are obliged to work unceasingly, inactivity is if not sanctified, at least regularised.

CHAPTER NINE

Carts and Puppets

EVERY country excels in a traditional native craft, which occasionally rises to the level of a fine art. Not all of these can be related to the surroundings or temperament of the people. Thus, it is not easy to see why the women of Brittany rather than of any other country should make such delicate lace, nor why the Fair Islanders should excel at knitting multi-coloured wools. But the decorated carts of Sicily obviously reflect the temperament and tastes of the people. These carts, which range in size from small hand-carts to horse-drawn wagons, are two-wheeled vehicles with projecting shafts, and straight, low sides and back. Like most native tools and primitive machines which have been elaborated in the course of centuries, they are of excellent technical design and construction, the weight being fairly distributed over the two wheels, so that the man, donkey, or horse is free for hauling. The carts vary greatly in the extent of their decoration, but the most elaborate have carvings on wheels, shafts, sides, front and back, and are painted all over in crude colours traditional and unvarying: red, yellow, blue, and green to symbolise Sicily's oranges, sun, sea, and grass.

In cramped outdoor workshops craftsmen carve the back panels of these carts, talking together all the while, interrupting their own carving and others' in order to joke and play. The piece of wood for the back panel measures three foot by one and is two inches thick. Here on this plank a young man of twenty-six, acknowledged as one of the finest craftsmen in the whole island, is carving a battle scene, comprising five knights in armour, four horses and in the background a medieval fortress. These particular figures are of exceptional fineness and mobility; the horses are strong enough for their riders and yet gracefully executed; the bridles are decorated; the scene, a balanced and ordered whole, leaps to life from the craftsman's glancing blade. This is not always the case, and often the coarse flourishes and bloodshed which distinguish end-panels cover up a lack of art. One of these back sections requires two days to carve, and is sold at a price which ensures the craftsman a very modest livelihood but which is nevertheless far in excess of the mere cost of the wood. Why is it then that in this poor island the ordinary trader and small farmer continue to buy comparatively expensive carved and painted carts? Tradition provides an answer, though an unsatisfactory one: from time immemorial it has always been the dream of a small trader to possess a beautiful cart, and a man's status and taste are to some extent gauged by the decorations on his vehicle. But, at a deeper level, it is their intricate carving and flamboyant colours which have always appealed to Sicilian pride.

During carnival time competitions and parades are held to foster this tradition, the horses wearing cocked plumes, the carts themselves newly painted and decked with flowers. The scenes painted on either the carved or uncarved panels are taken from French and Sicilian history. In many cases they depict Crusaders battling with Saracens or the story of the Sicilian Vespers, and all are distinguished by violent action, gesticulation and bloodshed. These the owner can appreciate, for he is generally not conversant with the historical incidents depicted on his cart; it is the builders, carvers, and painters who hand on the historical episodes from father to son, history in the process dissolving into legend.

Suddenly the carved figures in the panel become alive, move out of their frames and begin battling in earnest. They lunge and parry to the death, their armour gleaming in the sunlight. They call for help and receive it; they run to the rescue of outnumbered companions. The most vital of all battles is being fought for the defence of Christendom against the heathen. Such is the immediate impression upon a visitor to one of the few remaining marionette theatres of Sicily. In shape and colour, in dress and weapons these knights, none more than three feet in height, are identical with the figures on the cart. In fact, the theatre represents the same historical incidents as many of the carvings: the French knights fighting to save Christianity from the Saracen, culminating in the battle of Roncesvalles.

The puppet plays go back to a knightly epic, the *Reali di Francia*, which stems not directly from the *Chansons de Geste* but from an intermediate group of Franco-Italian poems. The whole complicated cycle, which takes thirteen months to present, has something of the quality of the Homeric poems, and the parallel with Greek epic and drama is strengthened by the fact that every member of the audience knows the details of the whole cycle and will correct with great indignation any departure in dress, gesture or incident from the traditional story. Although one would not believe it to look at the spectators—dockers and road labourers and children of the poorest classes—this fact is confirmed by the silence in which they watch the play, attentive to every word and action. The theatre itself is of appropriate size: no more than a large room divided into two sections by an archway. A bicycle hangs on the wall between posters showing scenes from some of the plays, and plain benches give seating accommodation for some sixty people. During the day the room simply forms part of a private house and is used for domestic purposes. The stage itself is of necessity very small, allowing the masters to pass across their puppets from one side to the other without being seen, but the curtain is as grandly and pompously decorated as that of any full-scale theatre, with paintings of battling Crusaders. Beside it children are lounging and playing the fool with the intimacy and informality of young bloods at an Elizabethan inn-yard.

Now the tinkling piano which has been playing continuously falls silent and the curtain rises to show a backcloth of a mill in rolling country, and the rowdy talk ceases at once. The first puppet enters—it is Orlando, hero of the story—to deliver his virtuous lines; everything about him proclaims a lordly miniature. His chief characteristic is his armour, the beaten metal shining for all the world like silver. Visor, helmet, shield, breastplate, gauntlets, and greaves are meticulously and elaborately worked. Plumes on the helmet, skirt round the thighs and the faces themselves distinguish the characters one from another: all these parts are interchangeable so that with only a few coats of armour the innumerable personages of the cycle can be presented, since all the Christian knights appear dressed for battle. The Saracens on the other hand wear no such glorious accoutrements—they are simply rag dolls with turbans: no love has been put into their construction and curiously, while the knights are quite realistic, the Turks, seen from side view, are as thin as the boy in *Struwwelpeter* who would not eat his porridge. Their round faces with wide, grinning mouths are depicted in the same fashion and with the same primitive feeling of hate as the Gorgon's head on the earliest Selinus metope. Since realism is not an adequate style for depicting monsters, the puppet-master has turned to expressionism. But Orlando is declaiming his lines and the spectator must pay attention.

He sets the scene in a long monologue, and although he is alone on the stage for some time there is no lack of action, for he gesticulates appropriately at every phrase, and his armour repeats the expression in its own sonorous way. Indeed, though they derive from French history, these knights move in the tradition of Italian grand opera. Now three comrades-in-arms enter to join Orlando, boasting of their accomplishments and fighting verbally their future battles. Apprised of the large numbers of the latest Saracen army, and of the danger the Christians are in, their bravado disappears and they shrink back in fear. Is there no way of avoiding battle, they ask: traitors, they must die on the spot, and Orlando proceeds to fight and kill them all in turn. These contests, which display the puppet-masters' skill, are conducted with the greatest possible shedding of blood, and form as it were the purple passages which the dialogue merely serves to link together. Only the basic ideas of the speeches are set, so that within a certain framework the puppet-masters can improvise. Now the Saracens launch a sudden attack and when all appears lost Orlando comes to the rescue, takes on innumerable infidels single-handed, slays them all—"Con un colpo della mia spada faccio saltare la testa a cento paladini!" he cries—and saves the day.

The scenes all have this in common: they are short, concise and to the point, full of action, with the outcome continually in the balance. It is not difficult to see why the audience applauds this mixture of declamation and courage. The poor dockers and children are brought up in a living tradition of ardent Christianity and they know what glory attaches to martyrdom. As they watch the miniature knights battling, they themselves become French warriors dying to save Christendom from the Turk. It is glorious to shed blood in a noble cause—and easier than living their faith through long hours of drudgery. It is a joy to kill Saracens on the battlefields of France, it is a joy to swagger and swashbuckle—if they had been fortunate enough to live in another age, in another place, who knows but they too might have fought and won glory? So they troop to the little theatre, night after night, to live another, more adventurous life, and die another, less pitiful death. The proprietor has his own particular clientele who prefer the puppet plays to the cinema, and he claims that the tradition will persist. But the fact remains that a few years ago in Sicily there were three times as many theatres as there are today: the cinema has proved too powerful a rival. It is a commonplace to accept as a regrettable fact that such local traditions will sooner or later yield before the delectations of mass entertainment. Yet every night in this little theatre it seems possible that the spirit of the crusaders may yet gain its way over the shoddy, the base, and the spurious.

Wood-carving and modelling in metal—in these two specifically Sicilian crafts is it too fanciful to see a survival of Daedalus' teaching? Their treatment of medieval subjects is no proof that the tradition of craftsmanship does not go back much further, perhaps to prehistoric times: on the contrary, the persistence of those subjects points to a material as well as thematic continuity. Pindar, in a fragment, speaks of the deftly-wrought donkey-cart as being typical of Sicily: therefore one at least of the crafts flourished as early as the fifth century before Christ.

Many of the authors who describe Daedalus' work mention that he used wood and metal for his statues, not stone. From surviving archaic statuary this is exactly what one would expect of the earliest of all artists, for such materials are easier than stone to fashion and can be modelled with primitive tools. The skill and elaboration with which the Sicilians work them are more than mere peasant craftsmanship and suggest, at some stage or other, the teaching of a master. Surely it is more than a coincidence that the only two native crafts in Sicily which are known to have persisted for centuries are precisely those for which Daedalus was famed and which he is said to have introduced to the island.

If a consideration of the donkey-carts and puppets tends to substantiate Diodorus's story, it also brings out the continuity of Sicilian history, a characteristic confirmed by other evidence, such as the carnival processions and little customs of everyday life. Again and again the externals of Sicilian history take the same pattern of invasion, conquest, and revolution, while the day-to-day life, also, in whatever century, manifests the same traditions and the same skills. A theme from a Greek vase is enacted in the market place today; a prehistoric myth finds expression in a contemporary carnival mask; and Charlemagne's victory is acted out by Daedalean puppets. It would seem that here, at the cross-roads of the Mediterranean, the meeting-place of Africa and Europe, the central point of much of European history, there is a permanence and continuity as at the still centre of a turning wheel. Nothing in this country is ever quite forgotten: the all-pervasive sun allows no object, least of all one of beauty, to become obscured. If for a while it should be lost or destroyed, during a later age it will rise phoenix-like in a blaze of glory. In an island of continual renewal and elaboration of age-old themes, there is every likelihood that what Diodorus called the golden honeycomb of Daedalus, which in his time had endured for 1300 years, survives to the present day. Its form may be transposed, its structure modified according to changing patterns, but so important and sacred an element can hardly have disappeared from the life-stream of this conservative people.

Erice: the twelfth-century Saracen-Norman fortress which encloses the shrine of Aphrodite *(see p. 20)*

Erice: the last surviving traditional shop of its kind, with its distinctive half-door, dates from the twelfth century

Opposite: Erice: one of the winding, patterned, mist-dampened alleyways

Agrigento: the temple of Concordia, built by Greek colonists about
450 B.C. *(see p. 36)*

Temple of Lacinian Hera, fifth century B.C., battered by earthquake
and war *(see p.35)*

Segesta's temple alone with the hills from which it was made

Segesta: graffiti of wind and frost

Segesta: the Greek theatre, fifth century B.C.

Overleaf: Hilltop Taormina's Greek theatre, with Mt Etna in the
background *(see pp.50-1)*

Donkey cart: its side panels depict battling Crusaders and Saracens
(see pp.68-8)

Dramatis personae of a Palermo puppet theatre *(see pp.88-90)*

Christian knights and one of the enemy, from the complicated cycle of puppet plays whose hero is Orlando (see *pp.88-90)*

Mermaid and seamonster add fantasy to the Orlando sequence of plays

Fire and brimstone on Vulcano, the most southerly of the Aeolian Isles
(see pp.94–5)

The nymph Arethusa: (*above*) on a Syracusan tetradrachm; (*below*) her
fountain home amid papyrus, Syracuse *(see pp.104-6)*

The Ear of Dionysus, Syracuse: a ruler's device for hearing the subversive whispers of his prisoners, according to Caravaggio, who visited Sicily in 1588 *(see 114-17)*

The Aeolian Isles

CARNIVAL time is over: Lent has begun. The people who crowded round the volcano to celebrate the return of spring have shown in their own rites a renewal of an age-old pattern. Already the rocks off Aci Castello have suggested that Diodorus's story must be broadly interpreted, and that all Sicily must be scanned for the true correlative of the honey-comb. The Sicilians themselves are proof that the search will not be a vain one, but at what point must it begin? Odysseus, after his encounter with the Cyclops, sailed to the Aeolian Isles, and there are two good reasons for following him there.

In the first place, though falling under Sicilian jurisdic-tion and geographically closely related to the large island, they stand apart; like a group of artists, they belong yet do not belong to the main body. As such, they may afford, by contrast and aloofness, a good vantage-point for assessing the specific qualities of Sicily and its people. Secondly, the Aeolian Islands are all but barren. In Roman times, when Cicero accused Verres, the governor of Sicily, of having exten-ded his crushing rapacity even to these meagre rocks, he goes so far as to describe them by the adjective *jejunus*, which means fasting. They would be an appropriate destination for Lent.

Milazzo, port for the Aeolian Islands: a point of departure, a series of arbitrary impressions: a small provincial town, centre of the wine-growing industry of the province of Mes-sina, and itself an island like the Aeolians until the sea, piling up alluvial deposits from neighbouring rivers, gave it in adoption to Sicily, a town which witnessed two battles which changed the course of the island's history: the first Roman victory by sea over the Carthaginians—proof that after countless unsuccessful attempts the masters of land warfare had learned how to build and fight from ships; and Garibaldi's final defeat of the Bourbon troops in Sicily. But the town which guards the tenuous peninsula has never been important in its own right: it has always been and always will be a stage in a journey. For this reason the impression the traveller forms of it is necessarily ephemeral, even superficial and probably arbitrary; yet the nature of the place forbids any other form of analysis. One is left therefore with broken images: the difficulty of controlling undisciplined crowds; erection of barriers; threat of sacrilege; quays lined with innumerable barrels of wine destined for England, a drunkard's dream; flowers in the public garden filched overnight; clumsiness with machines; heavy jowled faces; difficulty in manipulating long words; startling incidence of statues to notable local men; preoccupation with newspaper advertisements; large babies with thick hair; curious stale smells; walls painted in thick, scrawling letters with misspelt political slogans; men's reverence for fine clothes and illustrated papers; people who, misjudging distance, knock into one another in the street; controlling voices from Rome on the radio, insistent but unheard; difficulty of organising civic functions; failure of electricity; the struggle against apathy gradually being lost; lack of tribal taboos; multiplicity of powerless officials—clerks and counter-clerks; shallow foundations; shifting, unsettled population; dust.

After a few hours of these urban impressions, the surrounding sea, inky under a cloudy sky, seems to possess a welcome cleanness, even a solidity, that are lacking on the promontory, and the little ship an enterprise and vigour as she plies her daily voyage to the Aeolian Islands. Land is never out of sight on the twenty-mile crossing: Vulcano, the most southerly of the islands, even on a dull day is visible from Sicily; and to starboard Panarea and Stromboli, erupting day and night at ten-minute intervals, rise sheer out of the sea like two floating mountains—dark-coloured icebergs in warm waters, whales generated from the sea-bed. The islands indeed are more akin to sea than land: from the sea they were born in a titanic explosion of volcanic activity, attempts at producing real earth, miscarriages constituted of strange hybrid rocks, discontented and neurotic: lava, pumice and obsidian. Like other ill-adapted survivals, like the duck-billed platypus, they continue to exist by dint of an unbroken struggle. They manage to hold themselves above water; puny, shaggy dwarfs in a world of giants, afflicted with hot blood and strange weaknesses, liable at any moment to destroy themselves in flame.

If the land of Sicily is a garden of Eden, the Aeolian Islands are a place of exile after the Fall, where man must labour all day for food in the sweat of his brow: rocky mountains where a few scattered olives are almost the sole trees, birds scarce and wild flowers almost unknown. Two of the islands, a modern version of Sodom and Gomorrah, are continually consumed by fire, and all have that ashen-coloured soil which betrays volcanic activity. Their name, which is very ancient, derives from that Aeolus who, according to Homer, was controller of the winds and ruler of the floating island of Aeolia. He entertains Odysseus, gives him a favourable wind and a bag in which the adverse winds are confined. To see what it contains, Odysseus's companions open the bag; the winds escape and drive them back to the island, where Aeolus dismisses them with bitter reproaches. According to Virgil, Aeolus dwells on Lipari or Stromboli and keeps the winds imprisoned in a vast cavern, while other authors identify him with Zeus, and his six sons and six daughters with the months of the year. These classical myths stress what to the sailors of that age would have appeared the most important feature of the islands: their savage coast-line and seemingly variable position, exposed to every storm. Like ships sighted by night, at this remote period their inner constitution and inhabitants were deemed less worthy of record than their potential danger.

A great part of the islands is rocky and sterile: in addition, shortage of water makes agriculture difficult in the extreme.

In order to collect what rain may fall the houses are built with flat roofs in a series of terraces, from which the water is drained into cisterns. These cubic buildings, whitewashed and standing out against the grey earth like rotting bones, constitute the most obvious difference between the islands and Sicily. The vine is the chief product and, as in the soil round Etna, produces good wine, the most celebrated being Malvasia of Lipari, thick and golden, and the highly alcoholic fiery wine of Stromboli.

The islands were inhabited in neolithic times and colonised by the Greeks: allies of Syracuse, they were even attacked by Athens during the Sicilian Expedition, but without success. It is as pirates that the islanders achieved fame in classical antiquity, at a time when piracy was deemed a respectable trade like shoemaking or fishing. So successful were the Aeolians in harrying the trade-routes which led through the straits of Messina and up the west coast of Magna Graecia that they were able to dedicate at Delphi costly trophies fine enough to vie with the magnificent gifts of the tyrants at Acragas or Syracuse. Under the Romans the islands became fashionable for their hot springs, and later even more important as a place of exile. They must have fulfilled that function perfectly, lying within sight both of Sicily and Italy, islands of regret, sterile dungeons for men who had failed, and later, with the advent of Christianity, their role as places of exile from the world was continued by the foundation of a monastery.

The inhabitants, however, far from being close and rapacious, are gentle, kind, and trusting, less quick than the Sicilians and harder working, but in other respects, both physical and moral, very similar. The most fundamental difference is hard to specify: it consists in an absence of all grace and refinement, as though the quickening breath of civilisation which animates Sicily had failed to touch these island outposts. The people's spiritual condition is typified by the appearance of the country; some islands, completely volcanic, shaggy and uncombed as wild beasts, without even a tree to provide a harmonious line; others partly cultivated but with very little vegetation and in colour remorselessly grey. The archipelago hardly maintains a level of subsistence; where Sicily is all flower and leaf, these rocks are merely root, and the life of their inhabitants reflects this poverty. There is less time for merely talking and standing, for that attitude of *dolce far niente* which a rich country can afford: all the people's energy goes into the rock. Depopulation is making inroads on the islands' welfare: whole families are leaving every year for the other side of the world—for Australia. The Aeolians have always been people of passage, but this new wave of emigration is on a far greater scale than any movement which has taken place in the past, so that the islands may one day revert to their original barren state— the volcanoes will have gained final victory: subterranean forces will have taken command, and the islands will be shunned even as nesting-places for sea-birds.

Here the struggle between man and a hostile nature, using every possible machine of war, is waged to the death. Nothing intervenes to mitigate the conflict: on land and sea naked flesh fights natural forces in everlasting warfare. Strong currents and a rocky, treacherous coast make fishing precarious; gravel and lack of rain doom the leaf's attempt to burgeon, and over all loom the smoking, unpredictable volcanoes. In Sicily a benevolent nature provides man's needs with open hands; here she is as mean and close as a stepmother. In the mountains of Lipari, especially, the people are on the brink of destitution. Men wear trousers so patched that almost nothing of the original material remains, and cover their feet with home-made shoes of sacking laced with string. In order to eke out a living they make expeditions into the wilderness to find the pumice-stone of which part of the island is composed. In their back yards they pile and guard as treasure huge blocks of this stone which, like the proverbial weight-lifter's dumb-bell, are as light as though made of papier mâché. The whole northern end of the island is rendered quite white by dust of pumice in the earth:

a sight which recalls an arctic snow-scene until one learns that the men and women who labour in the pumice-galleries, extracting the stone under appalling conditions, refer to it as "l'inferno bianco."

The fact remains that the islands are uninhabitable if a certain level of dignity and self-respect is to be maintained, a truth confirmed by nothing so much as a full-blooded gale. During stormy weather the Greek nomenclature is justified to the hilt. When a succession of waves, high as cathedrals, crash in a torrent of foam against the volcanic cliffs of Lipari, carrying in their wake the hardly identifiable remains of a fishing-boat wrecked during the night, the island reverts to its original form of existence under the sea. Then it becomes evident to what an extent the archipelago is a marine formation, totally at the mercy of the waves. The destructive breakers are the counterpart of volcanic eruptions, the spray of boiling-hot springs, the hysterical shifting surface of earth tremors. Land and sea unite in this dance of death which precedes multiple human sacrifice. Between the salt battering waves and the grey grit all existence, all life, vegetable and animal, is annihilated. The sea is gradually eating its own litter, destroying its own abortive attempt at creation, slowly wearing away the malformed rock in some places by water, in others by consuming fire. As the seas crash on the waterfront with a mass salvo as deafening as a volcanic eruption, so that a shout shrinks to a whisper, the island might be a ship, foundering with all hands aboard. The split coast at any moment may fall apart to form a wreck of jagged rocks and ledges; the wind which gave the islands their name carries the spray in a winding-sheet over the dead fields; wild sheep and goats cower in the ruined craters of past volcanoes; the lighthouse sends out its silent reiterated message of alarm, until even that is obliterated in total darkness. So the storm is consummated through the night. At dawn the islanders stumble out to discover the damage and estimate the cost of repairs, half thankful, half alarmed that they will be unable to make good their loss.

Under such conditions it is astonishing that the islands should have been for so long inhabited, not by retarded, brutish nomads but by a comparatively rich people, as the tombs and other remains on the archipelago bear witness. The vases which have been excavated on the acropolis of Lipari form one of the most complete and unbroken cycles in existence, stretching from early neolithic times to the Renaissance. In a network of trenches numbering no more than a dozen, none deeper than seven yards, the entire history of the island has been discovered, each civilisation having left its layer of ceramics, a crude signature in the island's visitors' book. The collection is extraordinarily rich and varied, yet it betrays one common characteristic unique in such a sequence: not one of the vases was manufactured on the Aeolian Islands, where the soil is totally unsuitable for making terracotta. Each one of these vases, many thousand in number, over a period of three millennia, was imported—from Italy, Sicily, Greece, and lands still farther distant. The natural question is how did the islands ever attain sufficient wealth to be able to acquire objects which in early times were highly prized. The answer varies according to the different ages. In neolithic times, and even to the arrival of the Greeks, the Aeolian Islands exported all over the Mediterranean the one material in which the rocks were rich—obsidian, a dark-coloured vitreous lava. This stone was shaped into glass-like blades with good cutting powers, and served in place of knives in every corner of the civilised world. When obsidian and flint began to be superseded by bronze and iron, the Aeolian Islands had already established themselves as one of the trading centres for Mediterranean shipping. Later still, when the Greek colonisation of Southern Italy and Sicily relegated the smaller islands to a secondary position, they adopted piracy as a trade. In this way they were able to buy from every part of the civilised world the finest pottery in existence, which until recently has lain buried in a common grave. Now obsidian and piracy are both outmoded; the islanders can no longer afford expensive wares from distant lands, and most of the utensils now in service would not have been out of place in a neolithic cave. It is pathetic to look upon these layers of broken sherds, scattered with decaying bones, knowing that they form the sole memorial to the hundred generations who have inhabited the island. They do, however, provide a valid memorial, a true record of past generations, a blood test which reveals unerringly the state of health of a particular civilisation, the extent to which art and formal grace entered into the people's lives. The pale blue garments which serve only to set off the nakedness of women on Hellenistic vases reveal the effete sentimentality which occurs when a civilisation has passed its zenith; the little lamps with a minimum of decoration reveal Roman efficiency and esteem for practical above aesthetic values, and so on, each people unconsciously manifesting its character in the little serviceable objects of daily life. How differently they might have modelled these vases had they known that they would be judged by them! It was so unlikely that such paltry objects as pots would alone survive. But it is that very characteristic which makes them so useful a piece of evidence —being held in tension between fine art and pure utility, they reveal the extent to which grace and the aesthetic sense have become second nature, for if a people will go to the trouble and expense of using utensils which are not only purposeful but decorative, they already prove themselves appreciative of a higher scale of values than the strictly material.

These sherds are as informative as any ancient papyrus bearing written dates of history. In the earliest bronze age levels of the acropolis, quite recently fragments of pottery have been excavated with thick diagonal stripes and large black discs on a neutral surface. They are broken, random pieces, yet their bold design reveals that they were made in Crete in the age known as the late Minoan IA, that is, about 1,500 years before Christ. They are similar to sherds excavated by Evans from the well within Cnossus, where liparite believed to come from the Aeolian Islands has also been found.

This discovery is of great importance, because it throws light on the pattern of Mediterranean history at a little-known period. Previously it had not been proved that Crete had expanded its trade to this area of the world at such an early date. Occasional bone handles, believed to be of Cretan origin, had been found in Sicilian cemeteries, but from such objects it was impossible to draw certain proof, and no Cretan pottery had ever before been found in Sicily or the Aeolian Isles. The new finds would be comparable, for instance, to the discovery in New Zealand, after a future dark age, of Staffordshire pottery, which would prove trade relations over a distance as long proportionately as that which separated Sicily from Crete in the second millennium.

But the discovery has a more immediate importance. At a single stroke it makes plausible Diodorus's story that Daedalus had come from Crete to Sicily before the Trojan War. Here is tangible proof of direct Cretan relations with the Aeolian Isles roughly at the period when the artist is supposed to have lived, and the cargoes unloaded by Cretan ships consisted precisely of objects of art. Past historians had known of no connection between Crete and Sicily at so early a period and in view of this not unnaturally dismissed Daedalus's voyage as legendary; but now, against a background of known trade relations, the voyage fits into the pattern of mercantile and artistic history.

Interpreting Diodorus's story in this light, emphasis must now be placed on the close interconnection between the coming of Daedalus and Minos to Sicily. Personal jealousy can hardly have been the motive for the king's full-scale campaign against a distant island, any more than the stealing of Helen was the true motive for the expedition against Troy. In both cases expansion of trade went hand in hand with an attempt at conquest. Daedalus and Minos therefore are the two sides, refining and destructive, of the extension of Cretan civilisation; the first welcomed, the second repelled. The death of King Minos represents the failure of the attempt at total conquest, yet the burial of the King in

Sicilian soil and the establishment of two Cretan colonies, which gradually expanded and introduced their own religion to the island, is proof that the new civilisation made steady inroads in Sicily. Daedalus, who arrived in the van of an invading army, remained as a benefactor, executing artistic and architectural masterpieces; the new style of vases, such as these on Lipari, preceded the arrowheads and long outlived them.

A few broken sherds have drawn Daedalus from the mists of legend into the half-light of prehistory. The first and earliest clue has been deciphered: it remains now to follow up the thread through succeeding centuries. Not long after the death of Minos the power of Crete declined, and soon the centre of power in the Mediterranean shifted to Greece, whence, centuries later, colonies were once again sent to Sicily. Of these the most important is Syracuse, the Greek city *par excellence*. Here the search must be continued, here another civilisation must be scrutinised and interrogated, in the hope of getting back a chance word which will identify Daedalus and his honeycomb.

CHAPTER ELEVEN

Syracuse: The City

A WIDE, sheltered harbour, an island detached from the mainland by the narrowest strip of sea, and on that island a fresh water spring: such was the site of the second Greek settlement in Sicily, a colony founded by Corinthians, destined to be one of the world's great cities. These early foundations, like seeds scattered at random, flourished or declined according to their geographical position. Naxos, for instance, the first Greek colony, was an injection which did not take. Good soil alone did not ensure the city's growth; sometimes rock was more favourable because it afforded protection; but above all it was grain sown beside a natural harbour that yielded an abundant harvest and increased a hundredfold. No place on the east and south coasts of the island—at this time the only area accessible to the Greeks—was naturally so strong or so well-sited for trade as Syracuse. The limestone formation which dominates the site to the north is continued downwards in the island of Ortygia, which resembles a hand pointing, the index finger showing south. To the west and south lies the port, sheltered at the south-east corner by a projecting ridge of land, which almost completes the circle, leaving only a space of half a mile between itself and Ortygia. The city site dominates a plain some ten miles in diameter, and is finally shut in by the Iblean Mountains. Its exceptional feature is the island which was later to be developed into a self-contained fortress. Here the first colonists, having driven out the Sicels who already held the site as a trading centre, founded their city, giving it the name of Ortygia, after one of the epithets of Artemis. Soon the city began to be known under the name of Syracuse, after a neighbouring marsh called Syraka, itself in turn derived from a Phoenician word meaning "western place," while the name Ortygia was reserved for the island which, except in time of war, was linked to the mainland by a dyke.

That sense of beauty which perhaps unconsciously guided the Greeks in their choice of city-sites was never more unerring than in the foundation of Syracuse. The spit of land which is Ortygia stretches out into the Ionian Sea like a great ship proceeding to sail away: the peninsula has all the scenic advantages of an island with none of the strategic disadvantages. To the west the impression is of an inland lake, dominated in the distance by the almost straight, low line of the Iblean hills, along which, immediately before it sinks, the sun lights a long beacon of forest fires. On the other side of Ortygia the prospect is unprotected: the sea breaks in spectacular waves against the sheer walls, for on this side the houses extend to the sea edge, and apart from the line of rocky coast stretching north the horizon is unbroken. From the mainland Ortygia looks like an extended dyke, a single street lined with houses rising out of the sea. There are in fact some six streets down the length of the island, and twice that number across its breadth: narrow, winding alleys, traced in an irregular pattern as though by a boy trailing to school and dividing chock-a-block houses that give the island the appearance of an over-loaded cargo-boat.

The new colonists found nothing in the fabulous island of Ortygia so difficult to explain as the freshwater spring which bubbles up in a continuous fountain at the south-east side, only a few feet from the sea edge, as though continually renewing the place, and it was this phenomenon which gave rise to a legend which linked the new colony with the mother country. Arethusa, so the story goes, a nymph attendant on Artemis, lived on the wild plains of Elis in the Peloponnese. One day as she was hunting she was seen by Alpheus, a river god of that country, who fell passionately in love with her. He gave chase to the nymph, but Arethusa ran away and, just as she seemed to be eluding the river god,

reached the sea. Here she believed herself lost and in desperation called upon Artemis. The goddess took pity on
her and gave the nymph the shape of a fountain; she leapt
into the sea and continued to flow under the waves, preserving her own identity:

> Under the bowers
> Where the Ocean Powers
> Sit on their pearlèd thrones;
> Through the coral woods
> Of the weltering floods,
> Over heaps of unvalued stones.

Finally she arrived at the island of Ortygia, where she rose
once more to the upper world. Alpheus, meanwhile, being
a river god, was able to follow the nymph's course from the
coast of Elis to Ortygia and, overtaking her, mingled his own
fresh water with hers. Thus the two lovers are united in an
eternal embrace, continually renewed. To corroborate the
story Syracusans aver that in the harbour a short distance
from shore there bubbles up a stream of fresh water, which
they claim as the river god Alpheus.

The Fontana Aretusa is a pool of clear water, a wide well
between high walls. Fish and geese preserve the water from
weeds: crystal water that is ever changing, welling up at one
side out of the rock and draining into the sea at the other.
Around the edges grow papyrus plants in clumps, imported
originally by the Arabs, thin reeds that explode in a network of intricate tendrils, fine as a spider's web. It is certain
that at least until the end of the eighteenth century the water
remained sweet, on the testimony of no less a man than
Nelson. In June 1798 the admiral sailed into Syracuse with
fourteen warships and remained five days, while from all
around the Sicilians came to admire the ships, to fête the
sailors and sell provisions. A fair was held for the crews and
there was much revelry and rejoicing, for in the British Navy
were placed all Sicily's hopes of avoiding domination by the
detested French, memories of whose occupation five centuries

before still haunted the Sicilians. In a letter to Sir William Hamilton from Syracuse Nelson wrote that he had taken on provisions and fresh water, and since the water had been drawn from the fountain of Arethusa he would certainly gain a victory. The prophecy was realised, for his warships sailed out from Syracuse to win the battle of Aboukir. A generation earlier Brydone had visited Syracuse and mentioned that the fountain of Arethusa had been given over to washerwomen, who would have preferred even this hard, calcareous spring to salt sea water. Until the end of the eighteenth century, therefore, the legend still rang true, and if it was difficult to believe the corollary, that cups thrown into the waters of the river Alpheus in Greece had been found later in the Syracusan fountain, the fresh water mysteriously welling up so near the sea seemed to authenticate at least the substance of the legend. Soon after Nelson's visit, however, earthquakes shook the island and the waters of Arethusa were discovered to be no longer sweet. Perhaps the earthquakes had killed the nymph or frightened her away; perhaps the rock which had separated fountain and sea was shattered. Now the waters of Arethusa are said to be salt, and since the fountain is guarded by lofty walls there is no way of discovering for sure. It is perhaps as well, for in the absence of personal proof, the Greek legend exerts its spell, so that it is difficult to believe that the waters are not fresh, that this is not in truth the nymph from Elis, transformed into another shape, continually renewing both her love and the ancient city.

Some people in childhood experience such success or happiness that their after-life is totally overshadowed by these primary events. Having tasted the sweetest fruit on the tree, the rest appears insipid: the years of maturity are a mere postscript to childhood, a period in which to reflect on the earlier glory. The same is true of some Sicilian towns and of none more than Syracuse. As a devoted mother after the death of her child may keep its room exactly as it used to be when the child was living, with toys by the narrow bed and brightly coloured paper on the walls, only occasionally dusting and cleaning it with reverence, so does the present town preserve the memory of the city she once was. It is not that she made no effort to forget and transcend the past—under the Normans and Spaniards she bid again for glory—but the tide of history was against her. The ties with Greece which had formerly favoured a port on the east coast were broken, while Palermo and Messina were judged more convenient links with the mainland. Earthquakes, pirates, and plague in quick succession reduced her to one tenth of the size of the Greek city. In the Christian era she seemed destined to fail, and discouraged by what she believed was an adverse fate she retreated to the past. The architectural remains of her glory are far fewer than at Agrigento, for instance—a theatre, an altar and an amphitheatre and one temple which serves as the cathedral—but the spirit of the past is incomparably more powerful and pervading. It is partly that her very position on the new-born island, overlooking the harbour which was the scene of her greatest triumph, immortalises those years of greatness, for she owed much of her power to that matchless geographical position, and partly also that the people still think in terms of the ancient civilisation. Theocritus and Archimedes, Gelon and Dionysius are far more real to the people of Syracuse than any of her citizens, however great, who have lived since the Greek period. At times, especially on a summer evening, when the stars are up over the harbour and the bustle and shouting of the vendors are quiet, it is possible to imagine the city still Greek, still one of the most splendid centres of civilisation, a ship laden with treasures of art setting out from the island to humanise the world.

The quarries from which the Greek city was built are themselves cities, vast unearthly regions cut in the sheer rock. Of these quarries the largest is the Latomia dei Cappuccini; so called because a house of that Order is the nearest landmark, cut into the sides of the Acradina, the high plateau to the north of Syracuse. A sloping path hung with bougain-

villea leads down to the subterranean canyon: in a minute
one passes from the hot, flat, noisy earth with its dome of
blue sky to a world as shadowy and as silent as the sea-
depths. Since there are almost no qualities common to the
two realms, a totally new language would be required to
describe properly these remote regions. The immediate view
is of the city walls, that is, the sheer sides of the quarry, sixty
feet in height, surrounding a site of uneven pattern. They
might appear natural rather than man-made walls, for there
are no gaps between stones, were it not for a rectilinear pre-
cision which nature never achieves. Ivy creeps up the sides
and prickly pears on the summit let a branch hang down, as
though trying to lend a helping hand. While the sides are
sheer and precisely vertical, in the centre of the canyon at
irregular intervals rise vast, vague megaliths, unshaped and
eroded by the wind to assume absolutely meaningless shapes.
On this monster one side is worn to a sharp, beak-like edge,
the other being squat and square, while that formation takes
the form of a pyramid, and still another is cut off short
before it has time to articulate its gibberish. What purpose
was served by leaving this uncut rock at intervals is difficult
to say: it may be that the pillars are composed of inferior
stone, useless for building, or that they supported a roof
which has long since fallen in. Between these pillars and
within the perimeter of the walls a garden has been laid out,
a garden of flowers and trees and citrus groves in the centre
of this hidden city: a sunken garden, but deeper than all
others like it, so profound that only a narrow ribbon of blue
sky is visible between the fortress walls. It is a protected,
secret garden, where one would expect curious and perhaps
deadly flowers to grow, the equivalent of marine, flesh-
eating anemones. Yet these plants are the familiar ones of
the upper world—geraniums and marguerites, arum lilies
and bougainvillea; and the trees are cypresses and olives,
lemons and oranges, palm trees and cacti. Only the last
seem appropriate, their squat, formless shapes representing
in another order of being the megaliths and pyramids. A

meagre thin soil has been spread on the rocky floor, yet the flowers bloom and the trees bear as spectacularly as in the upper world. It must after all be an enchanted, a marvellous garden to produce this fruit from the bare, prime rock, these yellows and pinks from the relentless grey. One almond-tree still in blossom, its rose-white petals for all their fragility getting the better of the walls, seems out of place as a bouquet of flowers brought by some benefactor to brighten a prison.

That word draws groans and sighs from the walls, uncovers memories best left undisturbed, for this city of fruit and flowers, this enchanted garden, was once nothing less than a prison: not for a few local malefactors but for the remnants of the greatest Greek army that ever went into battle. Here in this dungeon open to the sky, this stone sheep-pen, the seven thousand Athenian survivors of the expedition which set out to conquer Sicily were incarcerated for a period of eight months. Here, under appalling conditions, with a pittance of food and water, they were compelled to strengthen their own prison, to add to the already towering walls, to dig their own mass grave. Not slaves but Athenian citizens, not confessed criminals but cultured and enlightened men, turned a hillside into a canyon to provide more stone for the swelling city they had come to destroy. A few only were released before the eight months were up, not the wealthy or strong or influential, for Syracuse was a Greek city, but those who could recite by heart parts of Euripides's plays, the Athenian dramatist being so admired in the capital city of Sicily that his words alone could swing back an opening in the rock. After their imprisonment those who had survived the terrible conditions were sold into slavery, to languish as tutors and worse in perpetual exile. But they had left behind an imperishable monument, not a city as Athens and Acragas were cities, but a subterranean metropolis, built with the same sort of stone, encircled with even thicker ramparts. It proved no less costly in labour for having been hewn out of the earth. Marks of the thin pickaxe, a miserably inadequate tool for such gigantic work, cover the area of the walls: primitive hieroglyphics, a rudimentary arithmetic. Were these units calculated and translated into descriptive terms they would reveal the true story of the imprisonment: how, unprotected from the sun and parched with thirst, amid the stench of unburied dead, they were forced interminably to scale and level walls which, like the hydra, were continually re-created.

Gradually the orange and lemon trees conspire to hide those vestiges of the city's origin, and another aspect of the place becomes apparent: the silence which seems to lie in caverns, a stillness as tangible as the shadow itself, a counterpart to coolness. It is not, however, an ominous or brooding silence, for it is interrupted all the while by bird song, by the calls of chaffinches and tits and wagtails: it is the silence of a bird sanctuary. As the light shifts, the canyon calls up still another image: this is neither city nor dungeon nor enchanted garden but a forest: the same shadows and coolness, the same alternation of hushed and ringing sounds: a forest perhaps that has suffered a sea-change and become petrified: a forest of stone. In this glade between cool trees, the shadows always fall; dawn is continual, spring is continual, and the birds are never hushed by the heat of the day. In the patches of sunlight flies and bees make a murmurous music as they move, like the off-white colour of a page on which the birds compose their songs. One of them starts from a mandarine tree and flits soundlessly away to the north, out of sight, into the wall, so it seems. But the wall is a passage, and this first great canyon only the vestibule, the antechamber to others still more extraordinary. The way lies under a great natural bridge of rock, an architrave some sixty feet wide and forty long, at the summit of the walls: an uneven coarse block of stone which was left undisturbed as a roof or bridge, who can tell? It serves to increase the outlandish nature of the system, to co-ordinate it according to some incomprehensible primeval plan.

The second canyon is planted with lemon trees only, but

wild flowers, undiscouraged by the austere surroundings, make a garden here no less colourful than the first. Between the summits of the walls, on a river of blue a half-moon is floating, its ragged edges, its grey-and-white dappled complexion so like those of the canyon that it seems hewn out of the same rock, a light fragment that has risen to the surface of the waters and is gliding gently away. This image more than any other seems near the truth, conveying by analogy the ineffable qualities of the place. It is not a subterranean city, but a city under the sea, a lost, abandoned Atlantis. The blue above is the remote surface of the sea, the coolness imparted by invisible currents of water originating in the frozen north, and these shapeless megaliths ruined palaces, worn away by a waste of waves. The silence in this second canyon (for no birds have ventured thus far) is that of death by drowning under the mountainous ranges of water. Everything that happens here is subject to that crushing weight; everything over-oppressed, futile and condemned to pettiness. The trees which elsewhere had seemed so magnificent, stretching up towards heaven, are pitiful absurdities, wasting their energy in a hopeless attempt to reach ground level, the flowers doomed to dance in an empty, provincial theatre.

Out of this sterile canyon a grotto leads to a third suburb, again a garden, smaller but richer in citrus trees, and the sea-vision, as inexplicably as it arose, now loses all conviction. A single lemon tree dispels it. Its slender trunk, so smooth and ungnarled compared with the neighbouring olives, grey as the limestone, seems to grow out of the canyon itself, almost to be part of it. Six branches, at various angles and heights, distribute the sap to a maze of subsidiary shoots and twigs, on which hang pointed oval leaves of delicate and unobtrusive green, a green which still retains a suggestion of its grey origin. Laid against these are the lemons, in such a profusion of clusters, in such abundance that they might have been crowded there like a myriad Japanese lanterns at an impassioned festival rather than slowly and arduously born from such narrow branches. The unripe fruit, its colour hesitating between green and yellow, seems still to be emerging from leaf, branch, and canyon, the process of growth illustrated in the growing brilliance of colour. The ripe lemons, a cool, moonlit yellow, are almost emancipated from the earth: they have already drawn some sweetness from the sun. This profusion of fruit is sustained quite effortlesly by the tree, the branches seeming light as the cascading jets of a fountain, and the fruit no more ponderous than drops of amber water. Some have fallen to the ground, in time to be collected in the deep basin, in time to be drawn upwards by the fountain, in time once more to gush and be caught for a single moment in the sunlight, urgent with that beauty which is flashed off ripeness everywhere.

From these quarries, a generation after they served as a prison, Dionysius the Great drew stone to fortify the city and erect some of its most magnificent buildings. This tyrant, the most famous of all Sicilian rulers, is a type not only of the many despots, from Phalaris to the Bourbons, who have stood astride the island, but also of the warrior artist who is to reappear, time and again, throughout the course of the island's history.

Dionysius was an upstart who during the Carthaginian wars gained absolute power as a military leader first in Syracuse and later over virtually the whole island. Curiously enough, he first discovered that he was destined for sovereignty one day while he was out riding, when a swarm of bees attached themselves to his horse's mane, an omen which he took as certain proof that he would attain absolute rule. Evidently within the island bees were considered symbolic of royal power, a notion which perhaps stems back to some such figure as Daedalus, who would have transferred to Sicily the Cretan belief that the insect had royal associations. Only later was the bee widely established as a royal symbol, being adopted by the Romans, by the French kings, and especially by Napoleon Bonaparte and his nephew. The connection between the swarm on the tyrant's horse and a flesh-and-blood

Daedalus is, at the most, slender, but in combination with other evidence even such a detail may prove significant.

War, defensive and aggressive, continued throughout the tyrant's reign of almost forty years, for Dionysius believed that military glory was the only way whereby a dictator who lacked birth and a winning personality could maintain his people's loyalty. The resentment evoked by his cruelty increased a naturally suspicious nature and he went about in constant fear of his life. Modelling his bedroom after the defences of his castle, around his golden bed he constructed a moat, crossed by a little draw-bridge. When one of his courtiers, a certain Damocles, spoke of him as the happiest of mortals, since he possessed all that a man could desire, Dionysius asked him whether he wanted to taste this life, an offer which was eagerly accepted. The tyrant then gave orders that Damocles was to be treated as himself and secretly arranged that whatever he was doing, whether feasting, drinking, or sleeping in the tyrant's golden bed, a sword should be suspended by a horsehair over his head. Damocles spent the day in a state of abject terror, too frightened even to eat or drink. In the evening Dionysius approached him with the words, "Now you know what it is like to be a tyrant," and allowed the panic-stricken man to return to his normal life.

By consolidating his own power he indirectly saved the western Greek world from the barbarian, but he consistently proved that he cared nothing for civilisation, forcing colony after colony into barren servitude. Yet his Greek birthright found an outlet in another side of his character. Just as his predecessor, Hieron, a suspicious, greedy, cruel tyrant, had a passionate love of poetry and made his court the greatest literary centre of the world, to which Bacchylides and Pindar, Simonides and Aeschylus resorted, so Dionysius, a man of low birth and no moral sense, was devoted to literature, and above all the drama. All his life he wrote tragedies and poems which failed to find appreciation either at home or abroad. It is said that a certain Philoxenus was sent to the quarries for refusing to applaud the tyrant's poems. Some time later when he was again received at court, Philoxenus was pressed for his opinion of a new poem by Dionysius. He answered by beckoning to an officer with the words "Back to the quarries!" But the story goes that on this occasion his wit won him forgiveness. At the Athenian festivals Dionysius frequently gained the second and third prizes, but always failed to win outright: for the mightiest ruler of Greece, for a tyrant whose power was no less than that of the great King of Persia, this was a galling humiliation. At last, in his old age, his tragedy *The Ransom of Hector* won first prize at one of the lesser Athenian festivals. Dionysius was so jubilant that he ordered a public holiday and provided food and wine for the people. A monumental feast was set out before the successful tragedian, rival of the greatest playwrights of the past, even of Aeschylus and Sophocles. Far into the morning the tyrant banqueted, his life-long ambition at last fulfilled, triumphant on the stage as he had been in his life, but so intemperately did he eat and drink that at dawn he suffered a stroke and died.

All his plays and poems have perished with him and the tyrant is chiefly remembered in Syracuse for a curious monument which he probably did not construct. The Ear of Dionysius, as it is called, is an artificial grotto, its ground-plan in the form of an extended S, some sixty-five yards long. Its width, nine yards at the base, diminishes gradually to less than a few feet near the top, so that the entrance has the appearance of an inverted pimento. Its height increases from twenty yards at the entrance to thirty yards at the far end. Its walls are sheer, comparatively smooth and marked with the indentations of pickaxes, so that the cave cannot, as some would suppose, be a purely natural construction. It is remarkable not only for its curious ground-plan and the marked tapering of its side walls, but also for acoustical effects. A whisper or the faintest sound, such as the tearing of paper, near the entrance echoes back with multiplied intensity and all the way up the cave the slightest noise is returned with compound interest. No one knows its history or for what purpose it was designed, and its name is a comparitively recent invention. In 1588 the Syracusan archaeologist Vincenzo Mirabella and the painter Michelangelo da Caravaggio, who was to exercise an important influence on Sicilian art, were visiting the artificial grotto. Caravaggio, struck by its close resemblance to the central part of the human ear, conceived the idea that Dionysius, the tyrant of Syracuse, had constructed the cave in this shape to serve as a prison: by listening at a hole above ground, he would have been able to hear, thanks to the echo, even the hushed secrets exchanged by its prisoners. The theory is an imaginative one and although it savours too much of Caravaggio's notorious persecution-mania, it cannot be dismissed lightly. There are, however, many difficulties in the way of accepting it as the true explanation of the grotto's purpose. In the first place, the cave is so elaborately and even beautifully constructed that it is hard to imagine such care being expended on a mere prison. Again, Dionysius was a realist, not the sort of person to indulge in such extraordinary fancies. When he wished to extort secrets from political prisoners, he turned to more effective methods. Finally, such a prison would soon become so notorious that anyone confined to it would certainly avoid speaking of important matters. The theory is instructive, however, for it shows how a plausible story which is logically false but imaginatively true will gain credence and eventually become accepted as the proper explanation. This particular theory has the advantage of linking a great monument to a great historical figure, so that the visible and the legendary reinforce and substantiate each other.

Scholars and scientists have put forward explanations which, besides lacking the colour of Caravaggio's theory, are palpably absurd. The most far-fetched is that the cave served in some obscure way as a resonant sounding-box for the nearby Greek theatre. What precise function it had is not made clear: but the fact that it lies far behind and beneath the farthest tiers of the theatre—on the opposite side from the stage and at least a hundred yards from it—marks the notion as ridiculous. Another group of scholars believe that the cave is simply a quarry and that its peculiar, winding shape is to be explained by the fact that it followed the course of a subterranean stream of water. This theory has the merit of accounting for the curious ground-plan, but it fails to account for the equally extraordinary shape of the cross-section, tapering at the roof to an extremely narrow breadth. A more damaging objection is that there was no lack of similar stone at hand, which could have been obtained without a hundredth part of the labour required to extract material from this narrow seam. To find a more satisfactory explanation it is necessary to go either farther back or farther forward in time. There appear to be two plausible solutions. The most striking and unique features of the grotto are its acoustical properties and the dark, over-awing atmosphere imparted by its winding shape. It is not impossible, therefore, that it was constructed expressly to display one or other of these features: either for a scientific or a religious purpose. In the first case, Archimedes, the Syracusan scientist of the third century before Christ, may have been the architect: the practical demonstration of scientific phenomena would have been in keeping with the other facts known about his life. The grotto, then, a testing-ground for acoustical properties, would constitute the first surviving link in that long line of analogous workshops designed for scientific experiment which culminates in the wind-tunnel. If, on the other hand, the grotto is taken to be a religious sanctuary, its date would be much earlier—perhaps before the Greek colony arrived in Syracuse. Its winding shape and narrow entrance, obscuring the light sufficiently to induce awe, do not produce total darkness. The extraordinary echo may have been used by magicians to produce answers to the prayers or questions of worshippers, while a primitive attempt at constructing a lofty building—the sloping walls joining to form a pointed vault—would account for the unorthodox lateral shape. It may well be, therefore, that the so-called Ear of Dionysius was a terrestrial sanctuary: a point of communication with the forces of nature, where supernatural voices could be heard.

The history of Syracuse under Dionysius's successors reveals the decline and fall of the Greek ideal, and also has a highly relevant importance as showing the first transition of Sicily from one civilisation to another, a process which in later centuries was to be repeated many times.

The son of a tyrant is generally weak and dissolute, for not only does he lack the marrow of established traditions, but brought up in luxury at a court where his father is feared rather than admired, he learns to love his own way, despise discipline and mistrust rule of any kind. The son of Dionysius was no exception: in him the vigour and ambition of the father degenerated to dalliance and vanity. For example, one day the elder Dionysius found his son in an intrigue with another man's wife. He took the young man aside, and told him that if he did that sort of thing he would not be tyrant for long; it was by keeping himself from such deeds that he had been able to hold power for so many years. He then withdrew, while his son with a petulant laugh continued his love-making.

Dionysius II had an uncle named Dion, a philosopher and upright man of the highest ideals, a passionate believer in aristocracy. It was he who invited Plato to Syracuse in the hope of making a philosopher-king out of the most powerful ruler in Greece. Plato, though sixty years of age and enjoying at Athens the widest influence and respect, accepted the invitation: at last he had been given the opportunity to realise his long-cherished ideals in a great Greek city. But he reckoned without a ruler swayed by the ever-changing current of Sicilian politics. Dionysius listened to the philosopher for a while with pleasure; geometry became fashionable at his court; he talked of making reforms and even of giving up the tyranny. But these noble resolutions came to nothing. Party politicians set Dionysius against Dion, who was sent in to exile. Later he proceeded to confiscate the exile's property.

declared Dion's wife Arete divorced and gave her in marriage to one of his own courtiers. In disgust Plato decided to abandon the attempted conversion and returned to Athens. His departure was also rendered a matter of prudence by the hostility of the mercenaries, who attributed to his influence the fact that their pay had been curtailed. It was an undignified, almost ludicrous defeat for the lofty ideals of pure reason.

With the news of Dionysius's brutality towards his wife, Dion abandoned his hopes of reconciliation and prepared to avenge his wrongs by force. Raising volunteers throughout Greece and Sicily, he marched on Syracuse, where the citizens rose *en masse* against their dissolute ruler and opened the gates as to a liberator. Once in control of the city, Dion proceeded to organise the government on aristocratic, even Platonic lines, with himself as philosopher-king. As proof of his high ideals he granted a pardon to his democratic opponents, but with the passing of time he found himself able to retain power only by force of cruelty and assassinations. From that moment he was lost. Without a tyrant's temperament, he wavered uneasily between the dictates of conscience and the necessity for keeping power, and was finally assassinated by his enemies only two years after liberating Syracuse. Thus the intervention of two philosophers in practical politics led in one case to defeat and disillusionment, in the other to victory and tragic death. Dionysius returned as tyrant to the capital city and it was left to Timoleon, another high-minded Greek who, in addition, was a skilful general and an astute politician, to liberate the island from tyranny. Not, however, for long. A succession of upstarts who resumed the tyranny culminated in the benevolent kingship of Hieron II, who ruled Syracuse and eastern Sicily for over half a century, first in his own right, and later as a dependent ally of Rome, for it was during his lifetime that Rome emerged as the world's greatest power and tentatively established her legions in the island. The outcome of the first Punic War had been to give Rome a still disputed ascendancy over the whole Mediterranean, and Sicily, as always, became the most bitterly contested prize in the recurrent war between Europe and Africa. Under Greeks, Romans, Byzantines, Arabs and Normans, like a piece of choice food between two dogs, the island was to be continually mangled by the warring continents.

Hieron was perfectly free in the administration of his own kingdom, but in foreign policy he found it prudent to follow the lead of Rome. His rule was prosperous for the city; he built many public buildings, including a great altar, two hundred yards long, dedicated to Zeus in thanksgiving for the overthrow of one of the previous tyrants. This altar still stands, a long stone floor on three steps, approached by a ramp, up which bulls to the number of 450 were driven to be sacrificed, perhaps the largest altar ever erected by man. Even now, the interminable structure is an impressive sight; how much more impressive it must have been when, amid the shrieks of dying bulls, to the glory of Zeus, it became a steaming river of animal blood. The edifice reflects Hieron's character: in an age of growing disbelief he was dutiful and reverent towards the gods, mild and just; moreover, he controlled wide dominions, all land paid a tithe to the state, and Syracuse ranked among the wealthiest of contemporary cities. The tribute which his namesake would have expended on banquets and debauchery, he reserved for the gods, and the annual sacrifice of almost half a thousand bulls.

After his death, the city, in a mood of pique, exchanged her alliance with Rome for the camp of Carthage, at that time under Hannibal the Great engaged in their second war against the legions. The Romans immediately laid siege to Syracuse, a siege that lasted more than two years. Archimedes was still living, a very old man, and he devoted his whole powers to the defence of the beleaguered city: it was said that he alone was the soul of Syracuse. He pierced the walls with eyelet holes for sharpshooters; he lined the battlements with artillery of every kind; he constructed iron hands by which soldiers who came near the wall were caught up into the air. Against the devices of Archimedes the Romans could make no headway; eventually the attack was abandoned by land and sea and only a few troops left to continue the siege. It was an incident which symbolised perfectly the state of European affairs: Greece, grown old and dabbling now in science instead of writing poetry or running at the Olympic games, is still clever enough to resist the vigorous young Roman troops, lacking a little in confidence, not yet skilled in the subtleties of military technique. Archimedes declared that with a lever sufficiently long he could lift the world. In his last days he did almost as much: with his inventions he held back the armies of Rome from their most precious prize.

But Syracuse did fall eventually, as most decaying cities fall, by means of desertion and treachery, and with the body the soul too departed: the soul, so it seemed, of all Greek Sicily. The story goes that Marcellus, Roman commander of the occupation troops in Syracuse, sent for Archimedes. When the message came, the philosopher was busy with a mathematical problem; he asked to be allowed to finish it; the soldier deputed to escort him seemingly misunderstood and in his haste drew a sword and killed the old man. He was the last genius of Greek Sicily, a philosopher-scientist, but neither his philosophy nor his science was proof against that lack of self-confidence, that fear of a great new nation in arms, which issued in treachery.

The booty transported from Syracuse was enormous. For the first time Roman eyes were opened to the glories of Greek civilisation: a revolution took place in Roman art as momentous as that which occurred at the Renaissance, and in both cases the discovery was the same. Greek paintings and sculpture, buildings and temples became the rage of Rome, so that even before the Greeks, the Sicilians could claim to have enslaved their conquerors. Much that was best and most beautiful in Sicily, the flower of five centuries of civilisation, was transferred to Rome, to be patiently copied, to provide a pretext for endless pastiche, and eventually to be handed down to future ages.

CHAPTER TWELVE

Syracuse: The Arts

THE depredations of Verres and the Roman merchants, how-ever methodical, could not extend to the buildings nor to all the portable works of art, of which the smallest and most exquisite are the Syracusan gold coins. Just as pottery gives evidence of popular aesthetic values, these reveal the taste of the ruling class, and confirm that high appreciation of art which its patronage and interest in poetry have already sug-gested.

Among the most perfect are the gold coins engraved by Cimon, depicting Persephone and Heracles. These minia-tures miraculously concentrate the whole glory of an epoch within their small circumference: being gold, a metal rarely used in those days for coinage, they testify to prosperity; the portrayal of divinities gives proof of a firm religious founda-tion; while the fine modelling of the features, true to the last delicate detail, reveals a humanism and an artistry which re-deem even material wealth from baseness. Such work was imitated, but never surpassed, both in Italy and in Greece.

No such excellence can arise spontaneously, and just as the greatest folk tales are not evolved by the "people" but are made up in remote antiquity by individual story-tellers who may be peasants but are none the less men or women of genius, so this tradition of die-engraving must eventually be traced back to one craftsman of exceptional gifts. For two reasons it would be an unacceptable reading of the legend to say that Daedalus merely offered a gold coin engraved with a honeycomb. In the first place it is highly unlikely that coinage existed at so early an epoch in the Mediterranean, and secondly, the surviving coins of Erice, which would certainly have repeated such a significant emblem, reveal nothing closer to it than an occasional branch of honeysuckle. Nevertheless, the coins of Syracuse may well derive from the work of Daedalus the goldsmith and their perfection goes some way towards substantiating Diodorus's praise of the original master's genius.

Among the divine faces on Sicilian coins, Arethusa, Athena, and Persephone, one in particular stands out, that of Aphrodite, for in it must be sought a substitute for the missing head on one of the loveliest of Syracusan works of art, the statue of Aphrodite. This white-marble work depicts the goddess leaving the sea, where she has been bathing, her left hand grasping to her thighs a garment which falls behind and beside her feet like a shell. Her right arm, which has been broken off above the elbow, was held across her body in a gesture of modesty: the protuberances in the marble, designed to hold the arm in place, are still there, one just below the breasts, the other on the left arm. Beside her feet rises a dolphin, the goddess's own symbol, which serves here also to designate the sea. As well as the right arm the head of the statue is missing: a fact which Maupassant held to be of the utmost significance, for it seemed to illustrate his belief that in the final analysis woman is a purely animal creature, without rational or spiritual faculties: a figure of pure passion. Other less accidental features of the statue make nonsense of this shrill interpretation, but before considering them it is necessary to decide whether the subject is human or divine, imperfect or totally idealised. At first sight the proportions of the body suggest that the sculptor was creating his ideal: the tall undulant figure, a waist slender by Greek standards, firm legs with ankles that today might seem too robust but which in that age were admired as the sign of strength. Only the fingers and toes reveal the human nature of the subject. Far from being idealised, their peculiarity is realistically depicted: the fingers are thick and have flat, stubby tips, while both feet have very long toes, and in each case the little toe is placed far back on the side of the foot. Though the subject is beautiful, she is imperfect; human not divine; and in this the sculptor was conforming to the spirit of his age. Euripides had been the first great artist to portray the gods with purely human qualities and weaknesses; from there it was a short stage to treating them as mere mortals. So it is with this statue: the goddess, if her feet are not made of clay, at least reveals a human shortcoming in her unattractive toes.

While the sculptor was in respect of detail a realist, and of religion a rationalist, in all other regards he was transcendentally imaginative, ordering the work to his own original plan. In the whole statue nothing is more inspired than the line of the garment Aphrodite holds across her body. It is a commotion of light and shadow which sets off the white smoothness of the flesh, a crumpled stormcloud which menaces the figure's orderly lines, a stretch of undulating country separating sea and sky. It is the barest of coverings, this narrow drapery, and the half-modesty of the retaining gesture is calculated to accentuate its inadequacy, just as the right arm, which in the original was stretched across the body, extended below the breasts without hiding them. The line of that arm repeated in a higher octave the same note achieved by the drapery, while the diagonal line of the left hand obviates too stiff and angular an attitude.

The position of the drapery and the gesture which holds it raise the problem whether the statue was purposely designed as an aphrodisiac, along the lines of her cult at Erice. While the male figure ever since the early stages of Greek sculpture had been depicted nude, as indeed it was in the gymnasia and at the athletic games, until the late Hellenistic age the female figure had usually been shown more or less fully clothed. With the decline of Greece, military prowess and strength of body lost esteem, and women assumed an importance they had never had in the classical period. Romantic love became the artist's theme, and the goddess of love, no longer an ethereal divinity but the symbol of passion, replaced Zeus as the most important member of the pantheon. In proportion as this new fashion gained force and the old standards of morality between the sexes declined with the changing structure of society, so the veils were lifted from the female form. But they were seldom completely stripped away: one veil was usually left as a concession to the traditional moral code. In the Aphrodite of Syracuse this veil is given a purpose, and there is nothing about the rest of the statue to suggest that the work possesses more than the usual erotic overtones attaching to a statue of the goddess of love; in fact, the voluptuous aspects of the body are not emphasised or depicted with more care than the rest, and the milk-white colour of the marble imparts to the statue a tone of purity.

The figure, composed of sea-foam, rises from the waves: the whole body is smooth, but the legs have a specially polished surface to suggest the glistening of water. Indeed, at moments the goddess seems to be standing in the sea, such is the equivocal quality of the lower part of her drapery, which forms now a grotto, now a stretch of waves. It is this affinity with the sea which is the essential feature of the work, an extraordinary achievement gained entirely by suggestion, for only the dolphin is there to set the scene. The marble has a melting quality, as though it really were the snow its colour says it is; the flowing, liquid lines of the drapery are drawn up through the fingers of the hand into the body itself, which assumes the undulating lines of a breeze-swept sea. The fingers serve another purpose, also, for their alternation of light and shade dovetails with the drapery, so that the hand, arm and body appear to continue in a calmer form the line of water which under the aspect of the drapery was disarranged and swept by tides. More than any other part of the statue, the back has undergone this sea-change: the long wide expanse of smooth flesh, on which each muscle is delineated, is a Mediterranean seascape, moonlight reflected on the surface, shadows falling between the swelling waves. As for the head, each person who sees the statue must create it anew after the pattern of his own ideal. The qualities which constitute bodily beauty are agreed, but beauty of face and expression must find a kindred spirit to be admired. Yet, so skilfully has the sculptor expressed the inner in the outer forms, the character of his subject is already apparent in her body, from which it is possible to guess the main lines of the missing head. It is dignified without being divine, graceful without being ethereal, vital without losing tranquility, beautiful without limitation: the head of a woman whom the sculptor loved but did not fully understand. The mystery he glimpsed in her he symbolised in the oldest of all symbols of love—the sea, whose forms distinguished her face no less than her body: her wet and glistening hair, her ears whorled like shells and her eyes, which reflect the moonlit, untroubled depths of the Mediterranean.

Such perhaps was the picture in Daedalus's mind as he laid his offering in Aphrodite's sanctuary over a thousand years earlier, and such perhaps was the ideal figure which led Sicilians for so many centuries up the road to the island's watchtower. The cult of Aphrodite at Erice had an exceptionally long life. As Diodorus says, all other sanctuaries enjoyed a flush of fame, but frequently were brought low by some mischance, whereas Erice was the only temple which, founded as it were at the beginning of time, not only never failed to be the object of veneration but, on the contrary, as time went on increased its great renown. No people were more devoted to the goddess than the Romans, who through Aeneas traced their ancestry back to her. The consuls and praetors who visited the island embellished the sanctuary with sacrifices and honours, and, laying aside their grave manner, revelled with the temple priestesses, in the belief that only in this way could they make their presence there pleasing to the goddess. The Roman senate went so far as to decree that the seventeen cities of Sicily which were most faithful to Rome should pay a tax in gold to Aphrodite at Erice and that two hundred soldiers should serve as a guard to her shrine. Thus the elemental forces latent in a local sanctuary were harnessed and transmitted far and wide to serve a military imperialism.

In this statue the goddess stands at the height of her powers, in the full bloom of her beauty, surrounded by admirers, Sicilian, Greek and Roman. Her original statue at Erice may have been an unlovely and primitive object, for it is known that the holy of holies of many a magnificent Greek temple contained nothing more worthy of adoration than a crude wooden idol or an awkwardly hewn stone. Such a state of affairs would have mattered little to the original islanders, but it may be imagined that Daedalus, coming from a country of high civilisation, was dissatisfied and left his influence in this sphere as in others. Only his offering to Aphrodite is recorded, but since he was primarily a sculptor, doubtless he taught that art to the countrymen of his adoption, fashioning the prototype from which this Hellenistic work is directly descended.

For several reasons it is fitting that this statue almost alone of the great works of Greek sculpture should survive. First, since it represents Aphrodite, the work bears witness to a continuous cult which dominated Sicily down to the Christian era. That cult was to be taken up and sanctified under the new dispensation, and *eros* given a universal meaning as *agape*, but at this point Aphrodite still stands supreme, a sacrament mistaken for a goddess. Secondly, it shows that purely natural religion, left to itself, tends at its highest point to become a worship of human beauty and, however emancipated it may become from the primitive rites performed at Acragas, must always remain tinged with the elements of a fertility cult. If the greatest rite of the dark mystery cults was the secret unveiling of an ear of corn, the official religion could offer its devotees hardly more: the physical love of a beautiful woman. For all their proud liturgical display the truth, in both cases, was pathetically narrow, limited and human. Finally, this statue represents the end of a tradition. Christianity would produce sculpture but neither in Sicily nor elsewhere would it emulate work like this. The body would be clothed and spiritual virtues would require the more exact medium of paint for their expression. Of all that was most beautiful in a world still unaware of revelation, the Aphrodite of Syracuse is the final and ultimate symbol.

To turn from Greek art to Roman, which in Syracuse takes the form of a vast amphitheatre standing, significantly enough, close to the fan-like ruins of the Greek theatre, is to leave civilisation for crudeness, to realise graphically how little the Romans contributed, how much they marred. In most realms of art they were content to copy. In architecture they made use of the dome and arch—unknown to the Greeks but not Roman inventions—yet built for a utilitarian rather than aesthetic purpose; their painting was pastiche; one great poet they produced, but even he had to work in a borrowed form. Their philosophers were eclectics, their divinities discarded Greeks. They merely transmitted by force of arms a heritage which was not theirs: they gave a language and laws to Europe, but added little new beauty. As artists they lacked the creative spirit, and tended to accept unquestioningly materials and forms which had already been carried past perfection. Moreover, they lacked a balanced sensibility; whenever the aesthetic sense becomes apparent, it soon degenerates into luxury or sentimentality. Perhaps the possession of a great empire, with the consequent expenditure of talent and energy on administrative and military affairs, precludes great culture; perhaps, in order to civilise, one must deny oneself the refinements of civilisation.

No art is more representative of a people's total culture than drama, for it requires not only several enlightened patrons (as other arts do) but also a communal interest in and appreciation of crucial moral dilemmas. When drama declines into melodrama and comedy of situation, when clowning takes the place of high tragedy, when the hero is replaced by the ordinary man in the street, it is a sign that the people's taste has become coarse and their moral sense debased. This is precisely what happened when the Romans copied the New Comedy, but made of it degraded buffoonery. Soon there came a point when people could no longer be persuaded to enter a theatre at all: the sight of men and women work-

ing out their destiny no longer interested them; they preferred to watch wild beasts shedding animal and human
blood. It cannot be argued that this was a natural and even
healthy revolt against the insipid comedies of the time, for
they too had their admirers and it was precisely the lack of
wide public interest, the coarse taste of the people, which were
responsible for the closing of the theatres. Good architecture
can be forced on a nation, but not good drama; it scarcely
matters how many people admire a public building, but a
play cannot be performed to an empty house. Because the
people preferred gladiatorial shows, all over the Empire
amphitheatres were built. Their very size proves their immense popularity. They were the first buildings designed for
mass entertainment, for men and women who came not to
be exalted but to be degraded. Bread and circuses, it was said,
would keep the masses contented, and while Sicily provided
the capital with bread, Rome allocated money for provincial
circuses. The amphitheatre at Catania, a crumpled ruin
under a deep layer of lava, proves that the entertainment was
not exclusively reserved for the island's capital city. Where-
ever large crowds could gather to air their discontents and
perhaps foment trouble, an amphitheatre was erected to
appease dangerous passions with a sterile diversion.

Since Cicero does not notice it in his description of the city—
it is first mentioned by Valerius Maximus and Tacitus in the
Augustan period—the Syracusan amphitheatre must date from
the end of that reign, for in the first years of the principate
the Sicilian capital had fallen into such decay that Augustus
was obliged to send out a colony. It was Nero, appropriately,
who increased the number of gladiators at this amphitheatre,
a generation after its construction. The work itself is on the
purely pragmatic scale befitting a poor provincial town:
grandeur and graceful lines were deemed less important
than economy. On all sides except the south it has been
hewn out of the Temenite hill, and where necessary banks of
earth have been heaped up to support the tiers. It thus resembles the amphitheatre at Pompeii rather than that at

Nîmes, which is built up in a series of arches. The lowest tiers of seats, the podium, reserved for the leading spectators, is constructed in the Greek style, and the marble blocks which formed a back to the seats are still to be seen, each inscribed with the seat-holder's name. The arena, like the tiers of seats, takes the very unsatisfactory form of an ellipse, seventy yards by forty, at the greater axis of which are two wide entrances. Beneath the lower tiers runs a low, vaulted passage in which the wild beasts were confined. In the centre of the arena is cut a large rectilinear recess, some six feet deep, communicating by means of subterranean channels with a large pond from which after the gladiatorial conflict water flowed to wash away the traces of carnage. The recess itself, filled with water, may have served to vary the usual bloody routine: hippopotami and crocodiles may have been confined here to be engaged by gladiators in small boats, or minor sea battles may have been fought in the fashion that Nero made popular.

The usual spectacle was neither pretty nor edifying. Slaves armed with swords were set against hungry wild beasts: lions, tigers, and wild boar. The gladiator, by his skill and daring, attempted to provide sufficient diversion to win the crowd's applause; as a reward for which the proconsul, sitting in the position of honour, might very occasionally grant him his life and liberty. Oftener he was wounded in the combat, permanently maimed or so mangled that he had to be thrown to the waiting beasts to stimulate their appetite. Whether the human or animal elements conquered, the spectators had their fill of blood. If the gladiator triumphed they identified themselves with their hero; if he was devoured they derived a sadistic pleasure from the spectacle. In either case they were degraded to the level of beasts. Hour after hour the show continued, its crudities repeated with little variation, until the spectators were at last surfeited. The bloodshed ended, they trooped home to relive its horrors until the day of the next performance. Not all, however. The infirm and sick, epileptics and cripples tumbled down the tiers into the arena to suck warm blood from the carcasses and to pluck out the livers from the wild beasts, hoping thereby to infuse new life into their own decaying bodies. It was the summit of their participation, the climax of a sickly afternoon.

That same formation of limestone in which the Romans cut their amphitheatre served as the city of the Christian dead. Seven hundred years after Dionysius had quarried stone there on a mammoth scale the Christians began to burrow into the grey rock and after the fashion of moles to construct a subterranean metropolis. They were not pioneers in the underground regions beneath the sloping hill of Acradina. Already the Greeks had pierced the rock with a network of subterranean aqueducts, graceful constructions, their cross-section similar to a lancet window, high enough to allow a man to pass with head and shoulders slightly bent. Terracotta pipes carried water through these passages to the mainland city, and perhaps also to Ortygia, for natural springs could not be relied upon in time of siege. The catacombs were constructed under the ruins of former Greek buildings, for by Christian times Syracuse had declined from one of the greatest cities of antiquity to an unimportant town and contracted into its original island stronghold of Ortygia. They were sited about a mile outside Syracuse to the north: burial closer to the city being prohibited by the Roman authorities. The earliest were simply private vaults, where members of the family and close friends were buried together, sometimes in the grounds of a villa, sometimes in a piece of land belonging to the family. The original catacombs were therefore simple and restricted: a subterranean passage hewn out of the rock, on either side of which bodies were placed in niches and cemented over with a terracotta plaque. Wherever possible, they followed the line of disused aqueducts, merely widening the gallery to allow free passage. At this early stage, in the second and third centuries, no attempt was made to elaborate or decorate: the passage had a purely functional purpose. The highest niches on both

sides were the first to be used as tombs; later, when all the wall
space had been exhausted, the catacomb was made deeper to
provide additional room, and where this was impossible tombs
were cut in the floor itself. As these private burial grounds
extended and became more numerous, one would pass above
another, or meet and join a neighbouring passage, so that a
complex network was formed on several levels.

In the Syracusan catacombs of Villa Cassia and S. Maria
di Gesù, which date from the earliest period, passages run
at all angles, irregular as a tangled skein of wool. The ceilings are low and straight, the sides narrow, and stretching
from darkness into darkness deeper still the empty tombs,
row upon row, gape like the jaws of a toothless skull. Very
rarely does the terracotta plaque still cover the tomb, for
these burial grounds have been plundered by a succession of
pirates. It is still possible, however, to come across a newly
excavated wing in which the tombs are closed. Instead of
the skeletal and deeply eroded aspect of the looted catacombs,
such a passage has the appearance of any straight seam in a
quarry, the cement blending in colour with the stone ceiling
and floor. Occasionally these tombs are decorated with frescoes. On the side of one niche are pictures of Jonah being
thrown overboard by two stout mariners, and of Daniel in
the lions' den, while on the opposite wall is a fresco of a
donkey, which may have formed part of an Entry into Jerusalem. The commonest subject is that painted beneath the
terracotta plaque of this same tomb, two peacocks on either
side of a vase; the peacock with its fine tail feathers symbolis-
ing the soul and the vase from which it is drinking eternal
life. In another picture Our Lord is placing the crown of life
on the head of a girl, presumably the occupant of the tomb,
while an apostle stands on either side. Heaven is symbolised
by a few flowers; birds in the interstices denote the peace of
death. These frescoes are direct and simple statements in the
Roman style, executed in red, green, and blue, colours bold
enough to stand out even in the dim galleries. In the light of
day they appear crude work, but they were never meant to

see the light of day; by the flickering glow of an oil lamp they are adequate for their purpose. No coffins were used at that time: the dead body, wrapped in a piece of linen, was laid directly in the rock, in imitation of Our Lord's burial, while cement effectively sealed the tomb. The number of small niches, cut for babies and small children, is perhaps as much as a quarter of the total: evidence of conditions among the early Christians of a provincial town.

If it is a doubtful hypothesis that the Christians of that time were mostly of the poorer classes, the catacombs of Syracuse at least provide no evidence to the contrary. Certainly there is nothing in these passages to suggest wealth or even a moderate sensibility. The pagan sarcophagi of Greek and Roman times, by contrast, show a refinement of taste lacking in these crude vaults. A certain structural improvement, however, does appear in the catacombs of S. Giovanni, which were constructed between the fourth and sixth centuries, in a less urgent period when persecution on a large scale had ceased. The form of the passages is quite different: the ceiling is higher and arched, the width considerably greater, while the ground-plan takes the form of a criss-cross pattern, which shows that the catacomb was designed as a whole according to the plan of a Roman city. The largest gallery, the *decumanus maximus*, obtained by widening a Greek aqueduct, is intersected by many minor passages and capped by five *rotonde*, round domed spaces some ten feet in diameter, which perhaps served as chapels for requiem mass on the day of burial. Most of them were constructed by enlarging existing wells, the opening of which admits sufficient light to penetrate the adjacent corridors. Tombs are spaced round the walls of these *rotonde*, but if altars once stood in the centre, they have long since been overthrown. These are the mole-hills which provide communication between the dark warrens and the upper world. In the later catacombs, niches in layers along the walls are less common: instead there are recesses leading off the passage at regular intervals, where tombs are ranged one behind another, as many as twenty deep. Since the catacombs had by now become public burial grounds, members of a family were buried side by side in this fashion, the first tomb to be cut being the one nearest the passage, and the recess being gradually extended as need arose. It must have been a difficult matter to bury reverently bodies in the far-thest part, for there is no alleyway beside the tombs, and the alcove is so low that even to have crawled above the other tombs would have been awkward.

Some of the few remaining inscriptions are cut below a niche in these catacombs. In the centre is the sign ✗ with an alpha and omega on either side; to the right is a curious boat which is also a bird; the prow being marked with a large eye and turned upwards in the shape of a beak. Hovering above the beak is a small round disc marked with the same sign as the one in the centre of the tomb. Below the first boat is another, so worn as almost to be indistinguishable. These are evidently emblems of the soul's journey to the next world, the disc representing viaticum. The boat (or bird) represents a curious mixture of ideas, and the fact that all the small fishing-boats of Sicily have an eye painted on either side of the prow, so that they look like animals (whether bird or monster is uncertain), suggests that the boat could stand both for the journey and the traveller. Such symbols, the most important of which was the fish, originated in Greece and their wide adoption in Rome and elsewhere was perhaps due to the fact that they constituted a useful secret language, undecipherable by the authorities during times of persecu-tion. Such inscriptions are, however, rare in the catacombs at Syracuse; in general the name of the dead person was crudely cut on the terracotta plaque, a sententious phrase occasionally being added.

Christianity had revealed that the only offering worthy of God was God Himself: finished were the days when Daeda-lus had presented a votive offering of gold to the being he believed divine. Yet the Church, if she had refused his honeycomb under one aspect, accepted and perfected it under another. The first tentative signs of that acceptance are scattered around the catacombs, obscure and wasted by time: the peeling symbolic frescoes, here a fish, there a bird, testimonials that these first Christians wanted to devote their artistic skill, however inadequately, to the greater glory of God.

Only one object of beauty was rescued from the catacombs of S. Giovanni: the sarcophagus of Valerius and Adelphia, dating from the fourth or fifth century. This had been removed from its original niche and buried in the catacomb floor, where it escaped the attention of barbarians and Arabs bent on loot. It is a rectangular white marble sarcophagus with a lid, in a perfect state of preservation, both the front of the casket and the lid being carved with great artistry. Dominating the other carvings, in the centre, is a round medallion depicting Adelphia and her husband Valerius holding his symbols of office. The fact that he was a Roman official may explain so costly a mode of burial, in striking contrast to the tombs of other contemporary Christians. In horizontal rows on the lid and front are carved scenes from the Old and New Testaments, in no discernible order: Adam and Eve, the Entry into Jerusalem, Abraham about to sacrifice Isaac and other graphic incidents. The expressions are not very convincing, perhaps because of the miniature scale of the work, and there is a static quality about the scenes of action. The most curious feature, however, is that in all cases the bodies are too small for the heads: in consequence, the figures look like dwarfs or precocious children. This regressive characteristic of the carving appears, though to a less pronounced degree, in Carolingian work and even in some of the capitals in the cloister at Monreale, executed some seven centuries later—striking evidence of the poverty of invention during and immediately after the barbarian invasions. The figure of Christ is distinguished neither by a halo nor by any special physical characteristic, and since the scenes are not clearly separated one from another, the sarcophagus lacks any striking immediate effect and has to be slowly deciphered. In its fashion, however, it is an object of beauty and, if it was

executed by a Syracusan, probably many similar coffins have
been lost to vandals. Others may still lie concealed, for only
a small part of the catacombs has been excavated, miles of
corridors still remaining unexplored for lack of funds. Only
the catacombs of S. Giovanni have been completely unearthed since serious digging was started seventy years ago,
and all the tombs so far discovered number only a few
thousand, whereas at Rome, the only city which possesses
catacombs more extensive than those at Syracuse, it has
been found that tens of thousands of Christians were buried
in the underground passages. At Syracuse, unlike Rome,
there are no distinct chapels leading off the passages and,
apart from the crypt of S. Marziano, at the entrance to the
catacombs, no basilicas. It is unlikely, therefore, that they
were ever used as hiding-places during the persecutions; they
retained always their original purpose as burial sites.

One of the meanings of these subterranean hieroglyphics,
these winding passages cut into the rock, is that the Church
did not yet dare to build above ground. If they were not
actually used as hiding-places during times of persecution,
the dark galleries could have served that purpose excellently.
At a time when all was uncertain and shifting, life and death
dependent on an emperor's whim, when whole peoples were
migrating and civilisations collapsing, the very conditions of
existence were precarious, and the vital inner life, the faith
itself and its practices, more vulnerable still. To build a
church today was to leave ruin tomorrow; to parade the faith
was to invite reprisals. Yet all the while the Church was
growing underground, managing somehow to preserve unity
among its widespread members, spreading out extensive
mining-works under the barbarian cities, which, in course of
time, were to fall in beyond restitution. The catacombs are
links in that chain of mining-works: proof of persistent and
thankless resistance, a stonewall defence against the shifting
hesitancy of the age. They show, too, that concern with the
past and with tradition which is the mark of an eternal institution. Insignificant boys and girls, who happened to die for

their faith, were not forgotten: never before in history had quiet courage received reverence and honour, never before had worldly defeat and ignominy been reckoned fortunate conditions. In the caves, where spiritual man was going through a primitive phase with mental equipment as poor as the flints and bronze of neolithic man, the relics of martyrs provided tangible proof that it was possible to succeed. Such conditions were not without advantages. These early Christians were close in time to the Word: their grandfathers had perhaps listened to S. Paul preaching at Syracuse, and therefore the fundamental virtues of their religion were orders to be loyally obeyed. They had not yet been quibbled out of existence or spun into aspects of the unconscious mind: they were neither hereditary qualities nor dependent on environment, but straightforward commandments. Moreover, since these outcasts were leading a separate life, a hard and fast line divided them from the pagan majority: there was no great danger of gradually, imperceptibly compromising with the world. Again, the scrawled inscriptions on the tombstones of the catacombs, the simple frescoes and decorative devices, show that the truth was deemed sufficient in itself: beside it all human creations, crude or fine, were as nothing.

Yet the paramount difficulty lay precisely in this, that often the truth was hidden. Were these words to be used or those? Did orthodoxy lie in the genitive or dative case? In a Church that made appeal to tradition, a multitude of new problems was continually arising which could not be settled in this way, for no tradition had yet arisen regarding them. Time and organic growth would one day furnish a court of appeal, but meanwhile communication between scattered bishoprics was imperative for orthodoxy. At this crucial moment the barbarians swept down, turning the Mediterranean into a paradise for pirates and cutting off the young churches one from another. Thus pagan rites were sometimes carried on locally and later, with growing centralisation, had to be denounced as heretical.

The ancients, for example, used to smear the newborn

infant's lips with honey as a preservative, and this custom was carried over to their mystery cults, whose new initiates were given milk and honey as a sign of rebirth. Christianity adapted the existing symbolism to its own use. The custom in the early Church was to present mixed milk and honey to newly baptised persons after they had left the font. During the special Mass said for them, wine mixed with water, milk, and honey was consecrated, and the neophyte received a chalice of milk and honey as a foretaste of eternal life. The custom was discontinued after the sixth century, clearly because the addition of other offerings impinged on the pre-eminent position in the Mass of bread and wine, but during the centuries when the catacombs were in use honey must have been given to the newly baptised Christians just as it was to many contemporary worshippers of false gods.

This adaptation of what was good in pagan rites was also carried over to the realm of art and architecture. The cathedral at Syracuse was built by a Greek tyrant five hundred years before the birth of Christ: so intermingled are the civilisations of Sicily, so daring their cross-fertilisation. The Doric temple dedicated to Athena, which Gelon built to commemorate his victory at Himera, was transformed into a Christian church by S. Zosimus, bishop of Syracuse in the seventh century, and since that time has been the mother church of the oldest of all dioceses after Antioch. Sicily is full of churches which incorporate elements of Greek or Roman temples, but nowhere is the original more evident than at Syracuse. Almost the whole structure, including two lines of broad-based, fluted columns, is Greek, so that the newcomer believes himself in a temple before he discovers that he is in a church. Something about the building is known from Cicero's speech against Verres, for although Syracuse was one of the few cities which did not identify itself with the provincial complaint against the Roman governor, Cicero accused Verres of having despoiled the building. The walls were decorated with paintings of the kings and tyrants of Sicily, the doors were of ivory and gold and on top of the pediment hung the goddess's golden shield. This bright object served as a point of orientation to Sicilian sailors: setting out from the Great Harbour of Syracuse they used to watch the shield gradually lose identity in the mass of the Iblean mountains; when its gleaming rays faded from sight they threw honey and incense on the waves, invoking the goddess to protect them on their journey.

The temple of Athena was the glory of Syracuse, the city's landmark, a memorial to Sicily's greatest victory over the barbarian. Yet even this magnificent work did not rise as a wholly new construction: it has been discovered that an archaic temple, perhaps dating from pre-Hellenic times, provided the foundations for Gelon's building. The roots of this grafted tree were therefore themselves originally dovetailed into an older subterranean growth, and, as happened in so many other spheres, the Greek temple was christened in a Roman font. Conquered by Greek art, the Romans were handed over as slaves to the Olympians. The gods of Homer and Hesiod, of Pheidias and Praxiteles, the gods and goddesses of the Greek temples were too overpowering to be resisted. Athena continued to be worshipped under the name of Minerva in the same building, under the same forms, until some time in the fourth century, when the dual pressure of growing Christianity and imperial decadence caused the Roman deities to cower in fear. A century later with the coming of the Vandals and the Goths they toppled from their altars: the temple at Syracuse was stripped of its valuable ornaments and left desecrated and deserted. Finally Belisarius delivered Sicily to the Byzantine Empire, enabling Christianity to creep forth from the catacombs and suit the empty temples to its purpose.

This adaptation of a temple of Athena for Christian rites imposes itself as a figure of the Christian debt to Greece. Of the other early civilisations, in Babylon, Assyria, and Egypt and among the Hittites, were to be found mere crass superstition, astrology and idolatry; their languages were awkward and unadapted for spiritual concepts; in such a close and rigid atmosphere Christianity could hardly have been understood, let alone have flourished. In one country alone had the spirit of wonder, which Plato said was the beginning of all philosophy, broken the chains of superstition and magic, setting reason free to prepare the way for revelation. Within the framework of Greek civilisation, as within this temple of Athena, its broad-based, enduring columns supporting a lofty roof, Christianity was able suitably to express itself.

Art, no less than thought and language, was adapted to the service of the new religion. The time had not yet come to build anew, and S. Gregory the Great instructed bishops, wherever necessary, to take over existing temples, where the people, through long custom, naturally resorted, and, wresting out the pagan idols, to replace them with the Christian God. When the Church did possess wealth and leisure enough to begin decorating and refining, it drew here as in so many other ways on the Greek tradition, so that the continuity to be observed in Sicilian art all the way through the pagan centuries is carried on by the new dispensation. Just as the cathedral at Syracuse is an adaptation of a Doric temple, which in turn is based on prehistoric foundations, so the artistic tradition which is believed to have originated with Daedalus crosses the moment when eternity entered time and persists to this day. Since Christianity does not scorn to use the themes and forms which once served pagan religions, it will be possible to search for Daedalus's honeycomb, whether it be artefact or paradigm, through Christian no less than pagan centuries; indeed, whatever the original turns out to be, it may well appear more evident in a form perfected and fulfilled by Christianity, as part of some place and civilisation hallowed by the new faith.

CHAPTER THIRTEEN

Casale

THE scene now changes from the city of Syracuse to a lonely countryside, and the task of sifting Sicily's past for gold is resumed in a Roman palace, built at a time when the catacombs were being hollowed out of the limestone rock at Syracuse. Thus there is no advance in time: but the light instead of playing on the birth of a world religion illuminates for a moment a dying national cult.

Not far from the mean town of Piazza Armerina, near the centre of the island, hovels give way to hazelwoods beside the river Gela—like all Sicilian rivers, in springtime no more than a stream, but capable in October of swelling to torrential proportions—amid wooded country, soft and undulating. Here, in the fourth century, sheltered by hills, stood a palace, and here today lie the ruins of Casale. For sixteen hundred years they lay buried under layers of sand brought down by the flooded river, and it was only yesterday that they came to light: treasure directly mined from the hillside, jewels taken fully formed from the earth.

The palace is thought to have been built between A.D. 297 and 300 for the Emperor Maximianus Herculius. Born in Pannonia, between the Alps and the Danube, Maximianus made his mark as a soldier, became co-Emperor, with Diocletian, in 286 and ruled for nineteen years until, at the abdication of Diocletian, he too was obliged to abdicate. He is the last but one of the line of pagan Emperors, and his son-in-law was Constantine. Although the work of excavation is still incomplete, the site would already serve for a cathedral. Roman baroque columns with elaborate capitals form an arcade, beside which is a three-apsed triclinium, and a number of smaller rooms. The walls, the roof, the ornaments, were all swept away by the flooded river;

they have fallen and perished, but the glory of the palace remains, for its chief riches were buried in the ground—in the mosaic floors which pave the whole extent of the building and comprise the largest area of Roman mosaics outside Africa. There they lie, like an intricately devised garden of many-coloured flowers, a garden planted in Roman times, which is flowering a second time in a second millennium.

The first great tableau rises suddenly out of the ground to stretch in unbroken line for almost a hundred yards. This passageway depicts a number of interrelated scenes from country life, in particular hunting incidents, but it is difficult to see in them a complete unity. The pavement may well have been specially designed to commemorate events in the owner's life: certainly the subjects are not drawn from mythology. In one scene a peasant cart with solid wooden wheels is being drawn by oxen; in another a man on horseback is going up the gangway of a small boat; the sea being symbolised instead of realistically depicted. This symbolism extends in some cases also to the subjects: a leopard stands above what appears to be a cave in which lies a miniature leopard cub; the face of a man snarls behind the bars of a cage held in the claws of a ferocious griffin. Both these scenes are complete in themselves, and if they had a private meaning for their owner, it has been lost for ever. Many of the scenes show wild animals attacking their prey: here a lion is at an antelope's throat; there a leopard advances on a sheep, all vital with movement and tension. In the apse at the end of the same corridor is depicted a seated, dark-skinned woman, holding a tusk of ivory, flanked by an elephant and a lion. Whether she is meant to personify Africa or India or some more hidden subject is difficult to say. But this obscurity instead of detracting from the interest of the mosaics gives them an urgent and challenging appeal, as though one had stumbled on a bottle at the seaside containing a letter in an unknown language. No divisions separate the various incidents, which are united only by their rustic subject-matter, so that the passage stretches continuously like a rich allegorical diagram in a medieval romance, telling its secret story to the sun and stars. The colours have retained their splendour, reds, yellows, browns, and greens predominating, preserved from the oppressive sun, like the wealth of ancient Egypt, by saving sand, buried alive to be suddenly resurrected at this particular point of time.

The theme of wild animals is resumed in the pavement of the quadrilateral arcade, of even longer extent than the introductory passageway, but for the most part worked in abstract patterns, which the wild animals merely serve to decorate. In pairs, divided from one another and from the succeeding couples by an ornamental design, the heads of animals—an extraordinary variety, no two being the same—stretch round the cloister, lions and tigers, wild boar and wolves, hippopotami and hyenas, lizards and rats: the whole of creation as it was then known set out at man's feet. This dominant theme, together with the position of the villa in country which in Roman times was dense with woods and doubtless rich in game, suggests that the owner was a passionate hunter, so much so that he chose to reside for long periods in the wilds of Sicily, for this is too palatial a residence to have served merely as an occasional hunting-lodge. The lions and leopards in the mosaics suggest that he had hunted game in Roman provinces of Africa: perhaps he preferred that form of sport and came expressly to this remote part because the country was wilder and better stocked than Italy.

The remaining mosaics reveal a little more of his interests and even of his character. In one room, the least well preserved, Orpheus with his lute charms trees, hills, and all the animal creation, which is arranged, in imaginative rather than strictly evolutionary order, through the different species of birds and fish to the mammals. These are so clearly depicted for their own sake, the mythological story being merely a device designed to unify the details, that the owner, it seems certain, loved not only the chase but all animals in themselves, and delighted to be surrounded by pictures of them. One looks expectantly for the parallel figure of Daedalus, but he is not depicted here: with his usual cunning, he has outwitted the mosaic-workers.

Bulls and horses are added to the number of animals in the great pavement of the triclinium, which represents the labours of Hercules. The figures in this room are by far the largest in the villa, titanic forms that do indeed prove Hercules a demi-god. To see them to advantage one must climb and look down on them: a circle of pictures shows the hero and a succession of different monsters locked in eternal struggle, the separate scenes well balanced and integrated to form a total pattern. In the apse of the same great hall are figures of five giants—four of them with snakes instead of legs—struggling in their death agony, pierced by the arrows of Jupiter. The expression of pain not only in every line of their faces but in the gestures with which they try to staunch their wounds, and the tortured, twisted muscles of their bodies are depicted in realistic detail and with a force which betrays the artist's impassioned interest.

This fascination with struggle and with man or beast stretched to the limits of endurance, and the treatment of man as a natural animal of great strength and subtlety, can be traced in most of the mosaics. The subjects are straightforward, never oblique or brooding, seeking adventure and most at home in outdoor life. The gods are treated as strong men with fine bodies, brave and resourceful, but in no sense supernatural. The technical form is in complete harmony with the subject matter. Realism as regards movement, struggle and action; symbolism in respect of background and, occasionally, of certain subjects; very little imaginative detail, no rigidity or stylisation among the figures, no exoticism of colour, a style adapted to straightforward narrative rather than to nuances of expression. At this level they totally succeed: they tell their story vividly, with style and harmony, without blurring subject and background, without losing coherence by trying to say too much. If they lack the fresh naïvety of later mosaics such as those in the Cappella Palatina, they compensate for it with a boundless energy, and if they lack the golden background which suffuses the Byzantine works with light, their colours catch the full brilliance of an unsheltered sun. They delight in being true to nature, and turn sharp observation of the animal world to good account in pictures which are astonishingly graphic; beside them the Byzantine figures seem static and rigid: the emphasis there being on expression and gentle gesture, not on the snarling mouth and tensed muscle. In their general atmosphere, also, these mosaics afford a striking contrast to the Christian works. To come suddenly upon these Roman pavements, the hunters and the hunted, the tortured giants, is to return to a world where man is still a wild animal, superior to, but not totally distinct from other animals, to a world where there is no law but the law of the jungle. The Christian pictures, on the other hand, find order in everything, because they see all human action as a continuation of a particular sequence of events having infinite importance. The Roman mosaics are totally anthropocentric, the others totally theocentric. This appears, for example, in the treatment of animals. In the pagan work they are ferocious wild beasts, in one aspect killers of each other and of man, in another objects of diversion and sport, creatures to be hunted down for the banqueting board. The Christian mosaics, on the other hand, whether in the scenes of the Creation or in Noah's ark, show all animals as God's creatures, to be respected for His sake, to be studied as signs of His will.

The most fundamental advance, however, is from one order of reality to another. The Roman pavements depict natural, tangible and visual qualities, strength of limb and beauty of body, while the Christian pictures attempt the far harder task of representing the inner life, that other world which through the Christian revolution had come to be taken as the true centre of the universe. These mosaics are perhaps the last pagan achievement in Sicily executed under the old dispensation. Although they date from the Christian era, the new religion had not been received as a spiritual climate with which every artist, either by accepting or denying, would have to reckon. The mythology of the subjects is already outmoded: there is a hollow ring about the music of Orpheus. Because all truth in the last decades of the Western Roman Empire is relative, the symbolism is private: the wild animals are poised to strike: Europe is on the point of reverting to barbarism. Eight centuries will elapse before Sicily again produces comparable works of mosaic, masterpieces with an eternal significance and dedicated to a purpose very different from that of the pavements of Casale.

If the palace is primarily a world of heroes and wild animals, it is not exclusively so. One small room, a bedroom perhaps, departs completely from the dominant theme, and yet its subject has always, in aristocratic society, formed a complement to hunting. Beautiful women, in this mosaic, are playing with discus and ball and with weights; running and jumping, not frivolously, as maidens on Greek vases are often represented, but seriously intent on making their fine bodies lovelier still. It is surprising at first that they should be gymnasts: one would have expected rather languorous creatures clad in silk and reclining on couches. Yet under this form, they do, after all, harmonise with the hunters: arms and legs capably strong, and like the wild beasts poised to spring. They are women in a man's world, adapting themselves to his ideals, but also in a world where man is merely one among many strong beasts. Their faces are portrayed with little detail, for it is their bodies which chiefly interest the artist: well-formed, tall and graceful, naked except for two of the briefest cloths, they are the female equivalent of the hunters—fine animals adapted to a specific purpose. But these figures are in no sense decadent, as their scanty clothing might indicate. There is no excessive pre-occupation with the body as something desirable in itself, no diminishing of the size of the head: these portraits were products of a vigorous society, energetic, graceful, perhaps not over-concerned with the spiritual life, but certainly not indifferent to it.

Aphrodite is dead: the ideal goddess of beauty has been superseded by this plurality of particular girls, portrayed on a pavement where the feet of huntsmen can trample them down. The communal links, the old patriotism which directed and sublimated men's sentiments towards a lofty Venus who protected the state and from whom all Romans were descended, has fallen to pieces; and the old idea has run to seed in this bevy of bathing beauties. The world now is a world of flux, where no single ideal or person can remain constant for very long, for such girls as these are multiple and changing as those on the covers of present-day magazines. The Roman Empire is on the verge of collapse: soon the barbarians will pour down from the North as far as Sicily, and the Africans whom Rome has twice held at bay will seize their opportunity to bestride the island for two hundred years.

Can these mosaics, before they are engulfed by invading hordes, throw light on Diodorus's story? Taken with preceding works of art in Sicily, they do suggest the beginnings of a pattern in the carpet, a clue to the meaning of the legend. Not only these pavements, but the temple of Athena, the statue of Aphrodite, the theatre at Taormina, the splendours of Agrigento and the ruins of Selinus: every work of art extending back to the Minoan sherds at Lipari has been fashioned in foreign moulds. Looking forward, this characteristic would remain equally distinctive: Normans, Swabians, Spaniards, and Italians would in turn bring to Sicily their own particular artistic forms, each people disdaining to work in the modes set by its predecessor. The astonishing continuity of thought and theme and subject matter is offset by a total lack of formal continuity, as this palace bears witness. Here the Romans, content elsewhere and in other artistic fields to imitate Greek work, asserted their own civilisation in the mosaic art-form which they had brought to perfection. Each succeeding tide of invaders washed up a new style on the shores of Sicily, high-water marks which are visible still, alien and distinctive. Each invader has repeated the story of Daedalus, who, coming from a distant land, introduced to Sicily new and marvellous forms of art. If

Diodorus saw the original story of Daedalus as the embodiment of certain constants in the pattern of Sicilian art down to his day, then the legend was at least in one respect to prove prophetic over an even longer period of years.

What then has so far emerged from the quest? Erice was the point of departure, but neither there nor at Agrigento could traces be found of an actual honeycomb of gold. Selinus suggested one possible interpretation—that Daedalus brought to Sicily the craft of bee-keeping—but this reading was rejected as unsatisfactory. Etna proved a turning-point, for there it became clear that the legend might have to be interpreted more widely: the original honeycomb was perhaps something more permanently significant than a mere gift of gold. The carts and puppets tended to substantiate a historical Daedalus and so too did the Cretan sherds at Lipari, while the gold coins and the statue of Aphrodite at Syracuse suggested that Daedalus's offering stood rather for art in general, including poetry, symbolised by a honeycomb on the poet's lips. With the coming of Christianity Greek art forms were carried over and utilised for religious ends, thus showing that Diodorus's story held true for the Christian as well as the pagan era. Now Casale has revealed that each invading people has played the part of Daedalus, bringing new forms to the island. It remains to be seen whether a more complete view of Sicily will arrange these clues into a solution of the original legend.

CHAPTER FOURTEEN

Norman Palermo

With the decay of the Roman Empire, Sicily fell into a period of decline which is reflected in a dearth of new art. Its position as an island protected it for some time against the barbarian invasions, but in the fifth century it finally yielded to the Vandals. Not, however, for long. A century later Belisarius rescued it for the Eastern Empire, and there began a period of five centuries under Oriental rule, first by the Greeks of Byzantium, and in the ninth century by the Arabs, driven across the entire Mediterranean as far as France by enthusiasm for a new religion. Arab rule was tolerant of Christianity but in other respects made of the island a typical emirate. Palermo, as under the Carthaginians, became the capital of the island, a pre-eminence which the Norman kings, when they swooped gloriously down in the eleventh century, recognised and confirmed. For a hundred and fifty years the Normans turned Palermo into one of the great cities of the world, expressing their wealth and crusading faith in a riot of churches. But when the crown of Sicily passed to the Swabian Frederick II, and was later assigned by the Papacy to the Angevin and Spanish kings, Palermo no longer reflected the pattern of Sicilian life. During these turbulent years the arts were the arts of war, to be seen best in a fortress town like Enna.

In 1409 the island became a dependency of Spain, receiving a viceroy as governor: with a settled way of life and a wealthy aristocracy, Palermo again takes pride of place as the leading and representative city of the island. The chief works of art continue to be concentrated here, except for a period after the catastrophic earthquake of 1693, which laid south-east

Sicily in ruins. Towns such as Ragusa, Modica and Noto were then rebuilt almost in their entirety, and it is there, during the years after the Peace of Utrecht, when Sicily was assigned away from Spain, that the pattern of contemporary life is most evident.

Soon, however, the balance shifts back to Palermo; it was in the capital city that Nelson, who guarded the island from Napoleon, took up residence. Now, as under the Norman kings, Englishmen were to play a large part in shaping Sicily's destiny. Another Englishman, Lord William Bentinck, gave Sicily her first constitution which, although in force for only three years, fired the liberal revolutions of 1848 and 1860, and it was again British support which made possible Garibaldi's final liberation of the island.

In 1860 Sicily voted to be annexed to Italy. Like a satellite she was finally drawn within the orb of the larger body and absorbed. Yet there was nothing new in this—Sicilian history is a continual series of variations on one or two themes—for in the Roman Empire the island played much the same part as she was now to do under the Italian kings. Unwilling subservience gave way in the name of a revolutionary ideal to voluntary surrender of the rights of self-government, but the country was still to suffer from the oppression and neglect which have characterised her history since the days when Homer referred to Sicily as a source of slaves. But now insurrection was no longer possible—one cannot with logic rebel against a freely-elected government—and Sicily was forced to accept the fact that it was her destiny to suffer.

Such is the historical thread which will lead through time and place, pointing a sure way across an island where different periods of history, because they are still living, tend to merge and beguile. After Casale the search continues in the wake of the Norman conquerors. Their art, as well as their way of life, drew heavily on the Arab and Byzantine traditions which, in the course of five centuries, had become well established, so that while there are practically no works still extant in Sicily which can be dated between the fall of the

Roman Empire and the Norman invasion, the Oriental style and excellence are easily distinguishable in the later exotic mixture termed Sicilian-Norman art, which finds its most perfect expression in and around Palermo.

The story of Palermo as a great European city begins in Normandy, in the village of Hauteville, between Coutances and St Lô. The seed which flowered in the heat of the Mediterranean as the capital city of a great kingdom, crowned with some of the most sumptuous ornaments ever fashioned, originated in a group of small, grey farms clustered in a green valley where the sun is never too warm. In this village lived a petty *seigneur* called Tancred, of Scandinavian origin, one of the numerous Vikings who had populated this region of France since the tenth century and given it a reputation for independence and resistance to Christianity. Tancred had twelve sons by two successive wives, and since their father possessed only a modest property the three eldest decided to travel and make their fortune. At that time Italy, contested by Germany, the Papacy and the Greek Empire, offered greatest opportunity to young soldiers, and so the three brothers, with a party of other Normans, rode south to Italy in search of wealth and glory, just as their forefathers had swept down on France a century before.

They fought first against the Greeks and then against rival Italian princes, always with great distinction, and soon managed, in the ebb and flow of continual war, to obtain principalities for themselves. Their prodigious military success, now and hereafter, was largely accounted for by their use of the stirrup, which had been introduced to northern Europe a century earlier. This device permitted the Normans to wear extremely heavy armour, which rendered their bodies almost invulnerable, while from horseback they were able to use lance and battleaxe to advantage on the usually unmounted enemy. Their appearance has been portrayed for all time in the scenes of the Bayeux tapestry, which chronicles an exactly contemporary invasion. Their armour was matched by proverbial physical strength. Thus, one of

the Norman knights, Hugues Tue-boeuf, a comrade-in-arms
of the Hauteville brothers, once took the horse of an enemy
general by the bridle, caressed the animal's head and suddenly, clenching his fist, gave the horse such a tremendous
blow between the eyes that it fell dead on the spot. Such
armed might had not been seen in the Mediterranean since
early Roman days.

Having established their power in Apulia, the Normans
were on the point of losing their new-won principalities
through rivalry when a sudden attack by the Papacy, fearful
of the northern invaders, united them as never before. The
Pope, having suffered defeat and unable to persuade either
Germans or Greeks to drive out these upstart knights, was
obliged to recognise their Italian fiefs in return for their
respect of Papal territory. The *parvenus* had at last won
acceptance.

While the conquest of Southern Italy was the work of
many Norman knights in unison, the conquest of Sicily was
the personal war of two of the younger sons of Tancred
d'Hauteville, Robert and Roger, who at a later date followed
their brothers south. Of Robert a contemporary chronicler
wrote: "Homer says of Achilles that those who heard his
voice seemed to hear the thundering shout of a great multitude, but it used to be said of this man that his battle-cry
would turn back tens of thousands," while Roger was no less
ambitious and gifted a general than his elder brother. Since
expansion towards the north of Italy was not feasible, the
younger Hautevilles, discontented with their principalities in
Apulia and confident of their power to conquer against any
odds, decided to attack Sicily. At that time the island, more
than half Arab and as to the rest Greek, was ruled by three
Arab emirs, continually at war among themselves. While
Robert was obliged to remain in Italy to suppress revolt among
his dependent knights and to safeguard his possessions
against the Papacy and the Germans, his younger brother
conducted the Sicilian campaign. With no more than three
hundred knights, against odds of a hundred to one, Roger

harried the island for ten years in a succession of minor raids until in 1071 Robert was free to bring up large reinforcements, Palermo, the Arab capital, was captured and peace signed.

Robert and Roger divided the country between them. Robert was to be suzerain of the whole island and to keep Palermo, half of Messina and some land on the north coast; the rest, whether already conquered or not, was left to Roger with the title of Count of Sicily. Roger spent the next twenty years in conquering the southern part of the island and consolidating what was already won by the construction of castles at strategic points. By showing religious tolerance and treating the Arab chiefs with honour, he was able to gain the goodwill of an alien people who, having for centuries been subject to a succession of foreign conquerors, were willing to accept still another new power without national roots. His attitude of religious tolerance did not prevent Roger from doing his utmost to restore Christianity: he established bishoprics, settled monks from oversea and girdled the island with churches. After forty years of continuous war and ten years of peace and stabilisation, Roger died peacefully in his bed. His brothers had come south as simple mercenaries and against the three greatest powers of their age had become rulers of a vast, rich, and populous country; he himself, lacking birth and wealth, had followed them a distance of two thousand miles from his native land; he had virtually single-handed conquered an island of alien civilisation and several million inhabitants, establishing his power so solidly that his dynasty was to endure for over a century.

Roger II, the first Hauteville to assume the title of King of Sicily, was no less active a warrior than his father. He re-united under his power all the Norman possessions of Southern Italy, conquered part of the North African coast and made several punitive expeditions against the Greek Empire. But he was more than a brave warrior: he had been born in a court and raised by the most civilised of tutors. He loved art as much as battle and among other services to learning he

caused the writings of Ptolemy to be translated from the
Arabic into Latin, supervised the compilation of a geography
of the world, transferred the bones of Virgil from Posillipo
to the Castel dell'Ovo in Naples in order that they might
more fittingly be venerated, and called jongleurs and trouba-
dours from France to sing in his southern kingdom. Edrisi,
his court geographer, says he did more while sleeping than
most men awake, and a contemporary chronicler writes, "He
was a lover of justice and a most severe avenger of crime. He
abhorred lying; did everything by rule and never promised
what he did not mean to perform. Justice and peace were
universally observed throughout his dominions." Romuald
of Salerno describes him as tall, well-built with a loud voice
and inflexible gaze, but a mosaic in the church of the Martorana at Palermo depicts him as a frail ascetic, with dark
eyes and hair and a small pointed beard. It is probable that
the mosaic represents an Oriental ideal and that, like his
father and sons, Roger was in reality strongly built and handsome, with blond hair and blue eyes.

At the accession of his son, William the Bad, the Sicilian
kingdom goes into almost imperceptible decline. While King
Roger had known how to value the good things of the East:
Greek and Alexandrine science, Arab and Persian poetry,
and combined this appreciation with a life of action, William,
perhaps taking after his mother, a daughter of Alfonso VI
of Castile, in whose family fratricides and incest were not
uncommon, dabbled in oriental magic and astrology. He
ruled through a variety of ministers, including Moslems, a
Hungarian, two Englishmen, Walter of the Mill, Archbishop of Palermo, and Richard Palmer, Bishop of Syracuse,
and above all the gifted Majone, a native of Bari. The recurrent rebellions in Southern Italy were duly put down
but with noticeably less speed and vigour than in the old
days, as though the southern sun were sapping northern
strength, and as soon as they had been suppressed William
returned impatiently to his magic and cabals.

Under his successor, William the Good, the Hautevilles

suffered a major military defeat—the first in a century of almost continuous war—when a too ambitious expedition into Greece was cut to pieces. But this was as nothing to the diplomatic disaster of William's reign. In order to appease Germany, he gave his aunt Constance in marriage to Henry of Swabia and agreed that if he died without children Constance should inherit the Kingdom of Sicily: the hard-won island of the Hautevilles would enter into the patrimony of the Hohenstaufen, their life-long enemies. William was young and doubtless expected that the eventuality would never arise, but he died five years later without children. He is said to have lived in his pleasure palaces surrounded by Oriental slave girls; perhaps in a subtle way the Arabs had taken vengeance on the Hauteville dynasty.

Sicily, in accordance with the treaty signed by William, should have entered at once into the German heritage but the people refused, as long as there was still a Hauteville living, to submit to German rule. Tancred, a bastard cousin of the dead king, a man described by his chronicler as "semi-vir, embryo infelix et detestabile monstrum," astonished the island by rising to its show of loyalty. Having gallantly repulsed the German armies, he established himself in the throne, only to fall sick and die. Henry of Swabia took possession of the island. The Norman state of Sicily and Southern Italy, founded a century and a half before by Robert and Roger, existed no longer.

If the Normans were prodigious warriors, they were no less prodigious builders. Their rule is marked by the erection of castles, churches and cathedrals all across the island, and of palaces and lodges in the neighbourhood of their capital city. They came as northern warriors, Christian but slightly barbarian, to one of the most civilised countries of the world, and the stability and wealth they brought with them permitted the orderly flowering of arts which until then had languished amid civil wars. Just as the Norman kings recruited trustworthy ministers from all the peoples of the world, but especially from among the Arabs of Sicily, adapting existing conditions to their particular requirements, so they commissioned local architects, painters, craftsmen and mosaic-workers, formerly employed in the building and decoration of mosques, to erect castles and churches under the new dispensation. Craftsmen attracted from all parts of the world to the new court still further increased the already cosmopolitan nature of Sicilian art. Indeed, so varied and complex is the Norman artistic achievement that it can be studied only in its individual buildings.

Of their constructions in Palermo none had greater significance for the Norman kings than the Cathedral—where Roger II, wearing the tiara, mantle and dalmatic of a Greek Basileus, was solemnly crowned first King of Sicily amid splendour and pomp—a building which still dominates the capital city and, despite its deformation in modern times, remains one of the triumphs of Norman architecture.

A fine building, like a large canvas, is best viewed from a considerable distance. In a city as old as Palermo, it is rarely that one can get far enough away from a church to see it whole: but the adjacent houses, grouped as close as the crowds milling in the streets, allow a full view, on one side at least, of the Cathedral. Half way up the Corso Vittorio Emanuele the right side of the street gives way as though stage scenery had suddenly been removed to reveal the backcloth of sky and garden, and beyond a long mass of stone which in the present light seems quite fawn. Not fawn, for it is evident almost at once, as the sun plays truant from the clouds, that the walls are volatile, ranging in mood from a dark earth-coloured brown to an almost golden luminosity, and this changing colour of the walls makes the building appear, as the clouds close in, now a sister of the surrounding mountains, now a creature of the sky and sun.

It is the changing colour of the stone which first of all startles and holds the attention; only after a little while does the eye wander to take account of form. In general appearance the cathedral is that strange mixture of Norman and Byzantine which is so peculiar to the island: the crenellated roof and arabesque mouldings on the side walls contrasting with the rounded arches of the apse and the finely wrought tracery of the towers at the four corners. The dome in the centre is so clearly a later addition that there is no question of its belonging. It crowns the great fawn mass in colour partially yellow, partially dark brown, a cupola without any of the strength of the main building—a mere imposition. It is as though the architect, the Florentine Ferdinando Fuga, who designed the dome in his dotage, had twice tried to sing the right note and failed, reaching once too high and once too low. This eighteenth-century addition was meant to break the extremely long straight line of the nave; the intention was praiseworthy but by then men had forgotten how to build as the Normans built. Or was the dome perhaps a deliberate attempt at improvement? Fuga may well have been convinced that he could redeem the barbarous northern building which Archbishop Walter of the Mill had founded six centuries before. But the attempt fails hopelessly, just as the late cupola at Bayeux Cathedral fails, yet without being sufficiently incongruous to spoil the whole.

The apse is flanked by two twelfth-century towers, rising only a few feet above the line of the crenellated roof. The Gothic façade, flanked by twin towers similar to those of the apse, is a pastiche of all the decorative devices used by the Normans. Doorways and windows are ornamented with layer upon layer of zigzag, arabesque and other mouldings, like illustrations to a history of architecture. From the façade two pointed arches, like huge ropes mooring a liner, are flung far across the street to meet a massive belfry in the same style as the towers. The north side, the only one which can be seen as a whole, is broken by a wide fourteenth-century porch, composed of three Gothic arches surmounted by a sloping roof as of a Greek temple, so graceful that it saves from heaviness the long, unbroken wall. One of the pillars in the porch was probably taken from the mosque which had occupied the site of the original ninth-century church, for on it is inscribed a passage from the Koran. Thus even the exterior reveals a bewildering medley of different styles.

The doorway is made up of intricately carved dark marble, moulded to a pointed arch and surmounted by a golden mosaic of the Virgin and Child in the Byzantine style. This is the usual entrance to the Cathedral, an enchanted doorway which leads to another world. For passing through the fawn medieval walls one finds not the expected Norman work but a simple eighteenth-century interior without distinction. The Cathedral is two churches, an outer and an inner, bearing no apparent relation to one another and meeting only in the dome: it is as though a crusader, whom one would have imagined capable only of rugged sentences, had started to speak in the style of Voltaire.

The interior takes the form of a cross. The nave is divided from the aisles by pilasters, each composed of four grey marble columns, the whole finished in grey plasterwork. Nothing could be simpler than the lines of this interior, which was superimposed on the Norman original in the eighteenth and nineteenth centuries. Only the slightest ornamentation breaks the flat, bare Palladian lines: statues of the same period all round the nave, and above the side altars paintings which harmonise, adding just enough colour to redeem the whole from severity. Light falls on the plain marble floor, which is bare as a threshing stone. Of the outrageous details, concessions to popular taste, which so often mar an interior, there are in this building only two: the painted ceiling above the high altar, its too bright colours blatant in such decorous surroundings, and in the right aisle an enormous, over-elaborated reliquary of S. Rosalia, intricate to the point of losing all form, worked in silver during the seventeenth century, and imprisoned—as it deserves—behind bars closed with a massive padlock.

In the first two chapels of the south aisle stand six royal tombs, bearing silent witness to the disastrous years when Sicily exchanged Norman for Swabian, then for Angevin and finally for Spanish rule. The finest tombs, under rich baldacchini and mosaics, belong to Roger II and the Empress Constance, his daughter, whom William the Good gave in marriage to Henry of Swabia. Henry's tomb stands close by, out of place here, for he had no love for Sicily: when he conquered the island he roasted alive those who had shown any loyalty towards the bastard Tancred, and systematically despoiled Palermo, where he was known as the Cyclops. The neighbouring tomb belongs to Frederick II—his son by Constance—more ambitious and cultivated than the Normans themselves, the Stupor Mundi. In 1781, when the tombs were opened, his body alone was found preserved, small and ugly as in life, clad in rich clothes, with his crown and imperial orb. Nearby stands the tomb of his wife, Constance of Aragon, by whom the kingdom descended to the first of the Spanish rulers, Peter of Aragon, chosen by the Sicilian Parliament to free the country from the Angevin oppressor. His tomb, under a simple baldacchino, stands here with the others.

These monuments represent some of the authentic facts of Sicilian history. The way in which those same facts have been moulded by popular imagination is illustrated by a legend which seeks to explain the difference of appearance between this cathedral and that at Monreale, which is the most beautiful and richest building in Sicily. William the Good, so the story relates, was King of Palermo; William the Bad King of Monreale. Each conceived the plan of building a church in his own kingdom, and started to lay the foundations. William the Good built a church that was beautiful outside but not inside; William the Bad did just the opposite. They agreed that as soon as one had finished his church, the other should go and see it. As both churches were completed at the same time, William the Bad went to Palermo, William the Good to Monreale. William the Bad, before setting out for Palermo, buried his treasure at the foot of a fig-tree along the roadside. When he reached Palermo, seeing the beautiful exterior of the church and imagining it to be equally beautiful inside, he was so surprised that he fell dead to the ground like a load of cabbages. William the Good reached Monreale and seeing the church from the outside imagined that the interior was just as ugly. He did not even bother to go in, but he was puzzled for he knew that William the Bad possessed great wealth. Being tired, he lay down at the foot of a fig-tree and while he slept, the Madonna appeared to him and told him that treasure was buried at the foot of the fig-tree where he lay. When he awoke, he unburied the treasure and carried it back to Palermo.

It is an artless story: as in the case of the cycle of Charlemagne at the marionette theatre, the essential fact, in this case the royal foundation of both buildings, has been retained while names and other details have become hopelessly confused. But if the story is useless as history, it is significant of an important element in Sicilian tradition. Throughout the island the most popular folk stories are those which relate to the discovery of a hidden treasure of gold. Such a theme is found in other folk literatures but in Sicily it is so widespread and assumes such central importance that one wonders whether it does not reflect something more than the memories of a country torn by almost continual warfare, and therefore of hiding and looting. More curious still, the most frequent items of treasure are oranges, apples and other natural objects fashioned of pure gold. They are closely associated with the devil, who either in person or through a deputy guards the treasure, which thereby takes on a forbidden, unholy quality. Now of all the riches Sicily has ever known, the most magnificent were those of the pagan temples, of which Erice was the chief, and it is natural to see in these legends a memory of the hiding of temple treasure by pagan priests, as Christianity spread across the island. It is true that no honeycomb is mentioned in the stories, but in the course of time such an object may have dropped out in favour of the more familiar oranges and apples.

Such speculation, however, can never provide more than circumstantial evidence, and some more tangible clue must be found. On our return to the real world of Norman architecture, a diversity of styles even more striking than those of

the cathedral is to be found in the church called the Martorana or S. Maria dell'Ammiraglio. It was constructed by
Giorgio d'Antióchia, Admiral to King Roger. The son of
Syro-Greek parents, he and his father for some time served
under the Emir of Al Mahdia. In 1112 he came to Palermo
and entered Roger's service, for the population of Sicily was
still largely Greek and Arab, and the Norman kings did not
hesitate to employ Orientals in the highest positions of the
state. He distinguished himself in Roger's African wars and
was finally given the exalted rank of Emir of Emirs and
Admiral of Admirals. His office did not carry the naval
power alone: after the king, he was the most powerful man
in Sicily. He was a staunch orthodox Christian and particularly devoted to the cult of Our Lady: the dedicatory panel
of his church shows him prostrate at the feet of the Madonna.
The deed of the church's foundation has survived: the
church was erected from its foundations by the Admiral, in
honour of Our Lady and as a small thank-offering for the
gifts which she had bestowed on him; the founder endowed
the church, which he had built and decorated with lavish
munificence, according to the wish of the King, with ten
Saracen serfs, a village, two *fondaca*, a bakery and a garden in
Palermo to provide for the administration of the church and
the livings of the clergy.

Here, after the Sicilian Vespers of 1282, the barons and
mayors of the Sicilian cities met and decided to offer the
crown to Peter of Aragon. That turning-point in the history
of the island is reflected in the present remains of the church,
which looks backwards to the fruitful period of Norman rule
and forwards to the Spanish domination, during which King
Alfonso ceded the church to a neighbouring monastery
founded by Eloisa Martorana, whence it takes its familiar
name. During the sixteenth and seventeenth centuries part
of the original Norman structure was destroyed to make way
for baroque decoration: hence the dual nature of the present
church. From the Piazza Bellini the exterior is not particularly striking: the baroque west front adjoins a decayed

Norman campanile with four columned storeys. The entrance is through a simple courtyard and plain doorway.
Nothing outside suggests the riches within: the exterior, in
fact, is as dull, perhaps purposely as dull, as a bank or a mint.
But when the threshold is crossed one is in a universe of gold;
rich mosaics cluster above and on all sides, though almost
immediately it appears that the treasury has been robbed and
imitation work left in many places. The high altar is in
coloured marble and stucco work framing a dull painting
above a fine, large tabernacle of lapis lazuli; most of the nave
has been covered with eighteenth-century frescoes, to harmonise with and even to outdo (so, incredibly, it was believed) the mosaics of the centre.

The building takes the form of a Greek cross, divided by
four pillars supporting a dome, and it is these which are
encrusted with mosaics. They were probably executed by
Greek craftsmen, heirs to the Byzantine tradition, which
under the Arab domination had not been lost—the admiral
of Greek origin would have felt a special sympathy for their
work and employed them to decorate his church. The dome
itself is inlaid with mosaics of Christ with angels, and the
tambour with prophets and evangelists. Larger than these
are the figures of eight apostles at the sides of the cupola,
their long faces grave and reverent, with that totally spiritual
expression found in the sculptures at Autun, but with the
added force of inexhaustible colour, each one an individual
with a personality of his own, distinguished not by his clothes
or the name worked beside him in Greek lettering but by his
expression and the lines of his face. The gold background,
though it has gained rather than lost splendour in its eight
hundred years of continual summer, shows up rather than
dims the rich colours of the garments, green, white, rose and
lilac, mauve and blue, which soften the austere faces of the
saints who wear them.

The most interesting of the pictorial mosaics is a dual
scene. On the left of the nave under the dome is a Nativity,
Our Lady holding up the infant Jesus in swaddling clothes.

Balancing this on the right is the Dormition of Our Lady. Clothed in blue she is lying on a couch surrounded by mourners, while directly above Our Lord holds her in his arms, wrapped in a shroud, a complete equivalent of the infant Jesus in the other scene. A perfect symmetry of treatment does full justice to the symmetry of thought. There is no foreground or background, no past and present in these mosaics; everything takes place simultaneously and in one place. Such concentration of thought and imagery and colour, because one can never quite exhaust it, leaves a sense of mystery in fullest harmony with the subject-matter.

Compared with this Byzantine work the baroque painting and stuccoes which decorate the rest of the church (though admittedly not of the first order) seem superficial and ostentatious. They are in poor repair and the paint in places is peeling. Because they have not endured as the mosaics have, one fancies, but not absurdly, that the thought behind them was less vigorous and profound.

In this city of intermingled styles, almost every building is the joint product of two or more civilizations. Even Arab work has been utilised for what is perhaps the most picturesque exterior in Palermo. Set away by itself among trees and flowers, this disused church of S. Giovanni degli Eremiti, built by Roger II in 1132, not only combines Arab work but is unashamedly Arab in style. Surroundings of foliage are rare for any building in Palermo and in this case are particularly welcome for they set off the colour and form of the church to advantage, and isolate it from the rest of the city, to which it is in such striking architectural contrast. As one approaches it from the Porta Nuova, the body of the building is hidden by a line of palm trees, above which rises an undecorated grey stone tower, its thick walls pierced by plain arches and culminating in a smooth, rose-coloured cupola. A path leads up the surrounding garden to an eminence beyond, from which the church can be seen as a whole. Standing here at the angle of two walls one looks over at the west front and south wall of the nave. The building takes the shape of a T, the nave being surmounted by two large red cupolas, and the horizontal stroke of the T by the belfry tower and cupola, and two other cupolas equal in size to that which crowns the tower but smaller by half than those over the nave. The walls are of thick grey stone of the utmost simplicity. This oriental style of architecture is so unfamiliar to western eyes that instead of accepting its principles unquestioningly and going on to appraise the fine points of the building, as with works in a familiar form, one disputes the very conception of a church along such lines. In spite of oneself, first impressions tend to be of toadstools in children's picture-books, and even of coloured parasols, for these smooth domes are surmounted by thin, pointed stones. But soon the style sheds its novelty, and its power and simplicity are revealed. This is a church built for burning sunshine, its thick walls and small windows, now bare of their Arab lattice work, restraining the heat and glare. The rose-red of the cupolas is the one colour which can withstand and prove a harmonious contrast to the deep blue of a Sicilian summer sky. Other colours, other forms would be submerged.

The garden is crowded with flowering shrubs, fruit trees and flowers. Grapefruit, mandarines, lemons and oranges hang from the branches. Banana-trees and fig-trees are grouped luxuriously together with palms, cacti and prickly pears. One tree, close to the garden wall, is grafted, the branches on one side bearing lemons, on the other oranges: a figure of the building as a whole, for the church was built on to a mosque which formerly occupied the site, and even incorporates part of the earlier building, so that from the garden the red cupolas seem grafted on to the dark, lemon-coloured south wall, the remnants of the Saracen place of worship.

Still another age in Sicilian history—the Norman consolidation—is commemorated here. In the part of the garden facing the north-west corner of the church, still within the precincts of the mosque, stands a small cloister, a fine example of pure Norman work of the late twelfth century. By

then the conquerors were able not only to assimilate but to
impose the style of their native country: it was no Arab
craftsmen who built this airy colonnade with the light pillars
rising in pairs to support pointed arches. The view from here
through the graceful cloister to the powerful church and
coarse, ruined walls of the mosque beyond makes vivid that
tension in which Sicily has always been held, the pendant
jewel of Italy, catching the light from rising and setting sun,
poised at the centre of the Mediterranean between north and
south, east and west, and blending within itself in a riot of
styles, sometimes harmonising, sometimes conflicting like
the colours at a bazaar, the spirit of diverse civilisations.

The interior of the church is bare, containing only a few
Arab vases and strong Spanish chests bound with metal.
There still survive remnants of fine Byzantine frescoes which
the Spaniards covered up in favour of baroque decorations, a
Madonna and Child, S. James the Greater and S. John the
Evangelist, patron of the church. They are hardly visible,
however, and already seem to be receding like their com-
panion frescoes into decay and total oblivion. From the
ruined interior it is a relief to step out again into the garden,
and look down at the red cupolas, against which a tall cypress,
exactly equal in height to the bell-tower on the other side,
provides just the necessary contrast in line and colour. Dark
green, grey, rose-red, and over all the blue sky: it is a subject
for Dufy, not for mere words.

There are other Norman churches in Palermo to rival this
one: S. Giovanni dei Lebbrosi, with its crude octagonal pillars; S. Cataldo, with its three rose-red cupolas running the
length of the nave; and the most northern in appearance of
all Norman buildings, S. Spirito, which apart from its limestone and lava decorations might be taken for a contemporary church in France. Elsewhere, too, Norman riches are
to be found: on the Agrò, the brick lava and limestone
church with rectilinear apses, and at Messina, sole survivor
of the earthquake of 1908 and the only fine building in a dull,
modern city, the polychrome Annunciata dei Catalani, its

cupola garlanded with a colonnade. Each one is interesting, but where so much else remains to be studied, they must yield before work which is more likely to throw new light on the island, its artistic traditions and its people.

To the south west of Palermo the Norman kings created an immense park in which they built palaces, lodges, fountains and other works of art. Of the palaces two are standing today, but both are so stripped of their former splendour and stand among such squalid surroundings that it might perhaps have been more fitting had they died a sudden death, in battle or by an act of God, rather than linger on to such an old age. In Palermo it is only the churches that have managed to survive in their original or equivalent form, preserved by faith as buildings with a purpose.

The Zisa, its name taken from the Arab word *aziz* meaning splendid, was a magnificent palace, begun by William I and completed by his son. Today it stands massive as ever, in the same style as S. Giovanni degli Eremiti, but without the cupolas, a rectangular building flanked by two towers and crowned by a crenellated roof. The walls are moulded with slight recesses, only a few inches deep, to form the outline of great pointed arches in three rows, sufficient to lift the building up and relieve its austerity without detracting from the mass. On the second and third floors the arches have been partially pierced to form windows, for today this is the home no longer of kings but of commoners. On the ground floor in the centre of the façade is a wide, arched doorway leading to the great hall, flanked by two smaller portals giving on to a passageway. It is this hall which still bears traces of its royal pedigree. It is a large, lofty room open at one side to a portico and beyond to the arched doorway. The hall itself is polygonal, for the three walls give way to rectilinear alcoves, at the corners of which are six columns, the capitals finely worked in the shape of peacocks, of exceptional grace, symbols no longer of the soul but of stately luxury. In the alcove facing the entrance is a fountain springing from the far wall, crowned by a mosaic eagle and the remains of baroque frescoes. From the fountain water used to flow down a carved marble plane inclined at an angle into a channel in the floor, and so down to a fishpond outside the palace. Above the fountain is a large mosaic divided into three panels, the left and right showing peacocks beside a palm-tree, the centre hunters shooting at birds with bow and arrow. Running round the walls this red and green mosaic work is continued in abstract form, and above, again, are the remains of baroque frescoes. The three alcoves are surmounted by stalactite roofs: their uneven design is mirrored fortuitously in the ruined, dilapidated state of the floor. The fountain which once flowed to make music for kings and their ladies is dry, and the channel leading to the ruined fishpond choked with dust. Only the inside walls retain their royal bearing.

The second Norman palace, the Cuba, is totally ruined within, but still possesses a magnificent and powerful exterior, the plain grey stone unspoiled by such brown stucco work as disfigures the façade of the Zisa. It stands in a barrack square, surrounded by army huts and garages, for the soldiers in their dusty khaki just another building in the square. The palace repeats the form of the Zisa, being rectangular with one tower at the centre of each wall. Round the top runs a frieze with an Arab inscription, stating that William II built the palace in 1180. It is thus a little later in date than the Zisa and an improved technique shows itself in the firmer, sharper moulding on the walls, again in the form of pointed arches, and in the even greater impression of power. Despite their changed condition, both the Cuba and its sister building possess a majesty which proclaims that they were, no, that they still are, royal palaces. The buildings are still highly enough charged to illuminate the days of their glory when the Norman court took its pleasure here: like all ruins they are not an occasion for regret but a challenge to the imagination.

From a violet sky a hot sun is beating down on the Conca d'Oro. All day the king has been out hunting; now he has returned to feast off delicacies and listen to the Arab poets eulogising himself and his splendour: "On the darkness shines his brilliánt face, the sun might be envious of him; he has pitched his tent where the Gemini rise, its pegs are the two great lights of Heaven, and the Pleiades."

In the great hall the court is gathered—Normans who have marched two thousand miles to take possession of a new, rich land, Englishmen called from another Norman possession, Franks who have migrated south to build churches in this island newly wrested fom the heathen. They are the rulers, but they go to school with their subjects, bearded, dark-skinned men who are masters of sciences and arts the very existence of which the northerners had not dreamed. The talk ranges from mathematics to the geography of the world which is being prepared. For this new facts and many fables are now being recorded: Arab merchants give all they know of Africa, Arabia, India, Spain, and the Moslem world; Greeks at court describe the East and the Empire; returning crusaders are called in; Roger himself knows all Apulia and Southern Italy, and the King's uncle, Henry, describes his native Piedmont and Northern Italy.

These descendants of Tancred, transported by their own force of arms from remote Normandy to the very cross-roads of the world, from provincialism to the most cosmopolitan court that has ever existed, from shadow to sunlight, from parsimony to luxury, look round at the mosaic walls, at the perfumed fountain, at the musicians and poets, and wonder who and what they are, Byzantine potentates or upstarts, fastidious aesthetes or coarse Northerners, civilised princes or merely warriors with superior armour, and they are unable, as the dizzy evening advances and the revelry grows more impassioned, to distinguish between themselves and the parts they play.

The Palazzo Reale is a vast collection of buildings of many periods and divers styles erected on an eminence at the western side of the city. Here in the ninth century the Arabs constructed a military post which was later enlarged by the Normans and decorated in the Arab and Byzantine styles. This was the most productive period of the palace, when the Cappella Palatina was built and art flourished under the patronage of Norman kings. Under their successors, the Germans, the palace became a centre of learning famous throughout Europe, and here, especially during the reign of the enlightened Frederick II, himself the best of early Sicilian poets, flourished the first school of poetry in the Italian language. The cloistered courtyards have not yet relinquished the spirit of that golden age, when a second Athens rose on a more western stretch of the Mediterranean, and the conversation of artists still echoes through the arcades. During the vicissitudes of later history the building was subject to destruction and reconstruction so that, apart from the Chapel, of the original Norman epic there remains only a single stanza, the Sala di Re Ruggero. It is a small room in perfect condition, encrusted with mosaics of hunting scenes, of birds and trees and convoluted foliage, against a golden background, an image of the great hall of the Zisa before its destruction. The room was built fifty years before the Cappella Palatina, and the Arab influence, with its tendency to abstraction and aversion from realism, for example in the treatment of the peacocks, is much more evident. This room leads abruptly to civilisations which it is not yet time to regard, to eighteenth-century apartments hung in purple damask, and these in turn to a still later ballroom, in green and yellow, built by the Bourbons. Indeed, the great variety of styles so overlap that neither within nor without is it possible to be certain into which century one has strayed. In Sicily this simultaneity of time constantly bewilders, suggesting that all beauty exists in an eternal present.

The buildings composing the Palazzo Reale, which are fused to form a single frontage without unity, have a pleasing exterior which, however, lacks grandeur. To the south stands the oldest part, a courtyard built by the Spaniards in

the sixteenth century, surrounded on four sides by arcades in
three storeys. As framework and support stand Norman
foundations, for the staircase of these arcades gives entrance
to the Cappella Palatina, founded by King Roger and dedicated to S. Peter. Of all the glories of Sicily, this chapel is
among the most beautiful, a myriad-coloured miniature of
Christian civilisation. If the treasure-house of the Martorana
was pillaged, this casket is overflowing with all the jewels of
the East; if Palermo is loud with suggestions of Norman
architecture in the Sicilian manner, phrases as it were of a
fragmentary poem, here is the text written out in full, the
manuscript illuminated in gold; if the vicissitudes of history
have tangled the skeins of Sicilian art, here is a masterpiece
they dared not touch. It is royal, it is golden, it is Christian,
it is a home, one is blasphemously tempted to think, almost
worthy of God.

The building is not large—no more than a hundred feet in
length—for, intended as a court chapel, it has been incor-
porated in the structure of the palace, so that of the exterior
only the south wall is visible, facing the courtyard and the
sunshine. From dazzling light, reflected in the cream-
coloured walls of this arcade, one enters to darkness, which
in turn gives way to a deeper, dimmer, more mysterious
light. At first only the main outlines can be distinguished:
the form, which is that of a Greek cross; figures looking
down from all sides; and the golden eastern arch illuminated
from the cupola. Only after many minutes, when the eye has
grown accustomed to the dark, gilded light, does the chapel
rise from its own shadows to stand revealed in full splendour.

What is to be chosen first, for everything within these walls
puts forward its own particular mode of beauty to be admired? The more immediately evident takes precedence.
The nave is divided from the aisles by ten pillars, some of
granite, some of cipolin marble, exquisitely moulded and
with gilded capitals. The sanctuary, reached by five stairs,
is surmounted by a cupola. At the right stands the pulpit, an
integral part of the chapel, raised on columns, in front of

which soars a marble candelabrum, thirteen feet in height, designed for the Paschal candle. This ornament, undamaged, is a fine example of twelfth-century Norman carving, and depicts symbolic animals in convoluted shapes, intertwined with saints and a figure of God the Father. It is grey in colour and its tall, tapering form leads the eye upwards to the roof of the nave, to which it provides the ideal harmonic introduction. This roof is made of wooden stalactites in the Arab style, and its added dimension contrasts admirably with the necessarily flat walls. Moreover, while its dark brown colour sets off the golden mosaics, it is itself sufficiently elaborate to withstand their brilliance. The floor, also, is in Arab style, being of white marble, patterned with rose, green and golden tesserae in oriental abstract shapes. These are matched in the lower half of the walls. The lowest space is decorated by a frieze of mosaics and this is surmounted by white marble divided into alternating panels, one showing a Maltese Cross, the other slabs of porphyry. This, the main section of the lower walls, is in turn surmounted by an even more elaborate frieze of tesserae. Thus the whole of the lower walls, including the pulpit and its pillars, is a progressive elaboration of the motif of the floor, culminating in the tesserae which cover the entire upper half of the walls, the pointed arches and their soffits, the cupola and apses. The thickness of the outside walls is shown at the windows, five in each aisle, five on each side of the clerestory, and eight small apertures in the cupola. At the back of the nave, raised on steps, is a dais for the royal thrones.

All this is magnificent, but set beside the figured mosaics it is nothing, for the chapel is its mosaics, as the dancer is her dance. Largest of all are the three great figures of Christ. In the cupola looking down directly on the sanctuary is Christus Pantocrator, with large eyes, thick hair and beard, holding a closed book. The light falls directly on his face, revealing an expression of great power mingled with compassion. Before even one is aware of a reaction, it has compelled homage and abasement. In the central apse above the high altar is a figure of Christ blessing, with book open, and fingers of the right hand separated in benediction. This mosaic, by its half-vertical, half-horizontal position in the conch, admirably suggests the dual nature of its subject. Finally, at the back of the nave, between S. Peter and S. Paul, is a mosaic of the enthroned figure of Christ, the only one of the three representations to portray the whole body.

The oldest mosaics are those in the sanctuary, the scenes on the south wall being distinguished by the Greek lettering beside them. They are in five main panels. In the centre is the Transfiguration, on the left the Baptism of Our Lord, on the right the Raising of Lazarus. Above is the Flight into Egypt, and beneath, balancing it, the Entry into Jerusalem. All these Gospel scenes are intrinsically dramatic and lend themselves well to simple yet graphic representation. Because the modern world is so accustomed to Scripture as a written text, it forgets that to many people of the Middle Ages the Gospel was preached by picture and mystery play, forms more effective to some than the spoken or written word. Indeed, the image can be taken farther still, and in the gold background to this Scripture in pictures can be seen the equivalent of the great gold initial letters in decorated manuscripts of the same period.

This dramatic instinct is evident in such a scene as the Entry into Jerusalem. At the extreme left walk eight of the Apostles, not all fully visible, their faces tense with ill-concealed fear. In front of them Christ, his eyes shadowed with sadness, his hand raised in benediction, sits on a white donkey led by an eager S. Peter. The road, silver in colour, shows up well the green palm branches which have been scattered on it. A palm-tree divides the groups, and on the right stand six men and a woman at the entrance to Jerusalem, their faces betraying every sign of dissimulation. In the foreground four children, with all the enthusiasm and animation of youth shown in their rapid movements, are tearing off their clothes to spread before the donkey, and it is these figures which Christ is blessing. The colours are green, rose, and mauve on silver and white, the background as always being of gold. The road which at the extreme left is very wide in order to contain the large interlaced group of figures simply narrows to a point at the city gate: the road is not important. This concentration on essentials at the expense of logical realism is again evident in a scene above, where the angel is shown appearing to S. Joseph in a dream. S. Joseph is shown wrapped in something white, which, though it looks like neither, is both the bed-cover and sleep: no distinction is made in Byzantine iconography between the symbol and the thing symbolised. Thus, everything in creation can be used as a figure: bird, beast, flower, or fish.

The other main scenes in the building depict stories from the Old Testament and incidents in the lives of SS. Peter and Paul. On the panels below the cupola is a particularly dramatic scene, similar to one in the same position in the Martorana. On the left is the angel Gabriel, on the right Our Lady, and in the centre out of a blue, round heaven is stretched simply a hand, the hand of God the Father, from which speeds a dove in a line of light to Our Lady. The impact is instantaneous, because so simple and dramatic, yet there is nothing superficial about the work, and the details are finely executed. In these mosaics, as in mime and ballet, the position and gesture of the hands are all-important. Thus the angel Gabriel's outstretched hand at once delivers a message and commands; that of Our Lady, held close to the side, palm lifted vertically, protests her unworthiness. This feature reveals one of the great secrets of the mosaics: they appeal immediately and overwhelmingly yet possess such spirit, such subtlety both of form and colour, that they are never fully fathomed. The faces overawe, yet remain inscrutable: the scenes appear simple, yet their delicacy of colour and imagination of detail are highly complex and original qualities which would outlast a lifetime of marvelling.

This ultimate achievement of Christian art shows such an advance on the crude sanctuary at Erice that it may seem as

Aphrodite emerging from the sea: a late Greek marble statue in the Syracuse museum; the protruberances (below her breasts and on her left arm) supported her missing right arm *(see pp.122-7)*

Syracuse: the old harbour on the eastern side of Ortygia, its headland
protected by a fortress built c.1239 by Frederick II *(see p. 103)*

Syracuse: the church of
S. Giovanni stands west
of the Latomia dei
Cappuccini. One of the
town's oldest, it was
rebuilt after the 1693
earthquake, a fourteenth-
century capital and arch
grafted into its portico

Syracuse: a Catalan-style
window in a gateway of
the old harbour, dating
from the fourteenth
century when Sicily was
ruled by the Kings of
Aragon

Roman floor mosaic, Casale: fourth-century ladies keeping fit *(see p.145)*

Opposite: Cefalù cathedral: high in the conch of the apse, on a background
of gold, Christ the Omnipotent raises his hand in blessing. The book
proclaims: "I am the Light of the World" *(see pp. 174-5)*

Norman strength joins Byzantine colour on the twelfth-century apse of
Monreale cathedral, founded by William II in 1174 *(see p.184)*

Opposite: Monreale: (*above*) the Norman-Byzantine cloister;
(*below*) paired pillars, detail *(see pp. 184-5)*

Antonello da Messina: *The Annunciation*, c.1470 *(see pp.196-7)*

Death picks off unsuspecting victims in an anonymous *Momento mori* dated 1445 *(see pp.197-9)*

Serpotta's most ambitious stuccowork, in the oratory of Santa Zita, shows
cherubs rejoicing at the defeat of the Turks at Lepanto *(see pp. 203-4)*

Baroque balcony supported by grotesques, ideally suited to spying on the drama of Noto street life *(see p. 230)*

Overleaf: Noto, the cathedral: equipoise of steps and columns *(see p. 226)*

Charioteers atop Palermo's neo-classical theatre, the Politeama Garibaldi
(see p.244)

Opposite: The gorge of the river Calcinara at Pantálica *(see p.254)*

Pantálica: tombs of the Sicels, one of Sicily's earliest peoples
(see pp. 254-5)

though no comparison were possible. That certainly holds true for the purely religious truths embodied in each building: God the Creator has robbed the earth of its divinity; the Mother of God, successor to the Earth Mother, is a figure of charity not of passion; sub-rational awe and emotion have yielded to mystery which out-tops reason; historical episodes have replaced fancy and myth: such an advance, being infinite, defies analysis. But in respect of religious art, comparison is both possible and revealing. Here as at Erice man has dedicated his craftsmanship to God. The offering of Daedalus has blossomed out into this gleaming chapel, without losing its identity, for the Cappella Palatina is in two senses an enlarged honeycomb, not only in colour but in construction. The small polygonal tesserae of painted glass which were pressed home in a predetermined pattern to form the life of God and His saints are the exact equivalent of the cells in a honeycomb. The conclusion is not that Daedalus's honeycomb was a mosaic, for the art of inlaying glass had not been evolved, but rather that it may well have seen the pattern for this building.

It is not far-fetched to estimate so highly the importance of a single masterpiece, for an initial and original choice points beyond itself and starts a compound trail of consequences. Just as Adam involved all mankind in his acceptance of the apple, so too, perhaps, Daedalus committed all Sicilian art in his choice of gold as a material and a honeycomb as his model. His masterpiece stands high like a subsidiary sun, wherever possible calling forth from art a reflection of itself, now from a Syracusan coin and the shield of Athena's temple, now from a Pindaric ode, and here, under Christian auspices, from the golden mosaics of a royal chapel.

CHAPTER FIFTEEN

Cefalù and Monreale

THE mosaic decoration of the Cappella Palatina is reproduced on a grand scale in the only two Norman cathedrals outside Palermo which still stand in Sicily. The earlier, that of Cefalù, was founded by King Roger as a thank-offering. Caught in a sudden storm at sea, the king vowed to dedicate a cathedral in the place where he should be brought to safety and when, miraculously, he landed at the little Arab town of Cefalù, he fulfilled his promise. Both the vow and its fulfilment are worthy of a man who combined faith and works, love of beauty and love of battle. King Roger made his court at Palermo the most famous centre of art and learning in Europe, yet he repelled the continuous attempts of Byzantium to recover Sicily for the East, and extended his dominions as far as Corinth, Athens, and Thebes. The saints he admired most were Peter and Paul, supremely men of action and apostles of the faith; the arts he preferred were architecture and golden decoration to the glory of God. Not since the Greeks covered the island with Doric temples to the Olympian pantheon, did a conqueror achieve such opulent and refined building.

The exterior at Cefalù is no less imposing than the immense rock which dominates the town. Twin square towers linked by a porch constitute a façade sufficiently powerful to balance the lofty apse. The stone is pale fawn; the decoration serves only to reinforce a building which reflects the disciplined strength of its founder. The interior, on the other hand, reveals Roger's eye for oriental splendour. Only the apse and sanctuary are decorated with mosaics. Confined to this limited section, they nevertheless impose themselves on the whole building.

By far the largest figure is that in the conch of the apse, the head and shoulders of Christ. In his left hand He holds the Bible open at the text in Greek and Latin: *Ego Sum Lux Mundi.* The right hand is raised in blessing, the movement parting His blue cloak to reveal a golden tunic. A halo crowns the head in which the large eyes are set close; the nose is long and narrow, the mouth straight and firm, and the whole framed by a curling beard and hair, of which two wisps are swept across the brow. Of the three comparable figures in Sicily, this is probably the earliest and certainly the most oriental in appearance. Only the round line of the halo prevents the face, with its curling beard, from appearing unduly long. If the lines of the face suggest asceticism, this is confirmed by the attenuated fingers. The eyes, on account of their large size and their dominant position in the cathedral, are all-seeing: nothing in the church is hidden from them: they symbolise that light to which the text refers. They are inscrutable and severe, yet not without compassion and love, illustrating the inscription which overarches the figures, where Christ is described on the one hand as redeemer, on the other as judge. This is the essence of the impression: mercy mingling with justice caught in an archetypal image, and since the truth expressed is a mystery the mosaic is inexhaustible. Such an interpretation, however, does not gainsay the immediate effect, which is of majesty and overawing power. There can be little doubt that Roger himself selected or approved the design for this and the similar figure in the Cappella Palatina. He had dedicated the cathedral, before ever a stone was laid, to Christ Our Saviour; he was passionately interested in all the arts, particularly those of oriental origin; and this mosaic was the most important feature of the whole interior. Did he, then, as some interpreters hold, purposely choose a figure correlative of his own power to overawe and even terrorise the masses? These historians support their argument by claiming that the

Norman kings were unbelievers who deliberately fostered Christianity and the power of the Church within the island because they themselves were dependent for their rule on the goodwill of the Pope. Amari, for instance, describes Roger as a "baptised sultan" and historians of the same school claim that the prodigious scale of church-building under the Normans was occasioned not by devout apostleship but by a desire on the part of the northern upstarts to identify themselves with a permanent institution which had claims on the Sicilians more binding than those of the Patriarchs of Constantinople or the Arab invaders from North Africa. Such a theory, however, looks with modern eyes on the medieval conception of royal power. The true state of affairs is made clear by the two thrones, of equal grandeur, on either side of the sanctuary in the cathedral at Cefalù, and by the mosaic in the Martorana at Palermo in which Roger is shown receiving his crown directly from Christ. The Norman kings, no less than the local bishops, held power by divine right, and this was a fact which the monarchs believed as wholeheartedly as their subjects. Moreover, the Normans at this stage were much too certain of their own force of arms and their ability to keep the island in subjection to have recourse, as it were, to psychological warfare of an order which in those days would have been blasphemous. What, then, is a more likely interpretation of this huge, overpowering figure of Christ, dominating the cathedral not from the Cross, but from the glory of heaven, no less forcibly than a gigantic statue of Buddha, which imposes by sheer mass? Perhaps simply that Christ occupied just such a dominant position in the lives of Sicilians of that time, including King Roger, and that craftsmen were at hand to express a contemporary fervour, denied its outlet during the Arab domination, in works of the greatest power and majesty.

For there can surely be no questioning the fact that these mosaics are among the supreme examples of Christian art. In scale as in conception, in line as in colour, which, thanks to the excellence of the materials, remains undimmed, the

Pantocrator at Cefalù is unsurpassed by any other representation of Christ. Moreover, since this figure was created in the tradition preserved from apostolic times by the mosaic-working hermits of Mt. Athos, it may be taken as an authentic portrait of the Saviour. Like the inscriptions, partly Greek, partly Latin, the mosaics are the fruit of the fusion between Eastern and Western Christendom, resultant upon that curious historical process whereby the Normans surged down from Hauteville to act as the fertilising insect between two cultural flowers. The humanism and compassion of the West are in this figure linked to oriental majesty, austerity and unlimited power; and corresponding to this psychological fusion is a stylistic combination of idealism in the facial expression, symbolism of gesture and a formal treatment of the garments. Yet there is nothing of eclecticism about the figure: the vision and vigour of the artist have not only fused but transcended the constituent styles.

Beneath the Christ, on a much smaller scale, stands Our Lady without the Child, her arms parted and fingers extended in prayer. Two archangels bear witness on either side, and below stand the twelve apostles. On the presbytery walls are patriarchs, prophets, and saints in several rows, single figures only, without landscape or architectural setting, of a very statuesque quality. The figures stand in stereotyped positions, differentiated not so much by facial expression as by the lines and colour of their garments, which range from pink and lilac to several shades of blue and green.

More curious and more immediately striking are the figures which decorate the presbytery vault. Can these truly be what they first appear, a solution to the whole problem, representations of Daedalus and Icarus, ready to take flight? Each figure is equipped with wings more powerful than those of an eagle, substantial yet light enough to bear him four hundred miles or more across the Mediterranean. If this were a pagan building the guess might be correct and in any case it is not far wrong. Daedalus's manufacture of wings from wax and his flight are the mythographer's way of describing how the artist spiritualises life, and these figures continue that symbolism in modified form, for they are angels.

Each compartment contains a six-winged figure described in two cases as Cherubim, in two other cases as Seraphim. In addition each of the two broader triangles contains a pair of two-winged angels, portrayed in the orthodox fashion, their human bodies covered by flowing white garments. It is the six-winged angels, whose heads alone are portrayed as the central point for the radiating wings, which are so curious. If they bear less resemblance to the human form than the usual Western pictures of angels, it cannot be said that they appear more superhuman: one would say they belonged to an animal rather than to an angelic order. On the other hand, the portrayals which follow the New Testament description have the disadvantage of being mere men, their wings appearing quite extraneous. The chief difficulty in portraying an angel is that the artist, unable to imagine concretely any being higher than man, is obliged either to depict fantastic hybrids, identifiable only by those versed in iconography, or to spiritualise a human figure in such a fashion as to be distinguishable from a saint. An example of the former is a pair of Tetramorphs at Monreale, with six wings and the heads of the four Apocalyptic beings, the whole mounted on wheels. In the latter event, the artist's difficulty is still further increased because he cannot with certainty go beyond the vague definition of an angel as a personal being intermediate in nature between God and man. What quality in man must he emphasise in order to give the effect of superhumanity? If spirituality, the angels are rendered invisible; if strength, they tend to brutishness; if beauty, they become effeminate. There is much to be said for Rilke's conception of angels as figures with a more intense being than man's, but these, clearly, would be even more difficult to portray. Christianity originally accepted current Jewish ideals of angels with their representation of Cherubim as winged bulls and Seraphim as the six-winged serpents of Isaiah's vision, but later tradition preferred to imagine them as *putti* or as young men, radiant and with wings to symbolise their role as messengers, being physically and spatially intermediate between heaven and earth. Here in Cefalù, at the crossing of the vault, the two traditions meet in the strict formula of Byzantine iconography: the soft-winged messengers stand face to face with the wild whirlwind.

Cefalù is a budding flower, narrowly limited but precise and vigorously defined, both in colour and form. At Monreale the same flower can be seen fifty years later, fully blown, its petals reaching out to the side chapels and up to the clerestory, until all the walls have been covered with a golden bloom.

The cathedral at Monreale formed one of a small group of royal buildings on the slopes of Mount Caputo, at the edge of the Norman kings' park, and overlooking the Conca d'Oro. It was founded by William II in 1174 and rapidly completed, being designed and executed as a whole. The founder lies buried in a white marble tomb in his own cathedral. He was a recluse who seldom appeared in public, and never at the head of his armies. He preferred to live in his summer palaces, surrounded by eunuchs, concubines, and negro guards, familiar with Arab speech and learning and patron of the arts. Yet he gives the impression of a great personality: he revived Roger's policy of conquest and directed a highly successful diplomacy. He was "William the Good," a king whom all classes revered and loved; to Dante he was in tradition numbered among the just men of the world; to Arab travellers like Ibn Jubair he was the very spirit of kingly generosity and tolerance. A contemporary rhymer has left his epitaph:

> Rex ille magnificus
> Cujus vita placuit
> Deo et hominibus.

The exterior of the cathedral gives an impression of strength but no hint of the decoration within. Indeed, it

bears traces, in its strong crenallated towers which dominate
the coast, of the turbulent age in which it was founded, when
every fine building like every eminent man had to look to
its own defence and carry its own weapons. The west front
is flanked by two bell towers (of which the left is incomplete), their thick walls pierced by tall undecorated arches,
while the sanctuary is surmounted by a simple square tower.
The lofty apse which faces Palermo and the sea from the
slope of a terrace, strong as a castle tower and as overween-
ing, is decorated with limestone and lava in a bold, highly
colourful pattern of intersecting arches, the whole being
supported by small, light columns. Against a violet sky it
stands out like a veritable honeycomb of gold, a reincarnation
on the grand scale of Daedalus's work. This part of the building alone bears a resemblance to the exterior of the cathedral
at Palermo, the nave lacking the decoration and fine colours,
the towers the intricate grace of Walter of the Mill's foundation.

In the sixteenth century an elegant portico was put up
along the left side of the cathedral, and in the eighteenth
the west front received a similar addition which does not
detract from the magnificent doorway, its layers of mosaic
and carving rising to a zigzag pointed arch. The bronze door
by "Bonannus civis pisanus," cast in 1186, is divided into
forty-two squares of bas-relief depicting Biblical events and
suggests in its own more durable medium the multiplicity and
dramatic interest of the mosaic interior to which it gives entry.

To cross the threshold is to throw a golden light forward
over the rest of one's life. Here, in a majestic pageant of
multitudinous scenes portraying spiritual history from the
Creation to the Redemption, is man's supreme tribute to
God. Here is the perfection of the Cappella Palatina writ
large, but far from having coarsened its delicacy of detail,
the craftsmen of the cathedral have added to and developed
the ornamentation, while preserving the freshness of the
chapel. If the smaller building is a medieval carol, here then
are *The Canterbury Tales*. The form has become tumescent,

the dramatic tension complete, and along a certain line the
point has been reached in the portrayal of men beyond which
no advance is possible. Decline and decadence lie on the
other side, but there are no decadent descendants of this
cathedral, no descendants at all, for the fall of the Hohenstaufen dynasty shifted the whole course of Sicilian art.

The cathedral takes the same form as the Cappella Palatina,
while lacking the cupola, and is three times the size. The
columns of grey granite were filched from Roman buildings,
and on the carved capitals the heads of Ceres and Proserpine
are prominent. This suggests that there was some technical
difficulty in procuring materials suitable for such vast pillars: certainly, judging from the rest of the cathedral,
economy was not the motive which prompted the use of
pagan remains. The ruins of Roman buildings in Sicily are
not extensive, but if, as may be the case, Byzantine mosaics
are direct descendants of Roman work in this form, then
these columns may originally have matched Roman mosaics
and, although it may be objected that grey goes poorly with
gold, they are not out of keeping with the surrounding Byzantine work. But the roof of painted wood is decidedly discord-
ant, being a late addition, erected in the nineteenth century
after the original had been destroyed by fire. Its rectilinear
beams do not go well in a building of pointed arches and
round columns, nor does its colour, a too-bright metallic gold
paint, harmonise with the delicate luminosity of the mosaics.

Round the nave from right to left in two tiers the mosaics
portray scenes from the Old Testament, beginning with the
first chapters of Genesis, while the aisles depict the miracles
of Our Lord. In the left and right transepts are the story
of the Passion and scenes from the lives of S. Peter and S.
Paul. Thus, many of these mosaics represent events also depicted in the Cappella Palatina, and a comparison of the two
buildings in this respect shows the development of the art
after an interval of forty or fifty years. Presumably no craftsmen, or very few, were employed in both churches; it was the
next generation, schooled by the creators of the Cappella

Palatina and profiting from their lessons, who decorated the cathedral. However, a total comparison between the two royal churches would be misleading, for one has the intimate, close atmosphere of a court chapel, the other the spaciousness of a public building, with a wider area to elaborate details and arrange figures, and, above all, with more light.

That, indeed, is the most immediately striking difference: the first, remotest scene in the nave is at once apparent: God commanding, Let there be light. In the Cappella Palatina these early chapters of Genesis are difficult to see on account of the obscurity, whereas here they shine, as if the words of the text were being read in a loud, resonant voice.

In one scene God is resting on the seventh day: He is sitting on the world, His body relaxed and leaning slightly forward, His head a little bowed with the effort of Creation; in another are Adam and Eve, the garden of Eden exotic with huge primeval plants such as could well have abounded there. Here is Eve, doomed to bring forth children in pain, sitting beside Adam as he labours with his hands, while she holds her belly, sitting askant in an attitude of suffering. In the scene of the deluge, beneath swirling waters the wicked can be seen struggling in desperation to save themselves; in another picture Lot's wife has been metamorphosed into quite palpable salt, her frozen form contrasting with the other figures hurrying away. The scenery is still minimal and symbolic, like that in the Japanese Nō plays. Two portals and a window serve for a house, and incidentally reveal oriental lines, just like the beds, which have come from the Eastern Empire. By now the Norman kings had adopted the comforts of the East, though it is possible that such details in the mosaics are a deliberate attempt to recapture the surroundings of the Old Testament story.

Who made the mosaics of Palermo and Monreale and Cefalù no one knows. Perhaps Sicilians, perhaps Greeks and Byzantines living in Sicily, perhaps Arabs at the court of the Norman kings; perhaps even, just as the great bronze doors were cast by an Italian from the mainland, the mosaics were made by Venetians. Certainly by this date the figures are decidedly less Oriental than in early Norman buildings. The earliest mosaic of Christus Benedicens at Cefalù is an oriental potentate with narrow face and nose and long fingers; that in the apse of the Capella Palatina, slightly later in date, is already less Byzantine, while here, after an interval of forty years, the figure is much less stylised and rigid, more human, and, so it would seem, more compassionate. The head and shoulders are almost sixty feet high, and the hand raised in benediction is itself six feet long, yet there is no suggestion of grandiosity or overpowering mass, nor, on the other hand, is the figure merely a man: the tension between the divine and human natures is exactly maintained.

The scenes in the transepts from the life of Our Lord chiefly represent miracles of healing, and the vividness with which the different diseases are depicted—the man suffering from dropsy has a huge, bloated belly, the lepers are wealed with sores, the blind men have transferred all their sensitivity to their outstretched fingers—shows how familiar that age was with suffering and sickness. The choice of these particular miracles was surely no chance, nor was the choice of saints to be seen in the apse, among them the first portrait of S. Thomas of Canterbury, who had only recently been canonised. That William II, despite the fact that through his wife Joan of England he was a son-in-law of Henry II, should have chosen to give veneration to a saint who had exalted the spiritual above the temporal arm argues a very close friendship between the Norman kings and the Papacy, on whom some of their power originally depended.

The development of style made possible by the increase of wall space is well revealed by certain details in the cathedral: for instance, the palm tree in the Entry into Jerusalem, undecorated in the Cappella Palatina, here has two white birds resting in its branches, and in the scene of Esau hunting, where the royal chapel shows two birds in the tree and two lying dead on the ground, the cathedral mosaics depict two birds actually falling from the tree—a much more vivid and telling detail. Again, in the cathedral there are five men working at the construction of Noah's ark, three handling great saws, as opposed to the three less striking figures without saws in the chapel. A still more important development is that here the walls have been conceived not only as the canvas for a series of scenes but as a complete whole. Scene is balanced against scene to obtain a total effect: the wall itself, not the individual episode, is the basic unit. The cathedral, planned and executed in a single burst of inspiration, is thus a homogeneous work of art, whereas the chapel, where the plans for the mosaics were several times changed, lacks this quality. But the most important advance evident in the mosaics of the larger building is one which can be traced in the development of almost every art within a certain genre and within a certain period of time: an increase of mobility, as though the winds of inspiration and technique had freshened, catching both faces and garments. Whereas the figures of the Cappella Palatina are to some extent still hampered by the formal aspect of the medium, here they are very much freer and more flexible, their movement more fluid and drapery more intricate, their faces less elongated and expression less stylised. The movement is towards complexity and realism, away from symbolism and naïvety. Not that the mosaics have been Westernised, far from it: they still belong to the Byzantine tradition, and the advance, which is purely relative and indeed only remarkable after detailed examination, has taken place within the limits of this tradition. The Norman and Romanesque carving of the period show that purely Western work, although sensitive and highly original in its treatment of nature, could depict human figures only quite simply and bluntly.

This remarkable contrast between Eastern and Western work of the same period can be seen in the capitals of the adjoining cloisters, contemporary with the cathedral. They stand at the south side, part of what once constituted a Benedictine monastery. They take the form of a square, whose sides are a hundred and fifty feet long, the pointed Norman

arches springing from 216 columns grouped in pairs, except at
the corners where they are in groups of four, and resting on
low walls. Each alternate pair is inlaid with mosaic work of
diverse patterns, and all the capitals are carved with foliage
or Biblical scenes, no two capitals being alike. In the centre
of the cloister a garden flowers, and in the south-west corner,
like the mathematical symbol which marks a right-angle, the
arcade projects from the cloister proper to form a tiny square
addition, in which a fountain plays. The outside walls of the
cloister are decorated in limestone and lava, yellow and
black, in the same fashion as the cathedral apse but on a
smaller scale. The simple harmony of these cloisters is the
result of complex imaginative planning: thus the inlaid
mosaics catch the black and yellow decoration of the outside
walls and add to them the strong red of the flowers in the
garden; while the fountain, a daring addition to monastic
cloisters, is yet discreet enough to be acceptable.

Certain details in the arcade no doubt caught the eye of the
Benedictine monks as they walked in meditation. On one of
the capitals William is shown offering the cathedral to the
Madonna and Child—an angel carrying the building on its
back—and all this carved on a capital no more than twelve
inches in length. Another feature is even more curious. The
fountain is composed of three diverse elements: the vase into
which the water falls is in the Pompeian style, the stem is
worked in Norman zigzag, and the top, showing dancing
Bacchantes, belongs to an age before Christianity: this diversity of styles serving, at the corner of the cloister, as a signature, authenticating the work as Sicilian.

By confining the mosaic work to every other pair of
columns the architects have avoided a sumptuousness which
would have detracted from the spirit of the place. The
Benedictine *pax* still lingers in these passages, beautiful yet
austere, imaginatively designed yet never diverging from
their set purpose: to provide surroundings which will lead
the mind to God. Indeed, of all the buildings in Sicily
this combination of natural and artistic beauty, where foliage

in the green square vies with foliage carved in stone, and graceful columns discipline a flamboyant garden and sky, is the one most conducive to devotion.

From the garden within these cloisters bees drew nectar to fill the monastery hives, hundred upon hundred of them, for honey-making was, until their dissolution, an important industry for most religious establishments, in Sicily as elsewhere. The honeycomb which Daedalus offered, the libations of honey poured before the gods of Greece and Rome, did not wholly disappear with paganism, for honeycombs found their way on to the Christian altar in the form of beeswax candles. The candle came to be considered a symbol of the Saviour and of the virgin body of Christ, because the bees carry the wax from the best and sweetest-smelling flowers. The wick denotes the soul and mortality of Christ, the light the divine person of the Saviour, and as the candle slowly consumes itself in light it symbolises Christ's life of self-immolation which illuminates the way to heaven. The candle stands as an offering not only on the high altar but before the shrines and images of patron saints, and there is competition on the feast days of Sicilian saints to produce the largest possible candles in the patron's honour.

If the honeycomb was of service on the altar, the bee itself and its habits provided many illustrations to enliven theological treatises. Such analogies as were made, however, are often inexact because the habits of bees were not always clearly understood; for example, even in the Blessing of the Paschal Candle on Holy Saturday the wax candle is said to have been formed by the *apis mater*. Bees are praised because they produce posterity, rejoice in offspring, yet retain their virginity, and the life of bees is compared to the life and duties of monks. As there is but one king bee in the hive, there should be only one king, one pope, and as the king does not use his sting, so bishops must be mild. The lay brothers of the monastic orders are compared to drones, and the slaughter of the drones to the scourging of the lay brothers, which took place occasionally. In the evening sudden stillness falls upon the hives, and so it should be in a monastery. The seven, or at most ten years of life which are granted to bees correspond to the sevenfold gifts of the Holy Spirit and to the Ten Commandments. In this way the bees whose marvellous habits had led the ancients to consider them in very fact divine were seen in their true light, as mere emblems, either of the divine itself or of the Christian life. Nowadays, since few people delight in symbolism, mistrusting it as ambiguous, the bee and honey no longer play their part in theological treatises nor point beyond themselves.

But among the people of Sicily they are still the object of curious popular beliefs. It is held that bees not only bring good fortune, but are so religious that they recite the rosary every evening. This is clearly a derivative of Christian symbolism, but two other beliefs go beyond Christianity to Greek and perhaps earlier times. The Sicilians, like the Greeks, believe that honey is a sort of manna which falls from heaven on calm nights and which the bees collect. More curious still is the belief that bees are hedged about with a rigorous code, and that if a man attempts to steal a honeycomb, he will incur some dreadful punishment. This belief, which is very rare in folklore, may well point to a time when a certain honeycomb on Mount Erice was sacrosanct and its violator guilty of sacrilege. But to the further questions whether that offering still exists, and if so where, popular tradition unfortunately provides no clue.

However suspect symbolism may be, the absence of bees here in this cloister garden does hold out one undeniable meaning: Monreale was the culminating point of Sicilian Norman art, the perfection but, no less certainly, the end of a golden age. With its completion, the Norman line succumbed to Southern heat and luxury, the era of peace and productive plenty came to a close, and Sicily felt for the first time, under Henry VI, the impact of German power and the rapacity of the Imperial armies. A new hierarchy of barons installed itself, amid the turmoil of war, imprisoning and torturing those of the old order who resisted. Henry's successor, Frederick II, though a patron of the arts, has left proof in the string of castles he built across Sicily that he was first and foremost a warrior. The city he preferred was no longer Palermo, lazing between sea and orange groves, but lofty Enna, the central stronghold of the island.

CHAPTER SIXTEEN

Enna

ENNA at twilight, a massive mountain fortress, a city of mist and bells. The new road from the north winds slowly up the rock face, edging now to this side, now to that, as though fearful of attaining the summit. The city is so completely a stronghold that to see it even from a distance is at once to feel the challenge of battle, and to move up the winding road is to storm the ramparts. At first it appears so high, so massive, allied even to the clouds, that the very attempt seems presumptuous, and as the road winds closer, there grows a sense of achievement—perhaps simply an effect of the finer air—to be fulfilled when the walls are passed and the stronghold falls. But, as in the taking of joy, the better part slips away: for the city has retreated further—into the clouds, into the mist and twilight. The walls, the foundations are here, it is true, thick, tangible, grey walls, but they stand like the ruins of an ancient town whose towers have toppled long ago. Nevertheless the occupation even of these ruins must continue—the street gives way to a piazza and here are the citizens, remote, grey, and ethereal as the city they inhabit. They huddle together, moving quickly in the thin, sharp air, the men (the taller figures) wearing great dark-blue hooded cloaks, like the habit of monks but made of thick, close-woven wool, the others bundled into cloaks and shawls. They do not speak, and it is this fact which makes clear what has already been half-divined: the city is quite silent, not as a village is, for the sound of birds and beasts is never altogether stilled in a village, but with the positive, defiant silence of a mountain height. Past the defeated ghost-like citizens, the street narrows between ruins—to the centre of government.

and farther still to the huge mass of the cathedral, itself a fortress, the great portals and minor doors closed, although it is not yet night, as though locked against loot and sacrilege. On all sides the houses refuse entry: guerrilla warfare and street fighting seem imminent. Still the silence makes its assault, ominous because so unnaturally profound, only to be thunderously broken by the one sound that can harmonise with the mountains, the mist and the muffled figures —the ringing of cathedral bells. They start to chime the angelus, these carillons in the clouds, with a loud, uncompromising, clear tone, emitting their message across the valley to the next range of rocky hills. But not only to the hills, for here and there in the street figures pause and make the sign of the cross.

All night the hard frost holds until the net of stars drags in a cold dawn, spangled and bright. In the cathedral, unlocked now, requiem mass is being sung, and the coffin lying before the high altar is draped in black, guarded by six tall candles. In the pew beside it kneel three old women enveloped in black shawls, indistinguishable from the one they have come to mourn. Soon they are joined by two others, one a dwarf twisted as an olive-tree and no taller than a child. They have brought with them a copper pot containing embers which they now place between their feet, allowing the warm smoke to mount between their skirts. During the singing of the *Dies Irae* the priest remains seated, and his server comes to the old women, takes the embers from them and hands them to the celebrant. He in turn puts the copper pot beneath his chasuble, and after a little while his breath becomes quite smoky: proof that the heat has been duly transferred. The cold is so intense that prayer is frozen before it can form: instead the breath of the congregation rises like an incense to heaven. Though this is still Sicily, the *Dies Irae* is the appropriate chant, awakening echoes of the previous night, so characteristic that it might be a local folk song. The spirit of this mountain fortress is almost the spirit of Brittany, and it would be no surprise to find a grey stone

ENNA   191

calvaire silhouetted against the sky by the cathedral porch.
The cold, the exposed position, the rock, the piercing, all-
pervading wind, all these, as in Brittany, show the precarious
hold life has on earth. The Stations of the Cross and requiem
mass are the two popular rites, figures of the people's condition.

Most Sicilian towns are poor in bells, perhaps because it
requires too much energy to ring them, but Enna, being still
northern and medieval in spirit, rings out the ceremonies of
the church with multiplied voice, as though to awaken an
echo from each of the surrounding valleys. All the churches
have their distinctive belfries: S. Francesco d'Assisi has a
sixteenth-century tower, pierced with round arches in three
tiers; S. Marco has a squat pointed tower of no great pre-
tensions; the Gothic campanile of S. Giovanni, formerly a
military watch tower, is the most graceful, with a lilting,
three-light window in its heavy walls; while on the heavy
Renaissance belfry of the cathedral, towering above all the
others, the mouldings, paying the price of their exalted
position, have started to crumble.

The history of Enna extends farther back in time than the
records of most Sicilian towns, with the exception of Erice,
to which in respect of its elevated position and medieval aspect
it bears some resemblance, for here in this town and in the
surrounding country arose the myth of Demeter, to spread
all over the fertile agricultural island. Thus Enna carries
on the religious influence of mountains inaugurated at
Erice and hands it on in the Christian era to Monte Pellegrino.
Even today the environs of Enna are celebrated for their
cereals, and the town's bread is made in peasant fashion with
maize, so that it assumes a yellow colour beneath the brown
crust. The seat of this cult of Demeter was on the extreme
north-east point of the city, on a great projecting rock dominating all the surrounding country and surveying in the distance the lake of Pergusa, important in the myth as the site
where Persephone was stolen away to the underworld. No
wonder the early Sicanians believed this rock the seat of a

goddess; hills undulate northwards towards the snow-tipped
Madonie, inlaid with ever-changing shadows of clouds, while
far to the east rises the white, moody pyramid of Etna,
modelling its form and colour on the cirrus clouds.

From this rock the pigeons flying high above the valley
look diminutive, and the hawk hovering patiently above its
prey can in its turn be surveyed. Across the valley immediately to the north rises Calascibetta, a Saracen town so married to the mountain that at first it appears to be a series of
cave dwellings cut in the rock face. From the summit houses
spill over the gentler slope of the mountain, so that one day,
it seems, the whole town will flow down the winding road
into the valley. Count Roger fortified the place when he
laid siege to Enna, and being the only town of comparable
height in the region, during the day it still has a menacing
air, while at night the lights of this citadel, reaching into
the sky, form new constellations of larger, more splendid
stars.

Of the two kings in Sicily who have loved Enna each has
left his monument at an extreme edge of the town. Frederick
II, the Hohenstaufen, built close to the temple of Demeter a
great castle with twenty towers, eight of which still stand.
This Castle of the Lombards, as it is called, though no one
knows why, is an immensely powerful, irregular building—
like its founder, conceived on a grand scale. The view from
its towers is such that although it does not extend to the sea,
it seems to include, on all sides, the whole of Sicily, justi-
fying Callimachus's description of Enna as the navel of the
island. On the opposite side of the town, as befitted a lesser
monarch, Frederick II of Aragon built a solitary octagonal
tower, which nevertheless has held out better than the castle
against the sharp winds. Enna at first sight instantly recalls
a Spanish mountain city such as Toledo, and it is not surprising that Frederick of Aragon found himself most at
home there, assuming the title of King of Trinacria at Enna
and ten years later assembling in the same city the Sicilian
parliament. That energy and sense of purpose which dis-

tinguished his life become apparent immediately one sets
foot in the hill fortress—and it continued latent down the
centuries to burst forth in vigorous revolutionary movements
during the insurrections against the Bourbons—unsuccess-
fully in 1848, triumphantly twelve years later. Those qualities are still impressive in Enna, so that to leave the cloud-
capped towers and clanging bells for the almond blossom
of the warmer valleys is a second time to travel from the
vigorous north to the languors of Sicily.

From the heights of Enna the road runs down to vineyards and almond groves, green pasture and the rich brown
earth of cornfields, amid which lies the lake of Pergusa,
probably of Plutonic origin (here, for once, geology joins
hands with myth), oval-shaped and some three miles in
circumference. By its waters the myth of Persephone was
born, that story which no poet could resist telling, Homer
and Pindar, Callimachus and Ovid adorning it each in his
own particular way. The maiden Persephone, with her
attendant nymphs, was gathering flowers on the banks of
Lake Pergusa. As she stretched out her hand, in amazement and a little timidly, to pick a wonderful bloom, a narcissus with a hundred heads, Aidoneus, lord of the underworld, came up through a cave near the lake (the gloomy
cavern still exists) with his chariot and black horses, and
carried off the Maid. In the plain of Syracuse, the nymph
Ciane rebelled against him and bade him let the Maid go.
Ciane as punishment was turned into the fountain that bore
her name and Aidoneus carried off his prize to the underworld. Demeter, the Maid's mother, distracted with sorrow, wandered in search of her daughter, but nowhere on
earth could she find a trace of her. Her sorrow prevented
the corn from growing; the human race was in danger of
perishing and the gods would then have been without
honour or praise, had not Zeus taken pity on her grief and
settled that Persephone should stay half the year with
Aidoneus as queen of the underworld. But she received
Sicily as a wedding gift and was allowed to stay for the

rest of the year with her mother as one of the two great goddesses of the island.

This legend, because it offers an imaginative explanation not only of the seasons of the year, but of the multiple pattern of human life, of the rhythm between sorrow and joy, has persisted longer and more vigorously than almost any other Greek myth. It is at once a particular, quite simple story and a universal truth susceptible of countless interpretations. The hundred-headed narcissus, like the fruit of the tree of knowledge or the Promethean fire, is the symbol of an ideal state, denied to man, but which, as he attempts to reach it, brings about his downfall. Persephone's wish to pluck the fantastic flower is every man's search for illicit or excessive happiness, while the god of the underworld is the "old man" lurking beneath seeming pleasure. Again, the myth illustrates every mother's grief at the marriage of her daughter, and apprehension of the pain and loss the Maid will experience in leaving her childhood state for womanhood. The compromise solution relies neither on the inexorable terror of tragedy nor on the sugared, fabulous impossibility of a fairy tale: instead, in highly imaginative form it expresses a strictly realistic view of life which, taking account of both laughter and tears, tries to strike a balance between them. Even today the people of Enna are proud to say that this legend originated within sight of their city; and that the temple at Enna was the seat of her worship. They call a street Via Persefone, not because the old gods are still alive, but because the story of Demeter and the Maid so admirably represents the essentials of human existence.

So the town's history has its roots deep in legend. Logically Enna is representative of the island's medieval life, of the disturbed period between the extinction of Norman rule and the age when Sicily became a Spanish dependency, but to isolate one particular layer of history from those before and after is virtually impossible in the case not only of Enna but of all Sicilian towns. In each the strands of multiple civilisations are interwoven, just as among the people can be glimpsed here a profile from a Hellenistic vase, there a coarse and swarthy African face, and in their speech now a Lombard, now an Arab word. Sicily is an island lying outside time, where past events endure in an eternal present, a beach on which the tides of successive civilisations have heaped in disorder their assorted treasure. But the very disorder favours a search such as this where the purpose is to identify an artefact, either literally or symbolically, either as a particular object or as some constant in Sicilian history. Identification nearly always takes place by contrast: the gold seam stands out not in a mountain of metal but against dark ore. If Enna itself has yielded no treasure, at least it has suggested that circumstances favour eventual success.

CHAPTER SEVENTEEN

Two Paintings

AMIDST the wealth of architecture and decorative work, of sculpture and mosaic, it is astonishing, at first sight, that there should be no comparable tradition of painting in Sicily. Time after time a church with a splendid façade will reveal above its altars pallid canvases by Novelli or frescoes by Vito D'Anna. If Sicily owes her artistic tradition to Daedalus, the shortcoming becomes explicable, for the Cretan was architect, sculptor and craftsman in gold, but he is never referred to as a painter, and painting is not one of the arts he introduced to the island. There are two undisputed masterpieces of painting in Sicily, both at Palermo: both are conceived in an alien Flemish tradition and were perhaps executed abroad. By contrast they bring out the distinctive nature of the Sicilian heritage.

The first of these paintings is the Annunciation, Antonello da Messina's masterpiece. In this work the realistic shading and detail which Antonello learnt in Flanders, already apparent in his portrait of an unknown man, are put at the service of a profound, almost visionary, insight. The work is a small wooden panel depicting with the utmost simplicity a single figure: indeed this perhaps is the secret of its greatness, for nothing, neither subsidiary figures, nor furnishings nor fine clothes nor background, stands between us and the Mother of God. To see the picture is immediately to be with her, in the same room, at the same intersection of time and eternity: she is there—we are as close to her as the angel Gabriel—looking up from her prayer-book, her dark, oval face at once strong and submissive, her eyes unsurprised and quite passive, her lips firm and untroubled. With her left hand she draws together across her breast the folds of her single blue garment, covering head and shoulders, for even an angel is an intruder. The gesture is simple and without urgency yet it reveals virtues which a whole litany could not list. Her right hand is lifted forwards and raised at a slight angle, fingers spread out towards the invisible angel, a gesture so mysterious that, while we seem to understand its purpose, in fact we know far less than its whole meaning. She is, before all else, simultaneously accepting and—without declining— hesitating: submitting at the spiritual level, hesitating at the human, but such are the gentleness and delicacy of the move- ment, it is certain beyond doubt that when the will of God has been made clear to her, she will already have accepted.

Yet there is far more than a hesitant acceptance in this manifold gesture. A certain tension in the hand betrays sur- prise: the outstretched fingers seem to be groping towards that more spiritual reality to which the angel belongs; the straight line of the palm seems already to have authority and to be imparting a blessing. All these things lie in that mar- vellous right hand, and many others too, more than the most clairvoyant of palmists could discover or interpret, and it is this unfathomable quality which makes the portrait a supreme work of art, this mystery lying in the single right hand, as enigmatic and inexhaustible in its expression as the smile of the Madonna of the Rocks.

If the Annunciation is a dedicated work, inspired by love and devotion, there is another great painting in Palermo, the Triumph of Death, which seems to have been blurted out in stark horror. It is a very large fresco by an unknown painter, inscribed at the bottom *O Mors Quam Amara Est Memoria.* In the centre, dominating the whole scene, is the skeleton of a man seated on a galloping skeletal horse, the legs of which form as it were a triumphal arch over the prostrate bodies of potentates, pierced by arrows discharged by the rider. To the left kneel sick and aged beggars petitioning the horse- man to release them from their sufferings; to the right are the rich, making music and going through the motions of amusement, but all of them surreptitiously watching Death out of the corners of their eyes. Details of dress, the fact that all the figures are on the same plane, the fair hair of the women and the forest which takes the place of the sky as a background, suggest that the artist may have been a Fleming of the fifteenth century. But the problem of the painter's identity and how he came to be in Palermo are less puzzling than certain other features. The subject, for instance, lies quite outside the Christian tradition, on the far side even of the *Dies Irae*. Death comes wholesale and irresistibly, with an aspect inspiring terror and even hysteria; a force in itself, not the gateway to eternity. This is the tradition of the *Danse Macabre* and the Camposanto di Pisa, but in the present work a still more gruesome and sombre note is evident. The artist, surely, had witnessed an epidemic of plague, not an infrequent occurrence in Sicily. Yet why should Death be symbolised rather than shown in a particular shape? The bodies of the dead, though jangled, are not treated luridly, as might be expected from an artist with an emotional rather than an intellectual concern with the subject. Indeed, it has been suggested that the painting is a visual treatment of Petrarch's theme in *Trionfo della Morte*:

> Ivi eran quei che fur detti felici,
> pontefici, regnanti e imperatori;
> or sono ignudi, miseri e mendici . . .

On the other hand, it may be that the fresco is less obsessed by Death than by contemporary social conditions, that it is in fact "committed" art. The dead figures are all of the ruling class: bishops, lawyers, princes, and other grandees, yet there are no young women, as might be expected if the artist's purpose were simply to lament that "tutti in un punto passavan com'ombra." It is the faces of the rich and their concern with death rather than the beggars that interest the artist. Moreover, the unknown painter is said to have depicted himself among the poor people at the left: he is thus taking sides against the ruling class. This interpretation might be supported by the inscription: the memory of death is bitter only for the rich, not for the poor, since only the ruling class lose honours, pomp and wealth when Death strikes them down. The artist's point, then, would seem to be this: only social justice will render the thought of death tolerable to the wealthy. The picture accepts as a premise the Christian tradition of an after-life, but instead of depicting the torments of Hell—a device to which the rich were then as now certainly immune—it emphasises with horrible intensity the actual deprivation effected by death on the material plane. Whatever the artist intended, the painting is a strange one to have graced a hospital, for the Palazzo Sclafani, which it originally decorated, was converted to that purpose in the fifteenth century. The very sick can hardly have been encouraged by it, and the doctors must have cast a cold eye on the structure of the skeleton, with receding pelvis and thigh bones extending in one piece over the knee. But perhaps in the fifteenth century in Sicily a hospital was little more than a mortuary. It has survived, this skeleton, while the human skeletons over which it galloped have long since crumbled to dust, because it is part of a highly imaginative work of art. The suggestion of disguised horror in the eyes of the nobles, the contrast between Death's skeletal horse and, nearby, a pair of intensely healthy dogs, straining at the leash, of all the creatures in the picture the only ones unafraid; the purposeful right arm of Death mocking the idle strumming of the musicians' fingers—these and many other details announce the resource and skill of this unknown master from the North with the apocalyptic vision.

Mary is portrayed at a moment of crisis; Death is reaping a wholesale harvest: both paintings, with their grave subjects and sombre treatment, their dark colours and deep shadows, stand well away from the Sicilian tradition. They recall the Aeolian Isles, not a rich and favoured land. Their alien qualities show up, by contrast, the light and laughter, the bright colours and essential joy which are the hall-mark of the island's art, brought to maturity, as it has been, by the steady, fruitful light of the Sicilian sun.

CHAPTER EIGHTEEN

Baroque Palermo

IF PALERMO enjoyed under Norman rule a golden age in both senses of the word, her glory was not extinguished with the Hauteville line. She was now an established city, a commercial port in her own right. Under Spanish rule her lot, like that of Sicily itself, varied with the fortunes of Spain and the character of the viceroys who ruled the island. In general the two peoples understood one another, and Spanish rule proved tolerant and tolerable. The positive achievements of the Spanish domination were the successful defence of the island against Turkish aggression together with the preservation of internal peace, and the building up of a system of conciliar administration. On the debit side, banks and credit were controlled by foreigners, so that Sicily remained poor, and excessive amounts of corn were sent out of the island, which more than once suffered famine. Palermo remained the capital, although a provincial capital, and the new Spanish aristocracy, which in course of time married into the great Sicilian families, gravitated naturally towards the seat of government. Since the faith was unchanged, part of their wealth, as in Norman times, was given to the Church and went to the building of cathedrals, convents and oratories. The Renaissance came late and lightly to the island, and it was not until the baroque age that Palermo evolved a new style which displayed the Sicilian temperament as exuberantly as the Norman mosaics had done.

The perfection of Spanish baroque work in Palermo suggests a general truth which holds good for every period of Sicilian art. Whatever forms were imported to the island, whether Greek temple or theatre, Roman mosaic, Norman cathedral and cloister, all ripened to their fullest and finest in the rich Sicilian soil, until they attained a magnificence unsurpassed by similar work in the mother-countries. That this should be so with regard to even one civilisation would be unusual; that it happened in each successive age without fail is quite unparalleled. Yet this truth is already implicit in Diodorus's story: although he worked in several other countries, it was in Sicily that Daedalus, importing foreign forms, achieved his finest masterpieces. Once more the original story has proved prophetic, pointing beyond itself to a general pattern in the island's history.

Baroque art in Palermo provides an exact figure of the aristocratic society, largely of Spanish origin, which ruled the island during the seventeenth century. It derives its forms from Spanish baroque, but carries them very much further than they were ever carried in Spain. It is characterised by stucco reliefs of immense complexity and by inlaid marble walls, enriched to such a point that every crevice of a church's interior may blossom with flowers of polychrome stone. On the other hand, in Palermo at least, little attention is paid to the exterior, which is dull and sober; in Sicily it is only at the cathedral of Syracuse and the church of San Sebastiano at Acireale that fine Spanish baroque façades can be seen.

Most distinctive of baroque work in Palermo are the little oratories to be found scattered across the old part of the city, their undistinguished exteriors lost in the close-knit pattern of walls and roofs. As their size and style suggest, they were built by noblemen who, wishing to patronise particular artists, commissioned chapels where they could worship privately and with decorum. It is a tribute to the devotion of the patrons that their family history is excluded from the sculpture and painting: the buildings were erected to the glory of God, although they may not be conducive to prayer. Now they are kept locked with enormous old double and triple locks, and are used only for an occasional mass or wedding. They are hidden away from the twentieth century, buildings with mean bodies and cultured minds, having lost their purpose in this day and age.

The Oratory of the Company of S. Laurence is a building no larger than the dining-hall of an English country house, its ceiling high and its walls decorated with stucco work depicting scenes from the lives of S. Laurence and S. Francis, the masterpiece of the seventeenth-century artist Giacomo Serpotta. These scenes are curious in being three-dimensional, and the figures are worked with extreme delicacy, even the smallest details being faithfully reproduced in the fragile stucco. The scene on the back wall depicting S. Laurence being placed on the grill is larger than the other groups and of exceptional fineness, the figures being modelled with power as well as with that grace which distinguishes all Serpotta's work, often to the point of weakness. The decorative stucco work on the walls alternates with ten symbolic statues of the virtues, the whole being interlaced with cherubs of the same material. The impression is one of lilting lightheartedness, and it is only the cloth of red and gold encircling the walls beneath the decorations and leading to the altar that stamps the building as a place of worship. The altar, of pink and green marble with a blue tabernacle, is decorated in gilt, with gilt candlesticks, and above it hangs a Nativity by Michelangelo da Caravaggio.

In 1606 the painter had been compelled, not for the first time, to leave Rome. Three years previously the protection of Paul V and Cardinal Scipione Borghese had secured his return to the city, but they were now powerless to help, for he was charged with murder. Taking ship for Malta, he was received there with favour by the Grand Master, Alof de Wignacourt. He painted several pictures in the island but it was not long before he insulted one of the knights outrageously and was ordered to leave. With hopes of returning to Rome, he sailed for Syracuse and eventually in 1608, a year before his death, arrived in Palermo, where he was given a commission for a Nativity, to include the two saints, Francis and Laurence. It is one of his most powerful pieces, filled with the turbulence of the conflict between good and evil which characterised the painter's life, but so far is it from being a religious painting that the Christ Child lies almost hidden in shadow. The Madonna, whose head, shoulders, and arms are alone visible, is the central figure of the canvas. She is dressed in red, leaning her elbows so that the shoulders are high and her hands drooping, and she looks down with a tender expression at the Christ Child.

It is no coincidence that this same expression was caught eighty years later by the young Serpotta in his figure of Caritas, the most beautiful of his allegorical figures in this or any other oratory. A girl is standing, flanked by two children, and holding in her arms a young baby who is sucking at her left breast. Her eyes are half-closed, and she is looking down at the infant with an expression of innocence and sweetness, dimples at her lips, her apple-cheeks rounded. So tenderly is the figure treated that one can imagine that Serpotta modelled it upon the memories of his boyhood mistress, the one woman he ever loved. If this is charity, it is a childish or angelic form, so spontaneous that one cannot imagine the face with any other expression: a love which flows as naturally as the milk she is giving to her babe. It is a blend of childish and maternal love such as one sees occasionally in a young Sicilian girl of fifteen or sixteen, so fresh and radiant that one imagines the infant she holds is a younger brother or sister until she starts to suckle it.

Round the walls are low wooden benches, inlaid with mother of pearl and supported at regular intervals by delicately carved figures in wood, an eighteenth-century addition which does not fall short of the earlier decorations. But, despite its particular excellences, this hall is misnamed an oratory, for of all places imaginable it is the least devotional. The stucco scenes are simply the playground for a gifted humanist, and the profane details are treated as lovingly as the saints themselves. This white plaster seems particularly unsuitable to sacred subjects, and its convuluted shapes, like the foam on a breaking wave, distract the eye instead of inviting recollection. Stucco is more fittingly used in a scene such as the Battle of Lepanto, on the rear wall of the Oratory of S. Zita, where each oar is depicted in web-thin plaster.

The Oratory of the Company of the Rosary of S. Domenico, a building twice as large, is altogether too elaborate and on too full a scale. The walls are surrounded not only with statues but also with vast paintings of the Mysteries surmounted by large stucco biblical scenes. The statues by Serpotta depict young women symbolic of the virtues, but these placed close to the dark paintings of the sorrowful mysteries seem frivolous and profane: such juxtaposition of dark, sacred canvases with light-hearted stucco work is common in baroque churches and weakens the effect of both. The ceiling, a Coronation of Our Lady, by the Renaissance painter from Monreale, Pietro Novelli, is an undistinguished example of his work. But amends are made by the large painting by Van Dyck (who was Novelli's master) over the high altar, of the Madonna with S. Dominic and the patrons of Palermo. It was commissioned in 1624 when Van Dyck was in Palermo, and completed by him four years later in Genoa, whither he had retired from Sicily to escape the plague which suddenly struck the island. In the middle of his work he was told to add to the centre of his canvas the figure of S. Rosalia, kneeling in intercession for the end of the plague: during this epidemic the city first found its beloved patron saint and no painting without her figure could have decently been hung. The result is a curious crowding of the canvas, with a very slim S. Rosalia just visible in the middle of the other saints —not the only time that the dictates of popular taste have marred a work of art. In the stucco scenes, which are large but placed too high to be seen to advantage, Serpotta has given a free rein to his imagination and illustrated such texts as "I saw an angel coming down from heaven." The statues are less good than those in the Oratory of S. Laurence, well executed but with little individuality, chaste Aphrodites without power to move.

Serpotta, the artist responsible for the decoration of the

oratories, was born in 1656, the second child of a sculptor of moderate talent in Palermo. He was trained in his father's craft and one tradition has it that he went to Rome to study. At the age of twenty he fell violently in love with a young girl of Palermo, who bore him a natural child, Procopio. He seems to have been greatly affected by this youthful escapade, never marrying, working fabulously hard and living a modest life almost in seclusion, unacknowledged by his contemporaries as anything more than a good local stuccoist. So little is known about his life that biographers are reduced to interpreting his character from his wills, in which he left a large sum to pay for masses for his soul, and asked to be buried in the habit of an Augustinian brother: perhaps out of remorse for the transgressions of his youth. Whatever the truth, Procopio became his ardent disciple and continued the school of Serpotta after his father's death. There is one other story about him: that he passionately loved music and would rest from his labours, standing on the scaffolding of oratory or church, by playing the lute. It is a likely tale, for about all his work, whether it be *putti* or saints in flowing robes, there is a lilting, melodic quality which might be the personification of an aria by another Palermitan, Alessandro Scarlatti.

The oratories which Serpotta raised to the rank of masterpieces, when taken in conjunction with the other artistic achievements of Sicily, point to a conclusion: that within the island, art, of whatever form, has been dedicated primarily to a religious purpose. None of the contemporary *palazzi* can boast artistic wealth to be found in even the meanest baroque church or chapel, and the same is true of other epochs. The glory of Sicily lies in its Greek temples, its statue of Aphrodite, its catacombs, its Norman cathedrals, its baroque chapels and churches; just as the Sicilians put on their finery and rise to the zenith of enthusiasm for their patron saint's procession. The sacred nature of the island's art is a counterpart of deep religious faith, which before the Nativity had no other course but to worship the local deities, whether Oriental, Greek, or Roman. But whatever the century, whatever the cult, that faith has objectified itself in consummate achievements.

Diodorus has put on record that the first artist to work in Sicily also dedicated his genius to the service of a cult, fashioning a votive offering for the mountain goddess of Erice. The original Sicilian work of art took a religious form, and since to originate in any field is also to start a tradition, the sacred element has remained dominant until the present day. The startling persistence of the tradition does not of course prove Diodorus's story true, but taken with the other confirmatory evidence which has already emerged, it increases the likelihood that Daedalus actually offered a sacred honeycomb of wide and enduring significance.

The masterpiece of Sicilian baroque is the church of S. Caterina, consecrated in 1664, facing the Martorana in the Piazza Bellini. As soon as one enters, one experiences that absolute satisfaction together with a penumbra of bewilderment which only a perfect work of art can give. Every visible square inch of this vast building (it is almost two hundred feet in length) has been cultivated to add its yield to the total harvest of beauty. A garden in full bloom, a granary heaped to the rafters with corn, an orchard teeming with fruit—none of these gives quite the same effect of abundance, for none has been harmonised and concentrated with deliberate and inspired art. The combination of colours—rosebrown, white and black—and the added dimension given by the relief work are the immediately striking features, conveying a sense of chiaroscuro and pale light which draws one into the nave. The interior takes the form of a cross, with a dome but without aisles. Pilasters run the length of the walls, separating the six side chapels, each of which is as richly decorated as the nave, and each having its distinctive pattern of inlaid marble. On a single pilaster there are carved as many as twelve cherubim in relief, each one perfectly executed, whether conspicuous or hardly visible high above the nave. At the base of each pilaster is carved a biblical scene—almost the only doctrinal evidence in a world of pure nature: one of them represents Jonah and the whale, with a magnificent Spanish galleon in relief, its rigging of metal wire. The richness of the meanest chapel here would dignify the high altar of many another church. That of S. Caterina in the south transept shows the *tour de force* at its highest pitch. Here the detail of decoration is carried to a point beyond which all form would disappear under the weight of ornament and the whole would be lost in the profusion of the parts. It is as though the flowers in a large garden had attained such luxuriance that it is uncertain whether the garden has not reverted to its primeval state; as though a snowstorm had been depicted in the medium of marble; as though a frenzied mind, the mind of a Rimbaud, were throwing out powerful and extravagant images before tumbling over the verge of madness. The first principle is that nothing shall remain simple: the straight line of a column must be twisted, or the flutings painted: the bases must be inlaid with bulging pieces of marble: the recesses must be filled with flowers: at all costs nothing must remain bare, lest it prove that other worlds exist, simpler and quieter than this extravangance of flowers and frozen fountains, abandoned to a perpetual state of tension.

S. Caterina used to be famous for its preserved pumpkin and blancmange, and the Martorana opposite for its *frutti* of sweet almond paste. If the taste for sweet cakes was introduced by the Saracens, it was the growth of the religious houses during the Counter-Reformation which developed cake-making into an art, and curiously enough the decoration on present-day cakes recalls nothing so much as the polychrome interior of S. Caterina—a significant sidelight on this form of baroque architecture.

Each religious house specialised in one particular form of confectionery or pastry, and since this was one of the principal means of livelihood competition became sufficiently intense to produce a wealth of designs and recipes. The fact that many daughters of noble parents chose the religious life perhaps accounts for the fastidious and elaborate decoration of the cakes. All are typically Sicilian in their extravagant colour and cloying sweetness. The simplest sort is the imitation of fruit or vegetable, smaller than life size, made in almond paste. As though in some fabulous greenhouse, strawberries and cherries, figs and oranges, apples and pears all ripen together in the confectioner's window, as they once did at the church doors. The small orange-coloured *nespole* which appear in May and taste half-apricot, half-orange, are shown cut in half, revealing the large seeds which resemble chestnuts. Wild strawberries and raspberries are fashioned with such cunning that it is almost impossible, before they are tasted, to distinguish them from the real. Heaped together in a wide bowl, their opulence of colour is as cloying as their tropically sweet taste.

If these almond-paste imitations out-colour nature, the actual fruits are candied to preserve what in the natural order of things would perish. As though embalmed in sweet spices, the rind of the fruit persists, its true essence lost in the taste of sugar. In this candied confectionery the colour becomes darker and autumnal, like the rich brown shade of heather honey. Both the imitated and preserved fruits, however, possess only a surface excellence, for they have that heavy, overpowering taste which Sicilians find pleasing in food.

The larger cakes are minor works of sculpture. Like severe Roman baroque architecture, the inside is of little interest: as in most Sicilian cakes it consists of a *cassata* layered with curds, enclosed in pistachio-marzipan. All the confectioner's skill and invention are lavished on the external decoration, which is as varied as three dimensions and a round shape will allow. Candied oranges halved with cherries on a chocolate base; a chequered carpet of cherry jam, in which are set waterlilies made of pistachio cream with petals of half almonds; a garden built up like a bas-relief with a succession of quartered preserved fruits; a coat-of-arms composed entirely of star-moudings in coffee and chocolate cream; a Catherine wheel spun with spirals of rainbow-

coloured icing: as varied as the pattern of snowflakes, as intricate, one can imagine, as Daedalus's golden honeycomb,
they present a carnival of colour, form, and materials. They
are new, exotic, perfumeless flowers, coloured stuccoes,
triumphs of architecture, their mouldings as finely worked
and fretted as any Saracen portal or window. They are
marble inlays more gorgeous than those of the church of S.
Caterina, vivid and intricate as the wheels of a Sicilian cart.
But, by contrast, they are as perishable as the butterflies and
flowers they resemble: no other artist unless it be the maker
of fireworks fashions such ephemeral materials as the confectioner. In the shop window his cakes attract the passer-by
as jewellery or silverware would, but to sell them is to destroy
his handiwork with his own hands: annihilation is the price
of success. As in an oriental slave market, in the confectioner's shop beauty is bought only to be consumed.

CHAPTER NINETEEN

Ragusa and Modica

THE development of Sicilian art has always been dependent
of the tastes of the ruling class, and nowhere is this more
strikingly displayed than in the early and late phases of
baroque. In the seventeenth century the great works were
built under Spanish auspices in the capital city of Palermo;
in the early eighteenth century political changes took place
which brought new influences to bear on the island's art.
The Treaty of Utrecht assigned Sicily away from Spain to
the King of Savoy, who in 1718 was obliged, in exchange for
Sardinia, to cede the island to Austria. The next change
came through the victorious expedition of Don Carlos, son of
Philip V of Spain and Elizabeth Farnese. By his recognition
in 1735 as Charles III, King of Naples and Sicily, the semi-
Italian line of Bourbons was established, and the island gravitated into the artistic orbit of Rome. The capricious and
highly worked interiors of Spanish baroque are now superseded by more sober buildings whose importance lies in a
façade based on the classical orders. As chance would have
it these new buildings were erected not in Palermo but in
the south-eastern corner of the island, devastated by an earthquake in 1693. The most important of the destroyed towns,
Catania, was rebuilt by Vaccarini, who studied at Rome in
the school of Carlo Fontana. He excels in circular churches,
like S. Agata, which display his sober virtues to perfection.
Much more impressive, however, and less dependent on
Roman tradition are the buildings in Ragusa, Modica and
Noto, designed for the most part by an architect whose full
importance has only lately been brought to light, Rosario
Gagliardi.

Ragusa is, accurately, two towns, not one, two hill-top towns, their bases joined by immensely long flights of steps, their roof-tops, in early spring, interlaced by ceaselessly soaring swallows, newly returned from nearby Africa, a day's flight away. The towns survey each other like two houses on opposite sides of a street, mistrustful and standing on their rights. Unlike Enna, which commands the province for miles around from a unique height, Ragusa looks over its own precipitous but limited valley on three sides to neighbouring hills of equal eminence, their skyline quite level: moors rather than Sicilian mountains, arid and uncultivated, whose limestone formation is articulated by the town's grey houses. Ragusa Superiore, the newer part, lies on the western side of Ragusa Ibla, so called because it claims, with little justification, to occupy the site of the ancient Sicel town of Hybla Heraea. The newer town commands a well-grouped view in the direction of its sister-foundation. The mountain falls away as far as the eye can see in a precipitous slope, which has been formed into terraces no more than two or three feet wide, planted with corn and beans. To the east houses take the place of fields, so narrow and haphazard that they seem at any moment in danger of losing their foothold. On the far side of the chasm lies the older town, at a lower level, but also built on the cone of a hill, its grey houses so tightly packed that the place appears to be one huge building, a fortress or prison. The town is dominated by Gagliardi's cathedral, of which only the dome is visible from this side, for the church faces west. Although the dome seems little more than a stone's throw away, the journey from Ragusa Superiore to the cathedral takes half an hour, the way being entirely by flights of steps: not an orderly, continuous stairway, but irregular, erratic goat-paths which wind like tangled skeins of wool in and around the houses and sweep under bridges; long, flat steps and narrow, steep grace-notes, tumbling down like a cascade, following the line of least resistance to the gorge below. When that is reached, a similar path up the farther slope zigzags through Ragusa Ibla.

The view back towards the newer town mirrors the previous panorama but looks upward, leaving no doubt which is the dominant of these two sister settlements.

The approach to the cathedral is up a long, steeply sloping road and an extensive flight of steps, above which soars the façade, entirely silhouetted. This has a convex central section rising to a belfry, which, instead of forming almost a separate unit as a half-tower, is integrated into the whole front. The dovetailing is effected by the subtle arrangement of the six central columns which are set in threes on an inclined plane and continued upwards in the second storey. In the third storey the columns are evenly spaced across the front on either side of the belfry arch, which terminates in a flattened square turret, rising to a point. The impression is of effortless height, depth as well as breadth, and grace on the grand scale, this last quality being affected by the outline of the second and third storeys which rise in a magnificent sweep to the tower. The lofty dome rests on a drum composed of sixteen columns, the lines of which are continued upwards on the dome proper and repeated on a miniature scale in the lantern, giving a light upward movement to the whole. In the last century the interstices between the columns of the dome were filled with blue glass which, however, does not detract from the dome's beauty. The interior is remarkable for thirty-two modern stained-glass windows, rare examples of an art which has never found great favour in Sicily. Reds and blues are rendered even more vivid by the southern sun, and the long nave, already flooded by light from the cupola, takes on the appearance of a gaudy patchwork quilt. The demonstrative canvases and gilded columns, the white plaster walls and sentimental statues, were perhaps already sufficiently cloying without the addition of this coloured cross-light, yet such is the cumulative effect of so many primary colours, sticky as sweets, that the interior gains rather than loses from this deluge of cherry water and lemonade. Nevertheless, here as in nearly all the churches of southeastern Sicily the interior is but a feeble reflection of the glorious façade: so disappointing, in fact, that there comes a time when one is tempted to remain outside an unfamiliar baroque church altogether.

The cathedral is more than a fine building; here, as in Cefalù and many other Sicilian towns, the tower, a figure of transcendence, of grace resisting the down-drag, redeems the grey hovels, lifting and dedicating them to a spiritual ideal, putting the whole town into touch with infinity. Just as Sicilians express their deepest feelings in religious forms which impart to them an absolute value, so at the purely aesthetic level their towns are often saved from meanness by the architecture of a single church. Ragusa owes more than it has ever acknowledged to Rosario Gagliardi of Noto.

Those towns in which one spends only a short time, like the characters in obscure periods of history, are remembered for one or more vivid and perhaps irrelevant pictorial incidents. So it is with Ragusa. The town lies torrefied: the sirocco has been blowing for two days, and although the upper town stands fifteen hundred feet above sea level, the surrounding mountains blanket it to such an extent that the region seems a desert. The time is four o'clock in the afternoon. In this doorway a lean dog sprawls sleeping, in that a beggar. Outside the clubs which line the main piazza— the Circolo Agricolo, the Circolo dei Combattenti and innumerable other similar institutions—are sitting the old men of the town—several hundred of them, each with his black cap pulled well down on his head (for even in the shadow the light dazzles), each with his straight-backed wooden chair, sitting in groups and talking interminably, as they have done for many years and will continue to do for the rest of their lives. All along the three walls of the piazza, like the elders of Troy whom Homer compares to crickets, they keep up their animated conversation and, when an occasional pretty girl passes by, a new Helen, watch her with dull admiration until she is lost from sight. Where are the heroes, the strong young warriors of the city, in whom the old men take their pride? Where are the bastions of Ragusa, gallant upholders of the city's noble traditions? There they are—in an adjoining street, sitting at *caffè*, watching the passers-by, talking, and teasing the pretty girls. The tradition is handed on loyally from father to son.

Suddenly there is a commotion, one of the eagerly awaited distractions of the day. The carved coloured doors of the *chiesa matrice* are opened and on to the stage of the church close, raised above the piazza by flights of steps, moves the advance guard of a funeral. The bell in the square begins to toll as the procession totters into the piazza. It is headed by a score of men, so extremely aged, bent double or hobbling on crutches, that it is a wonder they can stand, let alone walk, all the more so since each carries an immense, heavy wreath in the shape of an inverted heart made up of arum lilies interlaced with marigolds. The incongruity of the floral arrangement is matched by the next element in the procession, boys from an orphanage dressed in maroon, with navy-blue berets, each with a musical instrument. This is the brass band, playing a dead march so off-key yet so lugubrious that in spite of itself it excites pity. Behind the brass band follows a line of six priests, the younger ones scrupulously reciting from new breviaries, immaculate still with gold leaf, the older without books, perhaps praying interiorly, perhaps merely walking. The plain wooden coffin follows, borne by six youths, and they in turn are trailed by the mourners and finally the hearse which, once the outskirts of the town are reached, will bear the coffin to the necropolis. As the procession passes, the old men sitting outside the *circoli* struggle to their feet, take off their caps and cross themselves repeatedly. The cortège passes at a slow march: everyone in the piazza suddenly grows old—even the orphans, struggling under their drums and tubas like the children of Laocoön with monstrous beasts, appear to be staggering along, and their faces have the weary, resigned expression of old age. One of the leading wreath-bearers stumbles on a stone and almost falls. The brass band misses a note. The heat tightens its rack by still another notch. For a moment,

less and longer than a moment, of blind, irrational terror, it
seems that civilisation itself is being carried to the cemetery
—civilised man lies in the coffin and is being borne in procession by the last survivors. When the body has been lowered
into the tomb, they too will collapse and with them the whole
system: torpor, heat and decay will have their way at last.
Then the procession passes out of sight and sound, and with
it the moment of horror. One remembers gratefully and with
relief other scenes from the same town: children playing in
the shaded streets, flowering like the nearby corn out of the
very rock; infants being dandled amid laughter and admiration. Another generation is growing up to replace the ghosts.

The emotive quality of Sicilian funerals is purposely contrived: like all religious ceremonies in the island they are
spectacular pageants intended to overwhelm participant and
onlooker alike at every level of their being. Even fifty years
ago most people in Sicily belonged to a burial guild which
ensured an impressive funeral for its members, all of whom
paraded in white hooded dresses, with slits at eye and mouth,
to accompany the coffin to its final resting-place. If these
impressive costumes are now obsolete, the funeral itself, like
all the fundamental events in the human cycle—birth, marriage, and death—is still hedged about with all the elements
of mystery. The ceremonies which accompany them have
not been tucked out of sight, as has happened in so many
countries of Europe: since they are still acknowledged to be
significant and portentous not only to immediate relatives
but to the whole community, they have become clamorous
with music and fireworks, and beribboned with processions.

To the south of Ragusa lies a town which in many respects forms its corollary, Modica, a place renowned throughout the Middle Ages for its recalcitrant and independent
attitude towards the foreign conqueror. The county of
Modica belonged to the Chiaramonte, one of the most
famous and powerful families of Sicily, members of which
had once aspired to the throne. Covering an area of hundreds of square miles in very rugged country, it was for

centuries the strongest fief in the island and a constant source
of danger to the central authority. These inland towns, most
of them Sicel foundations, played little part in the Greek
history of Sicily, for that age was dominated by the sea. With
the coming of the Arabs and later when the great Norman
and Spanish families started to accumulate land in their own
names, they became the capitals of miniature private empires,
against which the nominal kings or viceroys were obliged to
wage almost ceaseless warfare not only to exact dues but even
as a means of self-defence.

The strongholds of Sicily are for the most part built on
mountains or on the coast. Modica is a notable exception, for
it lies unashamedly in a deep valley, stretching a short way
up both sides of a pronounced spur. At all points it is surrounded by high ground: city walls were never built, for they
would have been overlooked and easily scaled. The advantage of such a position is obvious. Although the town could
put up little resistance to capture, once fallen into enemy
hands it could soon be rendered untenable by brigandage.
From the surrounding hills marauding bands of guerrillas
could swoop down on the low-lying town, as indefensible
now by the enemy as it had been previously by its own citizens. The guerrillas were able to carry out their attack and
retreat with impunity to mountains more rocky and forbidding than any other Sicilian range, their grey stone never
entirely tamed by grass or trees.

The most picturesque approach to Modica is from the
south up the valley of the river which bears its name. The
spur dividing the two forks of the V shape, according to
which the town is composed, rises immediately ahead,
covered with innumerable tiers of square openings, arranged
according to no regular plan and apparently cut out of the
rock itself. At closer sight these take form as houses, built
of grey stone, ordered in terraces up the steep incline of the
spur, so neatly stacked that they seem two-dimensional, like
the backcloth of a stage town before the paint has been
added. The extreme point of the spur which dominates

Modica is occupied by a monument which in any country would be curious but in Sicily is quite extraordinary: a vast clock standing quite alone, not on a tower or any other building, but flush with the rock, as though it too, like the houses, had been excavated from the mountainside—a clock which shows the correct hour. In Sicily time is still the servant, not the master of man: the hours and minutes, far from assuming the important position accorded them by the rest of Europe, are treated with the utmost contempt. Time here is gauged subjectively, by the heart, not by clocks or watches. If an hour is appointed for a meeting or engagement, it is never to be taken literally: one attends when the spirit moves, which usually happens an hour or longer after the specified time. For this reason the huge clock in Modica, its face newly painted white, marking time accurate to the minute, seems as out of place as a sundial would be for timing a race. It is rendered all the more incongruous by the rhythm of the town, which, if possible, is slower than that of most Sicilian places. The carters stop in mid-street to exchange news or merely to drowse, the young men sit all morning drinking coffee and talking, the children make dust castles in the street oblivious of the regular ticking of the great clock, unhurried, without impatience, following a different, more leisurely rhythm than that of the mechanical age.

The church of S. Giorgio stands half-way up the central spur, in that part of the town known as Modica Alta. There are no fewer than 250 steps in its introductory staircase, arranged in four wide oval flights which, at the point of intersection, become landings. These landings coincide with side streets running horizontally between the houses along the mountain side: the intersecting alleys are composed of flights of steps. The naturally overwhelming position of the church is accentuated by the fact that one mounts, not in a straight line, but round the continually curving stairway, as though tacking in a boat, so that the actual time taken in ascending is considerably prolonged. After such a meandering introduction, which arouses hope to the highest pitch, all but the greatest building would appear to fail. The church of S. Giorgio does not fail. It is conceived and executed on the grand scale, with a broad base containing five doors and rising in three storeys to a great height which seems all the loftier for being silhouetted. The church's distinctive feature is the convex central section, which, rising with six Corinthian columns on each tier, assumes the character almost of a half-tower, narrowing to a belfry arch, surmounted by a clock and terminating in a half-cupola and decorated point. Thus the church, without losing strength, soars very high, combining the best features of a rounded tower with the power of an unbroken façade. The points of similarity between this front and that of the cathedral at Ragusa, known to have been designed by Rosario Gagliardi, make it probable that this church too was the work of the Notinese architect. In each case he has chosen to build on steeply sloping ground, an ideal site for a baroque church, which by its very nature is meant to be seen only from the front: the flowing lines which delineate the upper part are seen to best advantage against the sky, and the rest of the building blends harmoniously with the rocky background.

Another church in Modica—that of S. Maria di Betlem—has a particular interest, for on its west wall is nailed a plaque, about twelve feet above the ground, marking the level of water which in late September 1902 flooded the town, causing widespread destruction. The two *torrenti* which flow down on either side of the spur to form the River Modica had that year burst their banks as a result of heavy autumnal rains. For centuries the town had watched these streams, normally weak and docile creatures, grow furious in the autumn, like animals on heat. The habitual trickle of water, as though bearing fruit with the surrounding orange trees and vines, would rise in a week to the extreme level of the bank, while the still September nights would reverberate to the thunder of swollen waters. But though they raged every year at the same season, they kept within bounds, they did not attack. Like angry, well-bred dogs who manage always to retain self-control, they belonged to the community and were tolerated. Then one night, after particularly heavy rains, the dogs went mad, flew out of control, and ran amok among the people. They coursed through the houses and churches of the defenceless valley town, seeking human blood. They found it. Men, women, and children, to the number of a hundred and eleven, fell prey to the rabid animals. Neither church nor palace was respected: like a barbarian host the waters indiscriminately annihilated. When the flood, after three days, had receded, the people of Modica buried those dead who had not been swept downstream, and took a vow that no similar disaster should ever occur again. Since these dogs were immortal and inalienable, they would have to be muzzled. The torrents which formerly had been allowed to parade openly through the town, to breed and form canals so multiple that Modica was known as the Sicilian Venice, were now covered up with stone walls, hidden like sewers, buried alive. If Modica has lost her ancient aquatic beauty, she has gained her safety: the beasts will never more run wild. As the town expands to the south, the River Modica, a potential menace, is also being rendered harmless. Workmen are engaged in constructing walls strong enough to hem in and canalise its autumn waters. Great blocks of stone are being set in position on either bank, as high as the Spanish fortifications at Syracuse and even more formidable. In the centre of its wide, rocky bed runs the river, no more than a slow trickle from a household tap, as though purposely minimising its own size to prove the precautions quite unnecessary and rather ridiculous. But in September this river drains a whole range of the Iblean mountains, just as its sister river the Assinaros, in spring no wider than a rivulet, proved in autumn so turbulent a barrier to the Athenians retreating from Syracuse that they were cut down by thousands and stained its waters with blood. They are moody, seasonal creatures, these Sicilian rivers, dark terrestrial streams with insanity in their blood, inherited from antediluvian ancestors. Modica has learnt her lesson. Walls, which were never part of the town's military strength, are now being raised with urgency, double walls as though to form a moat, the town's first line of defence against the incursions of nature.

The other great church of Modica, S. Pietro, is remarkable chiefly for the statues of the twelve apostles which in the form of a square decorate its steep steps. The imaginative arrangement of these works almost redeems their blatancy, for they are all attitudinising and display their particular symbols too ostentatiously, as though to compensate for their uniform facial expressions. Only one feature about them is remarkable; their hair, which is fine and straight, reminiscent of an engraving, in contrast to the curls of most baroque statues, but this too is somewhat spoiled by the metal haloes which have been added to each head. The façade gains immeasurably by standing out against the skyline: it is a wide, flat front, only the pilasters and three doors being decorated, with four statues on the second tier, rendered anonymous by the blazing light.

In this church a wedding has just been celebrated. The bridal pair kneel in front of the high altar holding lighted candles. The girl's hair, parted in the centre and falling down to her shoulders, is covered by a silk handkerchief. She wears a pale blue dress with a train, embroidered with pink flowers of silk, and her neck is encircled with coral from which hangs a small golden cross. Benediction having been given by the priest, the sacristan comes forward to take the candles from the hands of the couple. He puts the two flames together so that they form one, then blows them out with a single breath. Everyone shows relief, for, if no precautions were taken and one candle were allowed to be extinguished before the other, whichever of the couple had been holding it would be the first to die.

The priest has returned to the sacristy and now the couple walk down the aisle and out of the church door, followed by the crowd. The new husband is self-confident as a peacock: the bride—she can be no more than fifteen—holds her dark

eyes downcast. Sunshine and conversation break out together; on the church steps friends throw nuts and corn at
the bridal pair, that their marriage may be fruitful. All is
laughter as the husband helps his wife up into the first cart
and they drive away, followed by friends and guests, some
in carts, others on foot.

The procession arrives at the bride's house, one of the dens
arranged along the mountainside. Before the newly married couple enter the house, they sprinkle wine on the door,
then break the bowl which has held the wine. They enter the
single room, decorated with flowers, and are followed by the
guests, who crowd round in a circle to watch the bride's
mother perform an essential rite, the presentation to the
couple of a spoonful of honey: the husband licks one half,
his bride the other. Then she distributes to the bystanders
broiled chickpeas, almond cake with honey and beakers
of wine, as a prelude to the nuptial banquet of macaroni and
sausages. Everyone eats heartily: for all save the young
couple this is the culminating point of the day.

Later, singing, dancing and music will continue until midnight, when the bridegroom will take home his bride. There
will be no honeymoon, only a week without work, but in
the marriage contract it is stipulated that within a year the
husband shall take his wife to some great celebration or
patronal procession, perhaps, appropriately, to the feast of S.
Venera in Avola. Also within the same period, the couple
will have to attend a further religious ceremony. They must
go and hear mass, kneel together before the altar, and each
again hold that emblem of their love, a lighted wax candle,
this time provided by the church, in order to obtain the
priest's blessing. That second ceremony is called the *spunsa-
liziu,* and is a confirmatory seal set on the marriage.

Beeswax candles and honey, ardour and sweetness: the
part played by these symbols reaches back past all written
records to remote antiquity. Just as the throwing of corn
directly carries on a Roman custom, it is likely that here is
a continuation of those libations of honey which were offered

to the goddess of love even before the Greeks held Sicily. As Empedocles writes in one of his poems, Aphrodite should be made propitious by an offering of honey, and that is precisely the unvoiced wish of all who have been attending this wedding in Modica. Here, in one of the towns which has been most shut off from change, where ancient customs have lingered on and on, the large part played by candles and the ritual presentation of honey may well be a survival of the rites which Daedalus knew and which he carried out in unique and inimitable fashion.

CHAPTER TWENTY

Noto

THE town of Noto, like Catania, was destroyed by the earthquake of 1693, and rose again in the baroque style. There
the resemblance ends. For while Catania has now become a
complex modern city, a great commercial port, its churches
side by side with shops, dominated by the smoking crest of
Etna, Noto has remained an eighteenth-century country
town of golden stone, standing on the slopes of a hill with
a view on three sides of almond trees, row upon row, their
leaves in March the most delicate shade of green, a shade
which springs new at every glance. The ancient town of
Noto lies some ten miles north-west of the present site, higher
up on the hills, a silent ruin of fallen masonry, more totally
destroyed than some of the Greek cities, with here and there
part of a wall erect, the only remains of a flourishing town
whose history goes back to the time of the Sicels and which
the Arabs established as capital of one of the three valleys into
which the whole island was then divided. After the earthquake
the survivors, unwilling to perpetuate the memory of so total a
disaster, and not obliged by considerations of defence or trade
to rebuild in the same position, moved farther down the river
and founded a new town on the slopes of a hill overlooking,
to the east, the Gulf of Noto. It was no insignificant town
that had been destroyed, but an important provincial centre,
with a strong architectural tradition going back to the time
of Matteo Carnelivari, the home of many noble families and
the seat of richly endowed churches and monasteries. As at
Catania, the disaster imparted a strong communal spirit
which, combined with the wealth and taste of the leading
citizens, helps to explain why the present town is such a

rich cluster of noble buildings: churches and palaces, monasteries, and convents.

Of all the towns of Sicily, Noto is perhaps the most uniform in period and style: nothing whatever, not even the earth beneath the buildings, remains of the original foundation: in its entirety it belongs to the eighteenth century. This uniformity—more complete even than that of Palladian Bath—is heightened by the unique colour of the stone from which Noto is built, a golden limestone, ranging from an almost crocus-yellow through fawnish sand to rose, yet keeping always within the limits of honey-colour. This stone possesses such a positive quality that even the simplest and most ordinary buildings are redeemed from plainness, as the faces of southern people are by their sunburned complexion. Thus, a façade of no great artistry which in the grey stone of Catania might well appear dull here seems pleasing and perhaps more distinguished than it is.

But Noto did not fail to produce artists worthy of its marvellous materials. In this comparatively small community, at the crucial moment of its history, a group of local architects, under the patronage of enlightened nobles and ecclesiastics, created, by patient work and self-sacrifice, without great resources, an entire town of distinguished buildings, in a style which deserved to be called the perfection of restrained baroque. One has only to look at the neighbouring town of Avola, rebuilt at the same time after it had been destroyed in the same disaster, a shabby, ugly, tasteless place, to realise the immensity of Noto's achievement. In one sense, it was an advantage to be able to build on virgin soil: an advantage which very rarely falls to a group of architects. On the other hand, simply because they were provincials starting from the beginning, there lurked a twin danger: either of pomposity and pretentiousness or of ponderous, studied pastiche. These pitfalls were avoided, and the advantage turned to good account, for Noto is a co-ordinated whole, its piazzas not mere widenings of the street, but designed to allow balanced views, its churches well sited to command the greatest possible effect from dominant positions. The town is extensive, the churches are conceived on a large scale, the convents are constructed to hold communities of a hundred or more—yet all this was achieved by survivors who had lost everything but their lives and land in the recent disaster. It would have been impossible without munificence on a grand scale, and in the case of at least one church—that of San Salvatore— such endowment is attested by documents.

Over and above the uniformity lent by its golden stone, Noto has a distinctive architectural style showing much of Rome and a little of Spain. The underlying principle of all the façades is the balance between imposing masses and classic columns, for Noto usually dispenses with carvings on the columns, cherubim, mouldings that have no integral part in the structure and, especially, with statues. The tendency to severity is counterbalanced by the colour of the stone and in several instances by the elliptical form of the façade. The harmony of each building in itself and in relation to its sister churches must be almost unique in a local school, such as the architects of Noto composed; there is in the whole town not a single instance of disproportion, and a newcomer might be tempted to attribute the various churches to a single architect of genius and mature experience. This intuition bears some relation to the true facts, which, however, have remained hidden in the archives of Noto and other Sicilian towns, and have never before been revealed. One thing is certain: an architect of Noto named Rosario Gagliardi was not only responsible for the Cathedral of Ragusa but also designed the chief churches of his native town and played an important part in planning many of the lesser buildings. In the light of these achievements, this hitherto almost unknown figure deserves to rank with the leading baroque architects of Europe. It will be many years before he receives the recognition which is his due, but since he has been denied it already for over two centuries, the delay will merely add to his triumph. Noto's golden stone, which provides a fitting monument to the golden age of baroque, will henceforth be linked in the history of art with the name of Gagliardi.

The largest piazza of the town is dominated by the Cathedral, which stands at the head of three flights of steps, extending the whole width of the façade and giving an impression of loftiness, majesty and calm. This spaciousness, a large-handed gift as though unlimited flights were there for the asking, adds greatly to the apparent size of the cathedral; and the chiaroscuro of the steps becomes a decorative feature of the front, no less integral than the vertical moulding on the façade. This spaciousness does not extend, however, to the sides, which look on to narrow streets. Such siting was deliberate, as though to hide a bad profile, and yet the walls are far from unattractive, being decorated with pilasters, ornamented windows, alcoves and renaissance-style doors, and the golden stone in the dark alleys takes on the colour of heather-honey. The façade itself has a simple, flat appearance, its plane broken only by eight columns on the lower and four on the upper storey. It is flanked by two *campanili*, which make the width of the whole façade greater than its height. Churches with two bell-towers are rare in Sicily: at Catania there is another, the church of S. Francesco, but it is marred by a dull and heavy central section.

On the upper storey four statues of the Evangelists—the only statues to grace a façade in Noto—crown the upward lines of the four extreme columns. The *campanili* are square towers, pierced by a single arch on each side, flanked by pilasters and surmounted by pediments, while the stone cupolas, rising from a square base and tapering to a point, soar slightly above the level of the pediment which crowns the central section of the front. The dome, erected in 1872 in place of the original which had been destroyed by earth tremors, is in keeping with the *campanili*, its eight windows being separated by pairs of pilasters, the lines of which are continued on the dome in mouldings which taper away as they reach the lantern. Lichen has modified the original colour of the stone from which this dome, like the *campanili*, is constructed, so that from a distance it appears to be made of beaten gold.

At left and right are elegant baroque palaces in harmony with the cathedral, and on the opposite side of this immense piazza stands the town hall, a distinguished building which has recently been disfigured by the addition of another storey, in the same style, but ruining the lines of the original, which is essentially a long, low structure. Along the straight façade, which curves outwards in the centre to form a convex projection, and extending to the two short sides of the rectangular building, runs an arcade of exceptional power. The wide round arches are divided by forceful Ionic half-columns which, above the cornice, support a stone balustrade. The elliptical form of the centre, which the arcade follows, is repeated at the two corners of the façade, these being softened by concave arches, and at the two remaining corners of the building, where the arcade finishes with a bold and most effective flourish of two concave arches at right angles to each other. On the three sides to which it extends this arcade hides the windows in shadow: on the fourth side they can be seen, large, stately, and quite simple, surmounted by pediments. This arcade, which combines the grandeur of a colonnade with the intimacy of a cloister, provides an ordered effect of light and shade: the graceful curves are exactly adequate to prevent solemnity, while the balustrade, which before the addition of a second storey stood out against the sky, provides the decoration necessary above the bare entablature.

The comparatively simple church of San Salvatore completes this square, among the most beautiful in Sicily, in which the various buildings balance one another as effectively as the different features of a façade. Yet the piazza is only part of Noto's wealth. Of the other churches by Gagliardi, that of the Collegio is the most elaborate, while S. Domenico, which takes the form of a simple harmonious mass, sweeping out in a wide curve to meet the sun, shows that the architect could create in more than one idiom.

But here as in Ragusa the baroque interiors fail to live up
to the façades. Yellow glass in the windows often stamps the
light so that the white stucco walls and roof are in every
corner gilded, and every harsh line and angular corner
softened. The effectiveness of this simple but revolutionary
procedure is undeniable, but after the first delighted impression, doubts give place to dismay. Gone now are the shadowy, evocative corners, pools of prayer, the subtle inter-
play of light and shade, symbols of grace and sin, gone the
sudden colour of the Madonna's dress in a painting at a
side altar, gone the mystery: this veil of yellow light has been
thrown over all, reducing the most individual hue to a common colour. It is as though a country in which money has
been scarce and highly valued were violently inundated with
a mass of inflationary synthetic gold, which, while giving a
false appearance of wealth, renders valueless all former
riches. This gilded light, which is such a feature of baroque
churches, is only one among a number of devices for human-
ising the interior, for reducing it, in fact, to a fashionable
drawing-room. The glass chandeliers, arranged in patterns
between the arches like so many dew-drawn spiders' webs,
are the exact equivalent of those to be found in fine houses
of the eighteenth century. The abundance of cherubim, or
more simply the faces of pretty boys and girls, executed no
longer according to a strict iconography but at the artist's
whim, are again of no religious significance—their counterparts grace the stairways of contemporary mansions. The gilt
frames, which hold canvases whose subject is wherever possible far removed from the essentials of religion, are in form
and detail the same as those which hold mirrors in my lady's
boudoir. The frescoes with their sumptuous golds and
pinks, like a feast of strawberries and cream and sweet little
iced cakes, are in almost every respect the frescoes of the
salon. Plain chant has been superseded by a string orchestra
playing in the gilded choir-loft music without words, lest the
vague feeling of mawkishness should be shattered by stern
doctrinal formulas. Even the very decoration of the walls—

the pilasters and rounded arches, gilded capitals and intricate cornice—serve to slur over the essential form of the
building, which is a cross. In these baroque interiors everything is designed to make the worshipper feel at home: everything must please the eye and excite the fancy. The Renaissance has come: all's right with the world. Suffering and
penance have not even a chapel remaining to themselves.
As for mystery, the golden light has sent it flying to the hills.
It is true that in every age there are points of resemblance
between secular and religious art—even the mosaics of the
Cappella Palatina have their counterpart in the Zisa—but in
the baroque churches the process has gone far beyond a mere
interchange of ideas: religion—the whole of reality, even—
is becoming secularised. There is taking place what can only
be called a softening of the spirit, evident in a neglect of
essentials. One of the elements in religious worship—beautiful decoration—has been singled out and made an end in
itself. It has even been distorted, so that theatricality and
trompe l'œil are now practised for their own sake. The life
of God is no longer depicted on the walls, but incidents,
imaginary for the most part, from the life of some more or
less obscure saint. There is no longer a dominant figure of
Christ in the apse, no longer lofty arches lifting man's
spirit heavenwards, no longer the austere plain stone to
symbolise man's imprisonment on earth: instead a pink-
and-gilded room which seems made not for prayer but for
dalliance.

There are other fine exteriors in Noto besides those by
Gagliardi: the church of the Carmine has a simple concave
façade, pilasters replacing the usual columns; so too has the
Monte Vergine, distinguished by its two wedge-shaped belfries, and its almost crocus-yellow stone. The Chiesa del
Crocifisso compensates for its unfinished façade with a fine,
steeply sloping dome, its stone even more gilded by lichen
than that of the Cathedral.

Of the many palaces the most richly decorated is the fantastic Palazzo Villadorata, built in 1731. Its façade is

rectangular, broken by a large doorway and two rows of windows, the upper with balconies. All over Sicily the balcony is the dominant feature of the houses. It is not built primarily as an airy terrace against the heat, for at midday shutters are closed and all life withdraws to the cool, dark interiors. Its primary purpose is to provide a vantage-point for observing without being observed. From a balcony the whole length of a street can be surveyed, conversation on the pavement below can be heard, passers-by recognised, transactions witnessed and, if the town overlooks sea or mountains, these can be contemplated without interruption. Yet, by a simple step backwards the observer—nearly always a woman—can lose herself in the shadow of the room, so that she steals her secrets without being seen. Balconies are little theatre-boxes, providing the best view of the stage and actors below. But the women who sit or stand in them wear no fine clothes, no flowers or jewellery: since the balconies often look out from bedrooms, they may step into their boxes wearing no more than a negligée in order to catch between dreams a glimpse of events below. Because in Sicily all business and most recreation and conversation are carried on in the streets, the advantages of a balcony are considerable: practically nothing can escape its surveillance. To look from a balcony is to possess temporarily an almost Olympian power: the women who sit knitting or weaving on their narrow sills might be the Fates themselves.

Balconies belong neither within the house nor outside it, but, like poets, exist beyond themselves, observing and recording a life in which they do not participate directly. They are lonely, attendant beings, for ever shut out from the intimacy of the house, for ever hovering like seagulls that encircle a ship at sea.

To the architect they present an opportunity for relieving an otherwise dull wall, an opportunity which in Sicily is generally neglected, the balconies, devoid of all grace, being simple rectangular areas of stone on stone supports, and the balustrade of crude metalwork. In Syracuse and Noto, however, and in parts of Modica, balconies are highly elegant features of the buildings, with a complex form: in many balustrades the metalwork curves outwards to give a pompous, inflated appearance in harmony with the eighteenth-century building. Flowerpots are sometimes hung in the curve of the metalwork, which may itself blossom into the shape of a passion flower at the corners of the balcony. On one palace in Noto the central supports are longer than those at the sides, and the balcony comes out in a half-circle of bulging metalwork, like a scallop shell.

The combination of balconies and window-decoration in the Palazzo Villadorata produces a cumulative effect of light and shade, ponderous weight and airy grace, of tension and agitation, to be equalled in no other baroque building of Sicily. For the most part the brackets are carved in monstrous grotesque shapes, perhaps inspired by the gargoyles of Gothic cathedrals. But where the medieval objects were purposely made ugly in order to frighten away evil spirits from the house of God, the baroque monsters have quite another function. The important thing is not that they should be ugly, but simply that they should appear fanciful, fantastic, extraordinary, anything but merely human or animal, for by now the normal has come to be considered dull. The cumulative effect of these creatures, however monstrous the individual combinations, is considered pleasing: the quaint and outlandish have been taken so far on the road of hideous ugliness that, going beyond this category, they arrive at a form of beauty. The two dangers are vulgarity and absurdity —both signs of a lack of control which is inherent in this extreme form of baroque decoration. Stability is found in preoccupation with detail: each cranny of these balcony brackets is carved deep and irregularly, to extend the chiaroscuro to the least noticeable parts. Just as in the frescoes which cover the ceilings of Sicilian baroque churches the figures themselves have become unimportant beside their constituent paints, to such an extent that the general impression, even after attentive gazing, is of an almost abstract colour complex, so in the external decoration of buildings, the monstrous composite figures serve only as surfaces to be encrusted with carving, in order to produce an abstract pattern of light and shade. The subject has been annihilated by the artist beneath a welter of form.

Of these general principles the balconies on the Palazzo Villadorata are a perfect example, for the richness and extent of the chiaroscuro are extreme. The architect has taken an ironic pleasure in conceiving the whole façade on classic lines: thus the central doorway is correctly Ionic and surmounted by a frieze (which, however, depicts a row of gryphons) and a cornice which serves as a balcony for the window immediately above. This in turn is flanked by pilasters and surmounted by an orthodox pediment. The lower windows are comparatively simple: a broad sill on florid supports takes the same form as a broken cornice above the architrave, which is decorated with floral devices. These windows are eclipsed by the upper row of larger windows which in extravagance of decoration could hardly be bettered. The sides are ornamented with garlands, and the cornice which projects above each is supported at either end by female heads, between which is a monstrous mask entangled with more garlands. But it is the balconies which display the most riotous carving: great bulging metalwork gives a graceful upward sweep to the rectangular stone bases, which are supported by five brackets. These supports are in two parts, a short vertical piece extending downwards and a long horizontal section. Each is usually decorated with monstrous head or body, human or animal, and while the brackets on each balcony form a unity, there is no relation between the six different balconies, each having a different set of figures, cherubim, Moors, lions, female heads, horses and old men. These carvings, in fact the façade itself, display southern baroque at its zenith, in the manner of the buildings at Lecce or some of the Jesuit churches in Brazil. The fantastic figures, caught in the act of taking flight, the bulging metalwork acting as sails caught by the wind, belong not with

Gagliardi's façades but to the world created by Churriguera and his followers.

Despite this exceptional building Noto as a town remains faithful to the Roman tradition, although it finds its own originality within that framework. The Palazzo Villadorata is merely a diversion, a brilliant display-piece included in a programme of more ponderous compositions. Because all are executed in that unique stone, its colour balanced between orange and fawn, the buildings of Noto remain in the memory after similar churches built of grey stone have been forgotten, like golden trinkets which endure long after their silver counterparts have worn away.

The town is a honeycomb of golden stone—anyone, even without the Daedalus myth in mind, would be forced to that analogy by the glinting domes, the varying shades of stone which suggest the different tones in the natural work of the bees, the uniformity and symmetry of the whole. At Acragas the Greeks had built in materials of similar colour, and both in the mosaics and exterior decoration of Monreale gold predominates: the colour of a golden honeycomb again and again makes its appearance in Sicilian art, a colour which matches the natural ornaments, citrus fruit and *nespole*, and even the whole countryside gilded by sunlight. Such a tradition of golden artistry must surely have a source, for nothing is so rare as absolute originality in choice of form or colour. Artistic excellence is not invented anew in each generation, but handed down as a heritage, and no great art can be achieved by repudiating the past. Perhaps, therefore, this tradition takes its rise from Daedalus's original masterpiece, which first tried to emulate the Sicilian sun, to distil the island's pollen into a form which would endure.

The various clues to the legend which have already emerged can now be resumed in two groups. On the one hand, such details as the giving of honey to Christian neophytes and the wedding at Modica have shown that in Sicily honey has had and still has a ritual significance stemming, perhaps, from a cult to which Daedalus was giving expression in his offering at Erice. These clues lend strength to a literal interpretation of Diodorus's story. On the other hand, it has become clear that the artefact can also be taken as subsuming such diverse arts as poetry, gold-engraving and sculpture, though painting seems to be excluded. These were carried on, after Diodorus's day, by Christianity, and were developed in characteristic form by each invading people. They were usually dedicated to religious ends and found within the island a perfection of expression seldom if ever achieved elsewhere. Now Noto has shed light on a further facet of the legend: the honeycomb seems to symbolise, either in its own form as a particular object or as allegory, a predilection for working in gold or materials of golden colour.

CHAPTER TWENTY-ONE

Monte Pellegrino

NOT since the days of Angevin rule, overthrown by the War of the Sicilian Vespers, had Sicily known such misgovernment as under the Bourbons, a régime which Gladstone, not without justice, called the negation of God. Rule from a great distance inevitably proved misrule, and the arts were left to languish, so that no notable works were produced in the nineteenth century before Garibaldi's liberation. Only one of the Bourbon rulers, King Charles, proved himself enlightened, and he has left behind a monument to his interest in the island, a golden cloak for the statue of S. Rosalia, which stands high above the capital city in the saint's own mountain-shrine.

The crown-shaped mass of Monte Pellegrino dominates Palermo physically and also spiritually. Perhaps the one is the consequence of the other, for spiritual forces must be actualised if they are fully to appeal at every level, or even to appeal at all to those who by nature or education are able to realise them only through experience of the senses. Few other peaks have such a memorable form and few are so well placed to be remembered, for the promontory neither overpowers nor loses effect, as Etna does at Catania, by lying too far away. The steep sides which rise not to a single point but to an irregular, slightly inclined plane are on the east and west, and the rose-grey south flank, facing the city, stands all day in the spotlight of the sun. The mountain is so called because of the pilgrimages made to its summit in honour of S. Rosalia, said to have been the daughter of Duke Sinibaldo, who was King William II's nephew. She was born in 1130 and lived in penance on this mountain for several years until her death at an early age. Her bones were found on the promontory in the summer of 1624 by some hermits to whom the saint had appeared in a miraculous vision; they were carried to Palermo where they brought to an end the plague which was then ravaging the city. Since that time S. Rosalia has been venerated in Palermo, the third of the great cities to put itself under the protection of a holy virgin, for Syracuse already counted S. Lucia as patron, and Catania S. Agata.

The mountain itself is calcareous, its grey stone acquiring a rose tint at the surface. Except on the south side it is rugged and covered with scrub, prickly pears and occasional trees. Pilgrims have for centuries climbed over a thousand feet to visit the sanctuary, and every year on the fourth of September a special procession winds its way up the slope to pay honour to S. Rosalia. Recently a modern road to the summit was constructed, so that pilgrims who even now climb barefooted to the sanctuary achieve a less heroic and penitential feat. This road, with its alpine, looping corners, for most of its length gyrating up the south side only, provides an uninterrupted view of the city. Half-way to the summit stands the Albergo Castello Utveggio, a pink stucco building playing at being a Norman-Arab castle and failing lamentably. To some extent it detracts from the prospect of Monte Pellegrino as viewed from the sea and the city: its colour is too blatant, its style too ostentatious. The Normans, who excelled in the construction of mountain strongholds, knew better, choosing for their castles a grey or brown stone and a style that harmonised with the surroundings. Nevertheless this modern castle does command an appropriately sweeping view at the south-west angle of the mountain, a view which includes every corner of the Conca d'Oro. In autumn when the groves are hung with citrus fruit, this sweep of country justifies its golden epithet, but even in spring the medley of sea, city and citrus groves is among the most beautiful civilised views in Sicily. The inventors of place-names, the primary poets, did well to call this bay Panormus, the harbour of everything, the all-harbour, for

not only does it give the impression of being wide enough
to shelter Europe's shipping, but it seems to embrace in a
single panorama the Mediterranean, the sky, and even the
sunshine itself—an effect produced partly by the mountains, partly by the extent of the city.

Almost at the summit of the mountain lies the sanctuary
of S. Rosalia, consisting of a convent and the celebrated
grotto, a deep, lofty chasm in the rock where the saint used
to meditate and pray. This cavern has been made into a
chapel, with an altar set deep into the rock. The water
which seeps from the ceiling and walls is held to be miraculous, and proofs of its efficacy are heaped near the altar in
the form of crutches discarded by men and women once
lame who have been cured by the saint's intercession; by
plastic reproductions of hands, arms, and legs, each brought
by someone who has been granted a cure in that particular
part of the body; and by paintings of illness or accident, such
as a man being knocked down by a bus, all cases in which the
saint has intervened to prevent or mitigate disaster. They
are talismans of a living religion, and if they are not beautiful
that is of slight importance beside the fact of faith.

Inevitably this rocky sanctuary recalls the grottoes of early
Sicilian nature cults. The holy cavern appeals to the same
profound instinct, but is not for that reason to be classed
with such sanctuaries as the one at Acragas. It is not simply
that the former is lofty and at least dimly lighted. Both
grottoes in fact offer an almost similar point of departure—
indeed they must do in order to satisfy man's urgent demand
in his religious worship for mysterious surroundings, for an
atmosphere suggestive of the supernatural—but the destina-
tions to which they give access are as divergent as possible: in one case matter, earth at its crudest; in the other
heaven, and the Infinite. The circumstantial resemblance—
impressive at first—is in the last resort superficial, and those
who dismiss the Christian grottoes as a relic of paganism are
mistaking the envelope for the letter, the binding for the
book.

Travellers to Sicily in the eighteenth and nineteenth centuries were genuinely shocked and horrified by this cave and its votive offerings, which they termed objects of superstition. Now we have learned better than dogmatically to label this particular action holy and meritorious, and that gesture superstitious and repulsive: the roots of faith lie too deep in human personality for any superficial judgment, or perhaps for any human judgment at all. Not that the censure of historians and scientists will alter one least detail of the tradition: however loudly they cry that the bones found on Monte Pellegrino belong to the neolithic period, the prayer of faith will rise louder still: for all time S. Rosalia will be the patron saint of Palermo, while the sick will continue to pay pilgrimage to her sanctuary and bathe in the water from her grotto.

Beyond the votive offerings and candles smoking in the damp air lies the central point of the shrine, a white marble statue of the saint reclining, clad in golden garments, the gift of Charles the Bourbon king. Above it an altar has been fashioned, so that mass can be said in the profoundest part of the grotto which is also a chapel, deep in the earth yet high above land and sea.

As at Enna and Erice, the people have gone up on to a mountain to be nearer heaven, to pray to their patron, to identify their faith with a huge and immovable rock, and the statue of S. Rosalia, with its gilded cloak, gift of a foreign king, is yet one more variation on the original theme of a stranger fashioning a religious offering out of gold.

CHAPTER TWENTY-TWO

Modern Palermo

PALERMO at the present day is a capital city and a provincial town, a metropolis and a village, a modern commercial centre and an Oriental bazaar set down between the mountains and the sea. A century ago it was still in the hands of noblemen—lordly with the palaces of princes and dukes—but today the rich Palermitans prefer the convenience and comfort of modern apartments—often in Milan or Paris. The hovels of the poor, however, have remained unchanged since the time of the Arab domination. It was they who made it their capital, and the Saracen town is still the centre of the city, as tightly packed as the rings at the heart of a beech tree. Here the markets are held all day, and, if there were customers, they would be held all night as well. The tables of fish and sausages, of mandarines and confectionery, of *panelli* and *quagghie* on both sides of the narrow street almost meet in the middle, so that the passer-by is more or less compelled to stop and by that fact to make a purchase. The hypnotic shouts of the vendors crying their wares in a sing-song voice descend, as soon as a customer approaches, into a cajoling, rapid patter, until a bargain is concluded. Then the sing-song starts again, untiring as the call of a bird. These vendors have pathetically little to sell, and many display the meanest, most untempting wares—a dozen diminutive and none-too-fresh fish or a few little syrupy sweets wrapped in coloured paper—and will spend a whole day trying to trade them. For selling is their traditional, their sole means of livelihood, and so all day long they will sit or slouch beside their little tables, hoping by their incantations to lure an occasional purchaser. After each sale, however insignificant, there follows a keen sense of satisfaction, of pride and even of achievement, related not so much to the material success, to the fact that the price of a piece of bread has been won from an uncaring world, as to the feeling of fulfilment: the seller of a few pieces of confectionery can identify himself in this moment with the merchant who trades by the shipload.

In and out of the tables and carts, a paradise of hide-and-seek, run the children, scuffling and fighting, playing with ball or coin, making a medley of shouts and laughter. They have no other home but the streets, these ragged, under-nourished waifs, and they resent the stranger as an intruder on their public privacy. According to their mood they beg or throw stones at him, inveigle or insult, and in any case are quite blameless. For in Palermo rich and poor live side by side, and although throughout the island there are many worse off, nowhere else are squalid conditions so juxtaposed with comfort and abundance, and therefore nowhere else so resented.

The passion for trading is not confined to the Saracen district. At dawn, simultaneously with the crowing cocks, throughout the city streets the vendors begin their cry—a sound which is quite Eastern, rising and falling in quick succession. The man selling fresh beans cries: "Miele sono queste fave!" "Beans sweet as honey"; and in similar poetical vein the fruitseller from Monreale boasts, "Pira butiti, si mancia e si vivi!"—"Pears like butter: you drink as well as eat." The call to prayer, a thousand years ago, from the thin, flute-like minarets of the Mahommedan city, cannot have been markedly different, for these vendors do, above all, entreat and pray—passionately so. Their goods comprise every imaginable commodity from goat's milk to cauliflowers, from baskets to brushes, from wine to olives, and even at the earliest hours women, responding like divinities in a primitive play, step from sleep on to their balconies and let down their shopping basket on a piece of string. When it reaches the street the tradesman takes from it the crumpled

paper-money and refills the basket with whatever the woman
orders; the wares are drawn up, examined and commented
upon; sometimes even lowered again, if they do not satisfy,
to be exchanged for better. Later in the day, but still at an
early hour, the street sellers take up their positions, in ranks
three deep, to launch an attack on passers-by, as they go to
work or simply promenade, with every variety of ammuni-
tion. Not only newspapers and soft drinks and ice-cream, but
ties and fountain pens, sweets and votive candles, paintings
of Monte Pellegrino and icons of the Madonna—every
assortment of decorative and useful article are offered for
sale. Sometimes, in the narrowest streets, two or three rows
of vendors completely block the pavement, so that pedes-
trians are canalised into the road, and the occasional car is
brought to a standstill. For in this city the car is deprived
by law from using one of its principal weapons—the horn:
it therefore becomes a relatively helpless creature in the face
of teeming crowds, often outdistanced by the prancing horse
and cart.

These swelling crowds are characteristic of Palermo, the one
large city in Sicily which, preserved from major earthquakes
and eruptions, has retained its old houses and narrow streets.
The basic living unit for the family is not a house but a single
room, in which as many as ten people eat and sleep, work
and play. The door may consist simply of a large piece of
wood propped against the entrance to block out light and occasional wind and rain. Because of the temperate climate the
poor suffer little from cold, and as noise and crowds please
the Sicilians in proportion as they approach the maximum,
these rooms are less insupportable than they at first appear.
Besides, when actual hunger is an ever-present menace, the
size of living-quarters assumes less urgent importance. Food
of low nutritional value keeps body and soul together, but
sometimes in a tenuous and almost animal condition. Here
an old man selling newspapers is being brought a bowl of
coarse pasta mixed with oil, which he munches like a soldier
at his post—greedily, for it is his only meal of the day; there

a child in arms is sucking a crust of bread to appease a hunger which milk alone ought to satisfy, were it less expensive. Sicily, in so many ways reflecting the social pattern of continental Europe a hundred or more years ago, is still a country of pitiable poverty, and in Palermo, where the Arab spirit is so evident, the hopeless, crushing condition of the poor suggests the cities of North Africa.

Because every activity, whether work, commerce, conversation or play, takes place in the narrow, closely packed streets, jammed with people, young and old, one has the impression of being present at a three-ring circus in which all the performers are going through their act at the same time. If comedy consists in the solemn juxtaposition of incongruous elements, then Palermo can claim to be the centre of comedy at its most ludicrous. The little boy who with one hand pushes a handcart with a newly painted coffin on it, and with the other holds a huge strawberry ice-cream cone; the vendor of carnations and roses in heated conversation with the fishmonger; the carter whose mule decides to sit down in the main street, holding up all the traffic and firmly refusing to budge; the policeman who for all his waving and semaphore makes the confusion in the narrow streets worse confounded; the man who sells brightly coloured balloons outside the most expensive restaurant in the city; the fortune-teller with her parrot in front of the street-corner icon: all partake a little of light-hearted lunacy.

In the last analysis, the distinctive characteristic of Palermo is something more than the sum of its incongruities, its crowds, its rhythm, its bazaars and that peculiar mentality which is the result of cross-fertilisation over a period of two millennia. This essential aspect of the city can best be described as an overflowing and intermingling of personalities. Passers-by in the street, instead of walking in a calm, anonymous manner, parade their personality and even their occupation. Everyone emits as it were a positive charge of electricity, like so many children reciting their names and vaunting their achievements in the playground. They have something of the primary colours they love so much; their whole essence is at once revealed in uncompromising fashion. Just as coffins are made in full view of the teeming crowds, so the Palermitan, by his mourning band, by eating in the street, by open marks of affection such as embracing and linking arms, and above all by his frank, public avowal of all that a northerner would regard as personal and even secret, displays all his wares to the world.

His love of talk of all kinds, conversation, sermons, speeches commercial, social and dramatic (Pirandello the Sicilian is one of the few modern dramatists worthy to rank with Synge and Yeats), is a characteristic the Palermitan—indeed every Sicilian—shares with the Irish. It is by no means the only one: deep religious feeling, a passion for politics, a distrust of books and dislike of reading are features common to both peoples. Like the Irish, the Sicilians also show a resignation to suffering which has been bred in their bones over centuries and amounts almost to fatalism. Worship, too, in the southern no less than in the northern island, has become a function of daily life, so that the crowd which interrupts a sermon to contest or approve, and the workman who rides a bicycle down the cathedral nave, far from showing disrespect, are on the contrary displaying affection by their familiarity.

The faces in the streets of Palermo are of a diversity to be found elsewhere only in great international ports. Here, at the heart of the island, blood from Greece, Phoenicia and Rome; from Africa, Scandinavia and Germany; from Anjou, Aragon and Catalonia, meets and intermingles with feverish activity. All the races of the world seem to be conducting and attending a Babel-like bazaar under the torrid sun, where the wares, holy pictures set above *nespole*, tunny fish juxtaposed with candies, seem purposely arranged to mirror the city's essential incongruity, a strident polyphony of colours, sounds and gestures which is appropriately caught up on a larger scale and matched by the diversity of architecture in the city itself.

A final element in the already confused background of Moorish houses, Spanish palaces, Norman and baroque churches, is the modern architecture which is the measure of material progress during the last hundred years. In the nineteenth century a wave of anti-clericalism together with the political union of Sicily and Italy were reflected in secular buildings which relied largely on the established or outmoded forms of the mainland, a tendency which in modern times has been successfully reversed to allow Sicilian architects and craftsmen to evolve an original style.

The northern part of Palermo was developed in a series of broad streets and blocks of apartments of neutral appearance, such as can be seen in any continental city of Europe. These are essentially middle-class buildings, stolid, comfortable and undistinguished. Not a lira has been spent on decorations unless either useful or ostentatious. In Palermo as all over Europe this rise of the commercial middle-class was characterised also by a great interest in drama, or more exactly melodrama, and two theatres were built in the single year 1875. Both are enormous, pretentious, stolid and without a trace of originality, modelled patiently on the buildings of Rome's greatness, thereby betraying the fact that at that time Italy was very far from being great—had, in truth, only recently come into existence as a national state. The Politeama Garibaldi, with hemispherical façade incorporating a triumphal arch, is a reproduction of the Pompeian style: its painted glass, its trite murals, its altogether synthetic appearance mark it out as pastiche and a failure in this city of successful buildings. Similarly, the Teatro Massimo, one of the largest theatres in the world (how often that epithet has an ominous ring), dismally fails because it is modelled on the outworn style of Augustan buildings. Steps lead up to the Corinthian colonnade, behind which rises a Roman dome, while at a higher level, and jarring outrageously with the round lines of the cupola, towers a hideous square mass with sloping roof. The colonnade does not extend the whole length of the façade, with the result that vast undecorated

windows of plain glass gape blankly at either side, disinteg-
rating any lines the theatre might otherwise have possessed.
The colour, a dark greenish-grey worthy of a gnome, lends
the building an air of solemn, brooding pretentiousness. This
in fact was evidently the desired effect, as is witnessed by the
inscription over the colonnade: "L'arte rinnova i popoli e ne
rivella la vita. Vano delle scene il diletto ove non mira a
preparar l'avvenire." Progressive idealism arm in arm with
materialism, the figure of social justice in bourgeois trappings! Art must be linked to social progress: art must be
strictly utilitarian. The stolid citizens of Palermo would give
their city a huge theatre, no, two huge theatres, not for any
frivolous purpose but to emancipate and educate the people.
Nineteenth-century idealists, they can see the answer of this
century in the placards posted round the theatre, announcing
Aïda and the operas of Rossini. In any case it is not the
realist art of nineteenth-century melodrama that will renew
the spirit of the audience, and the people know too much of
life already from the narrow, sordid streets to wish to pay for
the privilege of knowing more.

If the nineteenth century, partly because of its momentous
social and political changes, partly because of its temporary
shift of values, failed to erect effective buildings in Palermo, the
twentieth century has already succeeded. Today Italy leads
Europe in the field of architecture, and the new processes and
techniques of engineering provide her designers with an opportunity as momentous as that which followed the discovery
of the dome. It is a pity that some of the large, modern public
buildings of Palermo were commissioned by the Fascists, for
they betray, in consequence, a certain defiant assertiveness: they
seem to proclaim in a voice just a shade too loud: "Look,
here are the noble, useful buildings, symbols of Italy's greatness, which can be achieved under the enlightened dictator-
ship of one man." But behind the façade the cracks of
shoddy workmanship and cheap materials are all too glar-
ingly apparent. Previous civilisations in the island have
shown that nobility and grandeur in architecture are the

products not of government directives but of discipline, patient craftsmanship and above all a fine style which is also living—the expression of the beliefs of a distinguished mind reflecting the contemporary spirit.

The two most important public buildings erected by the Fascists are the post office and the Palazzo del Provveditorato. The former, built in 1933 to designs of Angiolo Mazzoni, is a rectilinear building entirely of ferro-concrete. The façade is dominated by ten vast columns, reaching almost the whole height of the building, without fluting and flush with the walls, topped by square abacuses too small for their purpose. At the sides of the architrave two angels, or more likely symbolic figures of vague purpose, provide the sole decoration. Flanking the columns on each side are twelve massive windows, while behind the colonnade low rounded arches give access to the public rooms, the chief of which has a low roof supported on groined vaulting and is dominated by three large semi-circular windows. These rooms, like the building itself, are simple and functional, yet none is sufficiently distinguished in line to succeed as it stands, without decoration. On the contrary, both columns and windows are unnecessarily large almost to the point of vulgarity, and the vast colonnade in point of fact supports nothing at all. Fittingly enough, beside this building stands the ruined symbol of Fascism, triple axes in brown marble, the blades broken off and only the mutilated handles standing.

The second Fascist work, again a Government office building designed to throw credit on the régime, is the Palazzo del Provved22torato, the project of Giuseppe Capitò. It takes the form of a rectangle on three sides, the façade being formed across the fourth side by three straight marble pieces supporting a cross-piece of similar material with an inscription. This front is totally rhetorical: an unintegrated attempt at grandeur, an unmasked pretence. At the sides are the usual symbolic figures, even less significant and attractive than usual: one woman holds a sword as though it were a

mirror in her boudoir, another, with wings, holds out the
olive branch of peace. These linked symbols of war (or
merely strength) and peace are a feature of Fascist buildings.
The inscription runs: "Tempio Munito Fortezza Mistica."
One can often learn a great deal from inscriptions on or in
buildings about the spirit of the age in which they were built,
for the phrases are concise telegraphic messages sent from
the past to future generations. This one is surely a classic of
empty abstraction, of a pseudo-ideology. One remembers the
inscription above the high altar in the Cappella Palatina, calling the sinner to repentance and prayer in face of the sufferings of Christ, a message valid for all eternity. However, the
attempt to found a mystical secularism, alien to the Sicilian
people, was doomed from the first to failure, and these
Fascist buildings constructed without love or faith will doubtless tumble long before the Norman churches.

One of the best examples of contemporary architecture in
Palermo is the Ristorante San Pietro, built in 1950–1 to
designs by a young architect of Spanish descent, Giorgio
Fernandez. It takes the form of two long, rectangular rooms
joined in the centre to make the letter H. These rooms,
which are below street level, have frosted windows stretching
the whole length of one of the shorter walls, additional lighting being provided by concealed fluorescent bulbs at the
angle of walls and ceiling. They are divided down the centre
by square pillars and reached by a flight of steps suspended
on cords from two piers. The two rooms are decorated each
in a distinctive way, one with purely abstract and surrealist
designs, the other more realistically. The abstract designs
take the form of painted geometrical squares and triangles;
the surrealist murals derive from Picasso's middle period,
and in the recesses let into the long wall are designs in cord
and metal. The ceiling, too, is recessed to form a non-
figurative pattern in which lighting is concealed.

The other room has niches along the most extensive wall
in which are set, to form bas-reliefs lighted from within,
objects such as a mandoline or a tree or glass pots arranged

on an inclined plane, while the pillars are decorated with geometrical patterns. The colour scheme throughout is pastel: tables and chairs are functional, a combination of light metal, marble, and wood. The harmony and vitality of the décor, the sense of space and light elicited from basement rooms, and above all the employment of modern materials and methods in an original manner in order to suggest new forms of beauty—such qualities show that the accomplished architects of Sicily do not all belong to the past.

These simple, bare, rectilinear rooms, with no decoration but the frescoes and bas-reliefs, austere, abrupt, and uncompromisingly essential, by accident or design recall some of the most ancient constructions of Sicily. There exist, on the other side of the island, at Pantálica, caves fashioned three thousand years earlier than these rooms, yet which might have been their matrix. Modern architecture, going back behind the Norman and baroque gardens, has discovered once more the underlying rock in shadow and sunlight, and if this clue is followed back to its source, at Pantálica perhaps Sicilian history can be brought full circle.

CHAPTER TWENTY-THREE

Pantálica

THE starting-point for the journey to Pantálica is the small
town of Sortino, standing high on the Iblean Mountains, not
far from Syracuse, an agricultural centre going back to Greek
times. The journey to the prehistoric caves possesses an uncommon significance for the inhabitants: they see themselves
as the sentinels of the past, and their town as the threshold of
time, the dark cave by which travellers to that other world,
older than theirs by three·millennia, must pass. They have
evolved a ritual according to which each detail of the departure is ordered. When a traveller tells the group of men who
soon collect round him that he wishes to make the journey,
they answer that they will attend to all arrangements, and
within a few moments a large crowd forms, offering advice
and pressing him to drink with them. In a quarter of an
hour, it is promised, a horse will be saddled and bridled
ready for departure. But a quarter of an hour, or any other
period, is in Sicily not a precise definition of time but an
evocative phrase suggesting that if one continues to wait
patiently the expected will finally arrive. In this case, the
phrase is used purposely and the wait prolonged, for these
people of Sortino are well trained in their rites and know
how anxiously the traveller attends, fearing now that there is
no suitable mount to be had, now that the guide is ill or
absent at wedding or funeral.

At last, when further waiting seems pointless, the party
arrives. The guide himself is a young man—too young, it
seems, to know the secrets of Pantálica—with laughing
mouth and serious eyes, a man conscious of his role as medi-
ator between past and present time; while the beasts are led

by an old, stoop-shouldered groom and a man with similar features who might be his son, joined in unceasing laughter. The horses are saddled simply with sheepskin attached by cords, bridled with long double reins and wearing blinkers and bells. Mounting, we take the road leading out of the town to the south. Already all the women and children of these houses on the outskirts are gathered to watch, cheering and laughing and shouting advice, while some of the older children run out to pull the tails of the good-natured horses, urging them on more quickly. The road comes to an end with the last house; henceforward it winds down the slope in hairpin bends or tumbles headlong in a series of ill-defined stairs, irregular as though they marked the steps of someone who had careered down the incline at full speed, its surface indistinguishable from the rocky bed of a *torrente*. Nothing serves to set off the path from the surrounding rocks but an occasional heap of loose pebbles. More often than not the way lies up and down the smooth stone of the mountain-side, and sometimes even over a rabbit-warren of eroded rock. Sortino lies at a height of over a thousand feet, and the road to the south precipitates itself almost half that distance down an all-but-sheer slope to the gorge below. Yet the beasts never once miss their footing, moving forward like the central section of a river which is never caught or thrown by the latent boulders at the edge. Indeed, the rider's impression is of being a river god, tumbling down in a cascade from infinity to nought within a few minutes, like the Sicilian torrents in October after the heavy rains.

At first the scenery, quite open to the sun, is characteristic of mid-spring, almond-trees already advanced in leaf and wild flowers in full bloom. To descend the gorge is to turn back two months in time. The almonds at this lower, more shaded level are still in blossom and many of the flowers still in bud. In the shelter of the chasm, in small terraces cut into the mountain-side, oranges hang on diminutive trees, like coloured balls juggled by a circus dwarf. In and out of the groves, goldfinches are looping in love-play, seen only for a

fleeting moment, gone in a flash of wings. The bird which
in northern countries astonishes with its brilliant red-and-
yellow markings, appearing almost to mock the pastel
flowers and delicate greens, is here perfectly in place: its
colours lie on either side of the myriad little suns, and the
black marking which divides them, like the pattern on
Mycenean pottery, answers to the dark shadows lying at the
heart of the orange-trees' leaves. Here, in this quarry of
fruit, in the garden at the edge of a gorge, the firebird seems
rightfully to take its origin, embodying the colours of the
wild flowers which bloom indiscriminately, here in the soil,
there in the bare rock.

Like drops from the fountains of the orange-trees, marigolds lie scattered on the grass; campions carry the colour
in one direction, yellow vetches and dandelions in another.
Speedwell and bugloss add blue, wild snapdragon a hint of
gold. Mallows and daisies, thyme and asphodel, crimson
sainfoin and wild stock flourish as profusely as though they
have been planted in a well-tended garden, their scent justi-
fying the Greek saying that in Sicily hunting dogs lose the
trail when the spring flowers are in bloom. Yet this abundance of fruit and flower is growing not in deep, rich, well-
watered soil but out of the rock, almost spontaneously.

Through this natural garden the path descends, crosses the
narrow bridge which spans the gorge some hundred feet
above the river and starts the long, difficult ascent of the
opposite side. The horses prove no less agile at climbing
than at descending, and though panting for breath they do
not pause to rest—indeed, there is not a single ledge which
could serve as a momentary stage. The layers of vegetation
change like the levels of a mine: in the heart of the gorge
pure gold of oranges; above this a less rich deposit of unripe
fruit and many-coloured flowers, surmounted in turn by
rock, divided into narrow terraces and already abundant
with young corn. Then the flat crest of the hill gives way
to another gorge, similar to the first, but with a dry river-bed
at the bottom, and cultivated all the way down with corn,

in little terraces and patches of field no larger sometimes than an outspread sheet.

The earth is worked with a hoe, and the harvest in June reaped with a sickle, threshed by hand and carried on mule-back to Sortino to be sold. There are no cottages on the land itself; in the morning labourers come out from the town on foot or mule, taking as long as an hour or even, in some parts of Sicily, two or three hours to reach the fields, and at twilight returning to their homes. The result is that the soil is poorly worked both because of the time and labour spent in travelling and because the labourer lacks that physical and moral attachment to the land which he feels when his home stands amid the crops. Since the land is feverishly fertile, this inadequacy is not disastrous. Methods which elsewhere in Europe would mean ruin to the farmer here produce good yields: so that the Romans said Ceres gave Sicily the power of producing corn without human labour. But for the agricultural labourer the system means a servile and crushing life. His mid-day meal is no more than a plate of pasta which gives neither nourishment nor stimulus, and when he returns home after dark he eats no better. His lot is the direct result of those historical conditions which made Sicily an island of large towns. Even before the first colonists arrived, the Sicels were settled in large centres as the surest means of protection, a procedure which the Greeks, Normans, and Swabians continued, for their rule too was continually challenged. The custom endures, and the Sicilian peasant is now so used to it that he would probably oppose bitterly any change which deprived him of civic communal life.

The path now arrives at a third gorge, that of the River Calcinara, a tributary of the Anapos, which marks the site of Pantálica. Approached from the north the prehistoric city rises up on the other side of the gorge, stretching along a terrace, guarded on the south side by the Anapos and on the northern and eastern aspects by the Calcinara. The first impression is of a multitude of square openings in the rock, row upon row, spaced irregularly, in several tiers, all along the length of the terrace. Because they are unique they at once bring to mind a flood of wildly divergent similes. They are like the caves of wild animals, and also like the most modern ferro-concrete buildings; they are eyries and hives belonging to colossal insects, windows and watching eyes. Their menacing effect is due not solely to the fact that they resemble concrete fortifications but also to their furtiveness —they are hidden and give nothing of themselves away. They terrify also by force of numbers: they are not confined merely to one section of the terrace but continue along the line of the mountain until they vanish out of sight on either side. Their efficient, straight-edged aspect, so unexpected in the midst of wild and remote surroundings where not even the precipices fall in vertical lines, enhances this effect. There is nothing whatever to detract from the primeval appearance of the place: everything remains now as it was when the early inhabitants were constructing their caves, or rather their city, since these caves constitute an entire metropolis in the form of a fortress. For, when the first overwhelming impression has passed and the traveller attempts to analyse the place, its impregnable position seems the most distinctive feature. On both sides this gorge rises almost vertically to a far greater height than in the previous two, while the Anapos to the south flows through a similar chasm. Only a narrow, easily defensible strip of land connects the terrace with high ground to the west.

At closer range it becomes clear from their inaccessible and cramped nature that the rows of square apertures which at first seem to constitute the ancient city are not all former habitations of the living: only a few of the larger openings where the terrace comes to a point at the spur of the mountain can have served as homes. The other smaller squares, which extend irregularly along the sheer cliff-face are nothing else than tombs, a multitude of sepulchres hewn out of the rock, a necropolis of colossal proportions. This fact once apparent, the whole place takes on an even more sinister aspect. The magnificent setting between sheer mountains,

looking over valley upon valley of green cultivated ground
to glimpse the sea beyond, the undercurrent of music sent up
by the river and augmented by deep grottoes, the scent of
innumerable wild flowers—all these seemed fitting surroundings for an ancient city that could be imagined as still living.
But now, as the framework to a vast and ostentatious cemetery, to a city doubly dead, to row upon row of gaping tombs,
these beautiful properties seem infected and limned with
terror. Loveliness degenerates to exoticism; the valley becomes so many traps leading to death; the river's music a
treacherous siren-song inviting the newcomer to throw himself down into the cool waters which will bring oblivion; the
multi-coloured wild flowers so many poisonous plants; the
square tombs expectant, waiting to close in on their prey.
The place is nothing less than a chasm of death, the final
stage, as the myriad sepulchres bear witness, on the route of
countless unsuspecting travellers.

The tombs themselves, built by Sicels of the second millennium are crude constructions. In the majority of cases an
opening three feet square has been cut two feet deep into the
rock; it's width at this point narrows to about eighteen inches,
and continues for another six inches into the mountain face;
then it opens out into the tomb proper, some six feet long
and three feet wide. The tombs have been sited in irregular
rows, wherever the cliff face falls sheer, and in many cases
must have been inaccessible without the use of ladders. On
either side of the city itself, and on the slope directly opposite
it, these apertures crowd everywhere. Though open and
gaping now like niches in the catacombs, they were once
closed, not with a terracotta plaque and mortar, but with a
single piece of stone.

This city of tombs provides a revelation of the island as it
is in its raw, natural state, as it was in the dark age between
the founding of the Cretan and the Greek colonies. There is
no artistic richness, not even a building above ground to prove
that man has raised himself from the earth, only the stark,
square openings dedicated to death, cut out of the brute cliff-

face. Here is Sicily of the stone age, intent on nothing higher than the taking of food and the burial of its dead. The pageant of nation after nation which was later to form a continual progress, the gorgeous trappings, the poetry and the palaces have not yet arrived: the stage is bare and empty.

Empty, that is, of civilisation, of man-made beauty, for all around, in the oranges and flowers and almond-trees, in the majestic lines of the chasm whose heights seem to dam and canalise the sky until it forms the torrent of water hundreds of feet below, throbs a natural, living beauty to be found in few other places of the world. If Pantálica, and Sicily at large, can boast no indigenous culture, if the island merely provides a theatre for other performers, something in the structure of that theatre, its own natural magnificence has called forth absolute perfection time after time, whatever the particular representation might be. The island possesses an intrinsic, though passive, loveliness which elicits artistic perfection no less surely than the golden sun now opens the wild flowers and turns the oranges into microcosms of itself.

Artists of all ages have found stimulus in Sicily, have matched its natural exuberance with works no less rich in number and design, have drawn inspiration from its innumerable wild flowers. Like the bees drifting over the hills to steal nectar from the canyon, they have come from afar to turn a natural and variegated beauty into the symmetrical pattern of art, and the honeycomb they formed was a direct result of a fertilising movement among opulent natural surroundings. Pantálica, by revealing both the open poverty and hidden wealth of the island, casts this light on Daedalus's offering: the honeycomb in gold which he presented to Aphrodite was the work of an alien who drew forth and stored in an enduring form the hidden nectar of Sicily: an initial act of artistry which at the same time fertilised succeeding civilisations.

Pantálica, therefore, city of crude, brute, indigenous barbarism, points the solution to part of the original legend. Sicily of herself has been unable to build or develop any of the arts, and had Daedalus never set foot in the island, she might well have remained another Corsica or Sardinia, a country of merely natural beauty, without any corresponding artistic achievement. The arts were brought by Daedalus and his followers, the peoples who have successively invaded Sicily.

The bees which make the far-famed honey of Hybla are drifting along the streaming sunlight, drawn to each flower either by its colour or scent, fulfilling an end greater than their own storing against famine. Most, when they are loaded with pollen, make off over the hills, but some, a tributary stream, turn away to one of the larger tombs in the rock face, as though, like the primitive Greek priestesses named Bees, to lay an offering before the dead.

To cross the cave-opening is to undergo burial and then, after a few moments, to revive in Hades, in a shadowy world of grey stone, of line without colour, of shape without form, where the flight of bees resounds like surf echoing through a coastal cave.

They are all purpose, these insects, and since this other world holds no pollen, presumably they use the cave as a hive. Yet there is no trace of honey either on walls or ceiling to explain the swarming bees. Although they enter continually, their numbers do not seem to increase, as though they take flight into the tomb only to die. But the true explanation soon appears: they are making their way into the far wall, through a narrow cleft at one corner. A ray of sunlight follows them in, illuminating the interior, which reveals itself as a deep and rough-hewn natural sanctuary, half the size of the cave which forms its antechamber. At the remote end hangs the object of the bees' resonant flight, the central figure of the chasm, clearly visible yet by reason of the narrowness of the cleft inaccessible as a kestrel's nest perched on the topmost branch of a Scotch pine, a wild honeycomb, glinting gold.

The moment of discovery strikes like a revelation and with all the force of surprise, and the gleaming treasure holds the eye no less surely than it draws the stream of bees. The pattern of cells, whipped like a whirlwind, convoluted as a seashell, glints from myriad facets, as sunlight finds in the alternating rows of liquid and solid its own self distilled and stored. One sun meets a hundred thousand suns in a torrent of light, until the honeycomb takes on the character of a golden prism. As a rainbow leaps astride the clouds of spray on a waterfall like some rare polychrome fish, so now not in any vision but in actual fact a golden spectrum is formed across the sun-struck honeycomb, holding in itself more than the whirled wax and nectar. Its colours, ranging through all the ranks of sunlight, are first to strike the eye: a galaxy of golds which not merely evoke but seem to hold in themselves (for all is real, in this wide spectrum, as though the buildings had been transported and reduced to miniature) the stone of the temples at Acragas and the baroque churches at Noto. As though with the bees there now come rushing back into the sunlight a crowd of other images which share this golden colour: the mosaics at Cefalù, at Monreale and in the jewel casket of the Cappella Palatina; the coins of Syracuse and gilded baroque interiors all across the island.

Now another feature of the honeycomb imposes itself, eclipsing even the colours: its intricate pattern, fashioned with all the skill and symmetry of a work of art. The coiled bas-relief, under the influence of sunlight, takes shape as the carved figures on peasant carts, as marionettes of beaten metal and as arabesque cakes. Lying within it, too, as the waves' beat lies in a shell, are the archaic metopes of Selinus and the statue of Aphrodite which takes a new form at Serpotta's hands; here is the honeycomb on Pindar's lips; and here too is S. Rosalia's golden cloak, the religious gift of an alien king. All assemble and find a unity, until it becomes apparent that the golden object at the far end of the cave is more than a mere honeycomb: it is the very essence of Sicilian art, a form which has been realised, now as a golden coin, now as a Pindaric ode, now as Norman mosaics, diverse beauties all stamped with one implicit yet distinctive pattern.

The golden honeycomb is nothing less than the archetype of all Sicilian art.

Pantálica has yielded up one secret, but there are others still to be discovered. As the bees drift in and circle round the gleaming prism, they seem to prove it a natural honeycomb, of their own fabrication. Yet does that, after all, necessarily follow? Since the treasure lies inaccessible for all time within the rock, touch can never prove the statement true or false. To claim, therefore, that it is not a natural object but a work of metal, the original offering which Daedalus made to Aphrodite of Erice, is not altogether fanciful, and can never, at least, be proved absurd. One point lends great support to the claim. Diodorus says that the original object in gold was indistinguishable from the work fashioned by bees, and if indistinguishable, then able to confound even the insects of Hybla.

The tradition of Sicilian art suggests the real existence of a paradigm such as Diodorus describes, and here, deep in the chasm, lies just such an object. To deny the honeycomb its true title as Daedalus's work simply because it is inaccessible would be the height of contrariness: rather, its inviolability seems in keeping with its holy nature. It would follow therefore that someone of the old religion centuries ago removed Daedalus's masterpiece from Erice to this cave, where it has endured as a living archetype. This is Pantálica's second, darker secret.

For such a claim the evidence is imaginative rather than logical, yet to see the gleaming, convoluted spiral is to know beyond doubt that the quest has ended. The absent, on the other hand, have a right to deny so improbable a discovery, but such a denial makes no difference to the conclusions which follow from Pantálica. Even supposing the cave holds nothing more than the work of bees, supposing Sicily no longer holds a honeycomb fashioned in gold, the accumulation of evidence none the less confirms Diodorus's story. Instead of being taken literally, it will have to be construed, after the fashion of many legends, as a symbolic statement of certain factors in the centuries known to the historian, factors which have proved constant in the Sicilian scene and persisted until the present day.

Daedalus, in that case, must be considered the prototype of the foreign invader who atones for his conquest by glorifying the island with works of art. The offering of his masterpiece to Aphrodite is an expression of the religious nature of those works, its unique form represents the introduction of new modes, and its consummate workmanship typifies the perfection of foreign forms on Sicilian soil, itself rich in natural beauty but altogether lacking an indigenous artistic tradition. That it was made from gold foreshadows a Sicilian predilection for that colour and metal, while the fact that it was indistinguishable from the work of bees is to be taken as an indication of that harmony between works of art and their natural surroundings which characterises all Sicilian building. In short, the qualities of this original work of art, its colour and intricacy and sanctity, have become the Sicilian heritage.

Furthermore, just as honey is the substance to which the bees devote their life, their sole monument, so it may be said that the Sicilians have displayed their qualities more excellently in their works of art than in any other sphere of activity. They remain, even the earliest, sometimes as perfect as when they were first fashioned, objects of beauty over which the eye can rove, fertilising the imagination, drawing images to be distilled as words and lines until another form of art is thereby composed.

The ritual of offering honey to Christian neophytes, popular belief regarding bees and the presentation of honey to the newly married—these and other details suggest that Sicily received from Crete a cult in which bees and honey played a significant part, at a date which corresponds with the Cretan sherds on Lipari. Such evidence confirms Diodorus's story. Daedalus must surely have lived, a man of flesh and blood and a supreme artist who set his mark on a country's tradition. But he is equally important as a prototype, a theme underlying all Sicilian history, a figure who is reborn now as a Greek colonist, now as Count Roger, now as a Spanish baroque architect. He is a man and more than a man, just as his masterpiece is both a honeycomb and the fountainhead of such rich and continuous beauty as can be found nowhere else in the world.

The chasm has revealed its seam of gold and thereby brought an end to the quest. Outside, the square openings of the necropolis stare as before, but no longer inscrutably, and another ancient music joins the humming of the bees. Devoid of the cover which an English spinney provides, the nightingale has begun to sing. Among the mottled mountains, against a bare, uncultivated background the notes form themselves into a spring of mountain water, issuing directly from the rock and flowing down to irrigate the valley parched with silence. In the soft surroundings of an English spring, the nightingale crowns the calls of a score of other song-birds, each one of which adequately celebrates the scene and season, but here, where birds are few, the nightingale is not a luxury but a necessity: the only bird whose music can match the profusion and abandon of flowers and fruit, of light and colour. Just as the goldfinch, by its plumage, proves its birth from some remote and legendary orange-grove of Sicily, so the nightingale, by that melody which surges up from earth to heaven in a string of crescendos on a single note, enunciates now and for all time the marriage between the island and the sun, a marriage symbolised in sweet, golden honey. Without the nightingale, the country would produce its beauty in vain; like the courts of Acragas and Syracuse without a Pindar to define and immortalise their achievements, the recklessly daring leap of corn and grass and clover; the old troupers, almond and olive, bowed down by their weight of fruit; the zany flowers, dressed in harlequin costume; the rocks, masters of magic, which produce a whole succession of brightly coloured festoons out of themselves—all these would perform to an unapplauding audience; their marvels would pass unrecorded; their rise and fall would pass unshared as a death without tears. But the nightingale is present and does not fail: in a continuous rhapsody it glorifies the island, gathering up all its aspects into a single essential melody, which in its abandon and abundance could be the spirit of Daedalus, responding to the delights of a sunlit Eden with his own form of beauty. The strong surge upwards does justice even to the mountains, the cascade of descending notes mirrors the petals of blossom as they fall from the almond-trees, and since of all birds it was the best loved of the Greeks it recalls those who brought the fairest gifts to Sicily and the civilisation which beneath all others has endured.

Index